William Blake

Songs of Innocence and of Experience

SARAH HAGGARTY and JON MEE

Consultant Editor: NICOLAS TREDELL

D0082644

palgrave
macmillan

© Sarah Haggarty and Jon Mee 2013

All rights reserved. No reproduction, copy or transmission of this publication may be made without written permission.

No portion of this publication may be reproduced, copied or transmitted save with written permission or in accordance with the provisions of the Copyright, Designs and Patents Act 1988, or under the terms of any licence permitting limited copying issued by the Copyright Licensing Agency, Saffron House, 6–10 Kirby Street, London EC1N 8TS.

Any person who does any unauthorized act in relation to this publication may be liable to criminal prosecution and civil claims for damages.

The authors have asserted their rights to be identified as the authors of this work in accordance with the Copyright, Designs and Patents Act 1988.

First published 2013 by
PALGRAVE MACMILLAN

Palgrave Macmillan in the UK is an imprint of Macmillan Publishers Limited, registered in England, company number 785998, of Houndmills, Basingstoke, Hampshire RG21 6XS.

Palgrave Macmillan in the US is a division of St Martin's Press LLC, 175 Fifth Avenue, New York, NY 10010.

Palgrave Macmillan is the global academic imprint of the above companies and has companies and representatives throughout the world.

Palgrave® and Macmillan® are registered trademarks in the United States, the United Kingdom, Europe and other countries.

ISBN: 978–0–230–22009–6 hardback

ISBN: 978–0–230–22010–2 paperback

This book is printed on paper suitable for recycling and made from fully managed and sustained forest sources. Logging, pulping and manufacturing processes are expected to conform to the environmental regulations of the country of origin.

A catalogue record for this book is available from the British Library.

A catalog record for this book is available from the Library of Congress.

Printed in China

3 4015 07114 5591

READERS' GUIDES TO ESSENTIAL CRITICISM SERIES

CONSULTANT EDITOR: NICOLAS TREDELL

Published

Jago Morrison	The Fiction of Chinua Achebe
Carl Plasa	Tony Morrison: *Beloved*
Carl Plasa	Jean Rhys: *Wide Sargasso Sea*
Nicholas Potter	Shakespeare: *Antony and Cleopatra*
Nicholas Potter	Shakespeare: *Othello*
Nicholas Potter	Shakespeare's Late Plays: *Pericles/Cymbeline/The Winter's Tale/The Tempest*
Steven Price	The Plays, Screenplays and Films of David Mamet
Berthold Schoene-Harwood	Mary Shelley: *Frankenstein*
Nicholas Seager	The Rise of the Novel
Nick Selby	T. S. Eliot: *The Waste Land*
Nick Selby	Herman Melville: *Moby Dick*
Nick Selby	The Poetry of Walt Whitman
David Smale	Salman Rushdie: *Midnight's Children/The Satanic Verses*
Patsy Stoneman	Emily Brontë: *Wuthering Heights*
Susie Thomas	Hanif Kureishi
Nicolas Tredell	Joseph Conrad: *Heart of Darkness*
Nicolas Tredell	Charles Dickens: *Great Expectations*
Nicolas Tredell	William Faulkner: *The Sound and the Fury/As I Lay Dying*
Nicolas Tredell	F. Scott Fitzgerald: *The Great Gatsby*
Nicolas Tredell	Shakespeare: *A Midsummer Night's Dream*
Nicolas Tredell	Shakespeare: *Macbeth*
Nicolas Tredell	The Fiction of Martin Amis
Matthew Woodcock	Shakespeare: *Henry V*
Gillian Woods	Shakespeare: *Romeo and Juliet*
Angela Wright	Gothic Fiction

Forthcoming

Brian Baker	Science Fiction
Nick Bentley	Contemporary British Fiction
Sandie Byrne	The Poetry of Ted Hughes
Sarah Davison	Modernist Literature
Sarah Dewar-Watson	Tragedy
Alan Gibbs	Jewish-American Literature since 1945
Keith Hughes	African-American Literature
Wendy Knepper	Caribbean Literature
Britta Martens	The Poetry of Robert Browning
Merritt Moseley	The Fiction of Pat Barker
Pat Pinsent and Clare Walsh	Children's Literature
Jane Poyner	The Fiction of J. M. Coetzee
Clare Wallace	Contemporary British Drama
David Wheatley	Contemporary British Poetry
Michael Whitworth	Virginia Woolf: *Mrs Dalloway*
Martin Willis	Literature and Science
Andrew Wylie	The Plays of Harold Pinter

Readers' Guides to Essential Criticism
Series Standing Order
ISBN 978–1–4039–0108–8
(outside North America only)

You can receive future titles in this series as they are published by placing a standing order. Please contact your bookseller or, in the case of difficulty, write to us at the address below with your name and address, the title of the series and the ISBN quoted above.

Customer Services Department, Macmillan Distribution Ltd, Houndmills, Basingstoke, Hampshire, RG21 6XS, UK

Contents

'Piping down the valleys wild'

This brief chapter acquaints the reader with Blake's *Songs of Innocence and of Experience* and outlines the aim and objectives of the Guide. It provides an overview of its treatment of the collection in subsequent chapters and introduces the reader to some of the unique bibliographical issues in relation to a text Blake printed and published himself.

Producing *Songs*: 'In a Book that All May Read'

This chapter examines the composition and printing process of *Songs*, from its origins in Blake's *Poetical Sketches*, *An Island in the Moon*, and manuscript notebook, to its inscription on copper as an illuminated book, copies of which were produced by Blake at intervals throughout his lifetime.

Blake's Contemporaries on *Songs*: Simplicity, Madness, Genius, and Swedenborgianism

Following a brief discussion of *Songs*' marketing and sale, this chapter surveys important, albeit miscellaneous, early responses by

Romantic-period writers, including Benjamin Heath Malkin, Henry Crabb Robinson, William Hazlitt, William Wordsworth, Charles Lamb, and Samuel Taylor Coleridge. It also contains definitions and discussions of these writers' critical vocabulary and affiliations.

After commenting on obituaries of Blake, this chapter considers early, broadly admiring, posthumous biographies by John Thomas Smith and Allan Cunningham, before turning to examine the first re-edition of *Songs* by John James Garth Wilkinson.

This chapter addresses landmark mid-Victorian celebrations of *Songs* by Alexander Gilchrist and A. C. Swinburne (an Aestheticist), setting them amid the context of further positive assessments by D. G. Rossetti (a Pre-Raphaelite), James Thomson, and James Smetham. The chapter closes by pitting against these the more negative comments of Henry G. Hewlett.

This chapter explores the endorsement of *Songs* by William Butler Yeats and Edwin Ellis in the 1890s, before moving on to the more ambivalent response of T. S. Eliot in the early twentieth century. It concludes with a discussion of scholarly responses by S. Foster Damon and Geoffrey Keynes.

This chapter addresses the foundations of post-war Blake criticism in the academy, focusing, especially, on the work of the three major

tranT

critics Northrop Frye, David V. Erdman, and Harold Bloom, and their development of Blake Studies towards systematic accounts, respectively, of the role of myth, history, and apocalypse in the poems.

Freedom and Repression in the 1960s and 1970s: Form, Ideology, and Gender

This chapter looks at the emergence of new approaches to *Songs* in the 1960s, including accounts of the formal qualities of individual poems under the rubric of Romanticism, and more ideologically inflected criticism that addressed Blake in terms of politics, psychology, and gender.

Blake's Composite Art in the 1980s and 1990s: Textuality and the Materiality of the Book

In this chapter, we address the influence of poststructuralist theory on ideas of Blake's textuality, the renewal of emphasis on 'composite art' in W. J. T. Mitchell's work, and the emergence of criticism focused on *Songs* as a book associated with Robert Essick and Joseph Viscomi.

Worlding Blake Today: 'Past, Present and Future Sees'

This chapter addresses the most recent trends in Blake criticism, including approaches to *Songs* that have developed issues relating to gender and the body, eco-criticism, and post-colonialism. It ends with a discussion of the emergence of critical interest in reception studies of *Songs*.

Acknowledgements

The authors conferred with each other throughout the writing of this guide, but the writing of the Introduction and Chapters 6–9 is Jon's, and of Chapters 1–5 is Sarah's. David Fallon for his help with the research for Chapter 6, Mark Crosby for his reminder about the 'single-' vs 'double-pull' method, and Tim Whelan for reading and commenting on the chapter section on Henry Crabb Robinson. We are also grateful to Jocelyn Stockley, our meticulous copy-editor, and Nicholas Tredell, whose advice on a first draft was both scrupulous and generous.

List of Abbreviations

Anns	Annotations
BIQ	*Blake: An Illustrated Quarterly*
BR	G. E. Bentley, Jr (2004) *Blake Records*, 2nd edn (New Haven: Yale University Press)
D	D. Dorfman (1969) *Blake in the Nineteenth Century: His Reputation as a Poet from Gilchrist to Yeats* (New Haven and London: Yale University Press)
E	Reference to page numbers in D. V. Erdman (ed.) (1982) *The Complete Poetry & Prose of William Blake*, rev. edn (Berkeley and Los Angeles: University of California Press). Commentary by H. Bloom
Experience	*Songs of Experience*
E-Y	E. J. Ellis and W. B. Yeats (1893) *The Works of William Blake, Poetical, Symbolic, and Critical*, 3 vols (London: B. Quaritch)
G	A. Gilchrist (1998) *The Life of William Blake*, ed. W. G. Robertson (Mineola, NY: Dover Publications)
Innocence	*Songs of Innocence*
Marriage	*The Marriage of Heaven and Hell*
N	Poems in Blake's manuscript notebook, as they appear in Erdman and Moore (eds) (1973)
ODNB	*Oxford Dictionary of National Biography*
OED	*Oxford English Dictionary*
Pl.	Plate
S	A. C. Swinburne (1868) *William Blake: A Critical Essay* (London: J. C. Hotten)
Urizen	*The [First] Book of Urizen*

All quotations of Blake's writings, unless otherwise indicated, refer to Erdman's edition.

INTRODUCTION

'Piping down the valleys wild'

'Piping down the valleys wild' William Blake (1757–1827) began his own 'Introduction', the first poem of what remains the poet, artist and engraver's best-known work. Perhaps with the exception of the lyric that has become the hymn 'Jerusalem', all Blake's most familiar poems, including 'London', 'The Sick Rose', and 'The Tyger', are included in *Songs of Innocence and of Experience* (1794). Like many collections, Blake's evolved over the course of his lifetime, but in ways very different from most other gatherings of poetry. *Innocence* (1789) had a few years of existence on its own, before being joined by *Experience* (1794), but the real distinction of *Songs* is that it was printed by Blake himself on his own press in the form of an illuminated book. Early responses to the poems tended be based on an encounter with the 'composite art' (a phrase that entered Blake criticism relatively early), but an irony of the wider dissemination of the poems from the mid- to later nineteenth century was that it required more traditional forms of typography and the sundering of the verbal and the visual. So Blake's songs have been mainly encountered in the classroom separated from the visual aspects of *Songs of Innocence and of Experience* as published by their author. This situation has changed of late with the internet Blake Archive (discussed at length in Chapter 7) making the illuminated books available to the reader in something like their full glory, but the issue of teaching *Songs* with access to their original form remains a vexed one.

There is a further complication. Part of the evolution of Blake's books was that they were reissued over the course of his life, even in its final decades, in ways that took advantage of the engraver-publisher's freedom to alter the colouring or ordering of different plates, and even the position of individual poems within the collection. So particular songs were moved across the two sections or omitted entirely, as discussed in our first chapter. The Blake Archive can bring comparison of different copies of *Songs* to the classroom, but the collection will always evade any simple idea of authorised form.

1

Most readings have understood the key to the collection to be the relation between Innocence and Experience, 'the Two Contrary States of the Human Soul' as Blake put it in his sub-title, but it soon becomes apparent on any close inspection that the two states are not absolutely different (as the movement of particular poems across them suggests). Many students have embarked on a reading of poems in terms of the signifying contexts of their place in *Innocence* or *Experience*, before realising that this position was altered later in the history of the collection, although this need not mean one cannot advance a reading of a particular 'edition' of *Songs*, to use Joseph Viscomi's terms discussed in Chapter 7. In this study, we have followed a convention of using the unitalicised Innocence and Experience to indicate the state of the soul, as it were, and *Innocence* and *Experience* to indicate the part or the freestanding book (where they were published separately). Where particular poems under discussion moved, we have tried to mention the fact when germane to any particular discussion, but it would have been tedious to have done it in every case, and the reader is duly warned before erecting any interpretative edifice of their own, based on position, or for that matter the colouring of any particular illumination.

Unusually for books in this 'Readers' Guide' series, a whole chapter is devoted to what might be called bibliographical matters to give the student a good sense of the unusual and complicated history of the production of *Songs* as a book (and its editions). One of the consequences of its unique production history is that *Songs* initially reached only a tiny audience. Chapters 2, 3, and 4 of the Guide give in some detail the early reception history of the poems, in a sense prefiguring what has been a recent important addition to criticism of *Songs* discussed in our final chapter, that is, reception history as an object of critical attention in its own right. These early chapters concentrate primarily on British responses, along with brief nods towards North America, although the question of Blake's reception in other places is starting to gain some scholarly attention, as we note at the end of Chapter 9. Chapter 2 surveys responses to *Songs* by writers during Blake's lifetime, including Benjamin Heath Malkin, Henry Crabb Robinson, William Hazlitt, William Wordsworth, Charles Lamb, and S. T. Coleridge. Chapter 3 shows an awareness of *Songs* still muted, but sustained and growing from the time of Blake's death, by obituarists, biographers such as John Thomas Smith and Allan Cunningham, and the Swedenborgian John James Garth Wilkinson. In this early period, key terms for understanding Blake emerged which have retained a surprising longevity in the criticism: 'simplicity', 'pastoral', 'childlikeness', 'genius', 'madness', 'enthusiasm', 'Swedenborgianism', 'mysticism'. Such terms, and others that emerged into prominence later but have come to play a similarly pervasive role in the criticism, like 'composite art', are registered in the index for readers to follow through the book.

With the responses in the 1860s of major literary figures such as Alexander Gilchrist and Algernon Charles Swinburne, *Songs* began to be known to a much wider public, as Chapter 4 shows. Chapter 5 picks up the tale with reference to W. B. Yeats, T. S. Eliot, the major bibliographical work of Geoffrey Keynes, and the systematic study provided by S. Foster Damon. Yet it took time even for Damon's study to be accepted by the academy. It was only with work by critics like Jacob Bronowski, Northrop Frye, David Erdman, and Harold Bloom in the 1940s and 1950s that Blake moved into the critical mainstream and secured a place as a major canonical figure within Romanticism, as Chapter 6 describes. Chapter 7 follows the ramification of this change in status in the proliferation of different kinds of criticism: the formalist studies of the 1960s, many taking the form of books entirely devoted to *Songs*; the development of criticism building on the tradition of Bronowski and Erdman of reading Blake against the ideologies of his time, as a revolutionary poet; other studies, often with a psychoanalytical approach, which understood his revolt against repression to be primarily a question of psychology; and, finally, the emergence of feminist criticism, often questioning how far Blake was in revolt against patriarchal authority. Chapter 8 looks at the major development of a deconstructive criticism much less invested in discovering a unified system in *Songs* and more interested in the way Blake's radicalism lay in the proliferation of meaning and the corrosive questioning of received patterns of thought. At around the same time, interest in 'the composite art' resurfaced, both as a hermeneutic relationship in the work of W. J. T. Mitchell, and as the material form of the book and its means of production pursued by critics such as Robert Essick, Michael Phillips, and Joseph Viscomi. Our final chapter looks at more recent developments, like gender studies, eco-criticism, reception studies, and more global perspectives, and provides some speculation as to where criticism of *Songs* might go from here. Given the complex course charted over the nine chapters of this book, it seems easier to be certain that *Songs* will remain an important text for literary studies than to be confident of what form future responses will take.

This guide is not a guide to Blake criticism in general, that is, its primary concern is with approaches to *Songs of Innocence and of Experience*. Nevertheless, some of the most influential critical responses, including those of Frye and Erdman, for instance, were embedded in works devoted to Blake's whole career. Often such works, following Swinburne, have

tended to use the long and more obscure works usually called 'prophecies' that Blake began engraving from around the mid-1790s as providing
a mythic template from which the earlier *Songs* collection is understood.
These include *The Book of Urizen* (1794), *Milton* (c. 1804–11), and *Jerusalem*
(c. 1804–20). The mythemes and aphorisms of *The Marriage of Heaven and
Hell* (1790) have also had a rich part to play in criticism of *Songs*, not least
because the two texts partially overlapped in their early development
and first printings. Necessarily, we have had to bring these other works
by Blake into the discussion when they are the basis of an interpretation
of *Songs*. Chapters 2 to 4 have applied the same criteria to discussions of
Blake's biography and temperament.

The work of making sense of *Songs* has gone on for some time now
in numerous individual articles and books. We do not presume to con-
duct an exhaustive survey here; for this, the student might consult
G. E. Bentley's *Blake Bibliography* and the various updates in *Blake /
An Illustrated Quarterly*. Our guide is essential in so far it covers what
we regard as 'essential', but the reader should not assume that everything worthwhile said about Blake's *Songs* is covered in these pages.
Furthermore, the general organisation of the guide takes a chronological form, a relatively easy decision for the criticism prior to the
proliferation of academic studies from the 1950s. Thereafter, we have
tried to map critical responses in terms of the emergence of key critical
methodologies, many motivated by changes in the academic study of
English Literature beyond Blake studies. These include, for instance,
the emergence of the deconstructive and post-structuralist criticism
discussed in Chapter 8, but also the powerful sway of the category of
Romanticism, especially in a consolidated form from the late 1950s,
more easily assumed to be simply a category of nature implicit somehow in the text, than another critical movement. The category continues to be a powerful one even now, and has played its part both in
consolidating Blake's importance to English Literature more generally,
but also in eliciting hostile responses that may or may not have more
to do with the sins of canonicity than with anything to be found in
Songs. Whether Blake himself would have wanted the sanctity of critical tradition is an interesting question. Certainly he tends to emerge in
nineteenth-century criticism as a counter-cultural figure. In any case,
the final four chapters of the guide do not rigidly adhere to the chronological structure. If some important later work seems more obviously
relevant to some earlier development than the other criticism being
written in its own time, then it has been discussed in relation to the
earlier development, but overall we have tried to show how different
responses to *Songs* have emerged in relation to each other.

In general terms, this guide is written with the idea that it will help elucidate criticism encountered by the student in the library, online, or from the bookshop, explaining the intellectual context of particular readings in terms of their own time and the development of Blake criticism. But it is not intended to replace an encounter with *Songs of Innocence and of Experience*. If the reader is encouraged to seek out the criticism we discuss, furthermore, then so much the better. Governing our selection has been the idea that students will want to know why and how, for instance, the idea of 'pastoral' has been seen as relevant to Blake or in what ways 'composite art' has been used as a term of analysis in relation to *Songs*. Blake himself once suggested: that 'which is made Explicit to the Idiot is not worth my care'. Our aim has been to elucidate the responses of others without treating anyone as an idiot: 'The wisest of the Ancients considerd what is not too Explicit as the fittest for Instruction because it rouzes the faculties to act' (E702). *Songs* necessarily will remain inexplicit, the complexities that lie within its seeming simplicity continuing to rouse the imaginations of generations of readers. Our hope is that this guide to the criticism of the most debated of Blake's illuminated books will make future readers aware of possibilities within the responses of the past which may provide the stimuli for their own faculties in their present.

CHAPTER ONE

Producing *Songs*: 'In a Book that All May Read'

Songs of Innocence and of Experience (1794) is a book of two halves. Its first edition brings together an earlier illuminated book of 1789, *Songs of Innocence*, with *Songs of Experience*, first issued as a discrete illuminated volume in 1794, slightly earlier in the year than the joint *Songs*. Two halves, then, or perhaps two wholes – for as we shall see, in the course of the next three or so decades Blake continued to issue copies of *Innocence* and *Experience* separately as well as together. Likewise some readers – for there were readers, even within Blake's lifetime – read one and not the other, and those who owned both *Innocence* and *Experience* could and did have them bound together, or have the combined *Songs* separated. Readers, including William and Dorothy Wordsworth, Samuel Taylor Coleridge, and William Hazlitt, could encounter Blake's poems and designs in other ways too, as we discuss in Chapter 2, and here our arithmetic of halves and wholes breaks down: individual lyrics or groups of lyrics from *Songs* were hived off, copied out by hand and circulated, excerpted and published in reviews and miscellanies, even sung and heard. Here we see Blake's illuminated book, a distinct, etched, hand-printed, and often hand-coloured artefact, turned to a variety of forms and uses. That said, a degree of adaptability is written into *Songs of Innocence and of Experience* itself, a collection of poems whose ordering in particular Blake was liable to change. Over the years from 1789 to 1827, working with his wife Catherine, he assembled some 25 copies of *Songs of Innocence*, 13 of *Songs of Experience* (pairing some together), and 16 copies of the joint *Songs*.[1] In the majority of copies, the order of poems varies, and as time went on some poems even migrated from one book to the other.

This chapter aims to give as neutral an account of Blake's productive processes as possible, albeit informed and mediated by the pioneering work of two recent studies, Joseph Viscomi's *Blake and the Idea of the Book*

(1993) and Michael Phillips's *The Creation of the Songs* (2000), whose approaches are discussed in Chapter 8. The chapter is in two parts. The first examines Blake's composition and drafting of some of the poems in manuscript in his first collection, *Poetical Sketches* (1783), an unpublished satire, *An Island in the Moon* (c. 1784–5), and his notebook (in 1793). The second describes the distinctive method of printing by which Blake produced *Songs* as an illuminated book, and also takes an overview of the run of copies that he produced throughout his life, noting some of the differences and similarities between them, and explaining how these might shape our interpretations of individual poems.

THE GENESIS OF *SONGS* IN MANUSCRIPT

Songs of Innocence, Poetical Sketches and *An Island in the Moon*

Before Blake's piper made a rural pen, before he sang, before he piped, even, the *Songs of Innocence* had begun. For four of the poems of *Innocence* had already appeared in earlier works by Blake. In 1783, Blake's first collection of writings, *Poetical Sketches*, was privately printed in conventional letterpress (and without illustrations). Handwritten in one copy is a version of 'Laughing Song'. Versions of 'Holy Thursday', 'Nurses Song', and 'The Little Boy Lost' appeared shortly afterwards in about 1784, in a manuscript satire by Blake, again unillustrated, known as *An Island in the Moon*. So remarkable and unusual is *Songs of Innocence* as a material artefact, and so celebrated, nowadays, are its poems that it is easy to chart its development only from 1789, the date that appears on its illuminated title page. To begin the story of its material composition earlier, though, in 1783, reminds us that despite the piper's spontaneity, and indeed Blake's own claims later in life that he raised up entire sequences of lines 'without Labour or Study', *Songs* was subject to drafting and revision (E729).

Relative to *Songs* and later illuminated books such as *The Marriage of Heaven and Hell* (1790), *America: A Prophecy* (1793) and *Jerusalem* (1804–20), *Poetical Sketches* and *An Island in the Moon* are little commented on today. Within Blake's lifetime the former was mentioned but seldom and there is no record of the latter being read – indeed *Island* was not printed and so not widely accessible until the early twentieth century (although its songs may have been sung by Blake at informal intellectual gatherings called 'salons'). Present neglect is egregious; the bold formal experiments of *Poetical Sketches*, the exuberant, carnivalesque dialogue of *An Island in the Moon*: both deserve attention in their own right, as well as for how they make sound strains of sensibility and satire, and an affinity to popular culture, that run throughout Blake's writings.[2] They are also, of course, significant as precursors to *Songs*.

Poetical Sketches comprises an array of materials – 'lyrics, seasons poems, dramatic sketches, created mythology, and experimental prose just one step removed from blank verse' (Bentley 2001, 79) – that according to the volume's 'Advertisement', written by Blake's friend and sponsor the Reverend Anthony Stephen Mathew, were composed by Blake between his twelfth and his twentieth year. Noteworthy for our purposes are the poems that show Blake 'working out his own voice within the English pastoral tradition' (Phillips 2000, 6), including two songs ('How sweet I roamed from field to field' and 'I love the jocund dance') quoted admiringly by Benjamin Heath Malkin in 1806 along-side, and indeed undistinguished from, poems from *Songs of Innocence and of Experience* (*BR* 569–70). These two songs belong to the printed text of *Poetical Sketches*; however, the 'Song 2d by a young Shepherd' that was to be adapted by Blake into 'Laughing Song' appears as one of three 'Songs by Mr Blake' 'transcribed in an unknown contempo-rary hand' in a copy of the *Sketches*, on the blank pages preceding the text. In the most comprehensive study to date of the genesis of *Songs* in manuscript, Michael Phillips calls Blake's 'choice of language' in both 'Song 2d' and 'Laughing Song' 'simple, native and unaffected in rela-tion to the still prevailing fashion for a Latinate poetic diction'. While the names in 'Song 2d' of *Poetical Sketches* are classical (Edessa, Lyca, and Emilie), though, they are translated in *Innocence*'s 'Laughing Song' into the vernacular (Mary, Susan, and Emily). In using native English names, Blake makes the same 'signal departure from convention' in *Songs of Innocence* as Edmund Spenser made in *The Shepheardes Calender* (1579) (Phillips 2000, 6–7).

By contrast, as a primary site of the largely pastoral songs of *Innocence*, the urban, domestic setting of *An Island in the Moon* is initially incongruous. In the manner of contemporary semi-scripted popular dramatic entertainments and witty literary magazines (see England 1970, 3–29, and Hecimovich 2008, 32–5), Blake's manuscript stages a skewed dialogue between a number of punningly-named characters (Quid the Cynic, Etruscan Column the Antiquarian, Obtuse Angle, Mrs Nannicantipot), variously interpreted by twentieth-century critics either as analogues of individuals known to Blake, or as caricatured social or intellectual types, examples of which, says the narrator of *Island*, would have been so familiar 'you would think you was among your friends' (E449). *An Island in the Moon* is part of a tradition of writing

that runs from Renaissance satires of learned folly, through Laurence
Sterne's *Tristam Shandy* (1760–7), to James Joyce's *Ulysses* (1922). It is
'something between a burlesque and a satire and a comic vignette of
a self-important society in which everybody talks but nobody listens:
"their tongues went in question & answer, but their thoughts were
otherwise employd"' (Bentley 2001, 81; E449). This dialogue is punc-
tuated by some twenty-one outbursts of song modelled by Blake on
urban ballads or popular pastorals. In Chapter 11, 'at the house of
Steelyard the Lawgiver' (E462), these songs include Obtuse Angle's
rendition of 'Upon a holy Thursday', which makes the company sit
'silent for a quarter of an hour'; Mrs Nannicantipot's rendition of 'my
grandmothers song' (which in *Innocence* becomes 'Nurse's Song'); and
Quid's rendition of 'O father father where are you going' (*Innocence*'s
'The Little Boy Lost').

The to and fro that we hear between conversational combatants in
An Island in the Moon is also inscribed in the difference between their
songs. In Obtuse Angle's 'Upon a holy Thursday', children walk 'two &
two' overseen by 'revrend men', while in Mrs Nannicantipot's 'grandmothers song', children 'go & play till the light fades away' and 'leaped
& shouted & laughed' (E462–3). 'Whether or not she realizes that it is
a counterpoint to "Holy Thursday", her song offers a Blakean contrary,'
writes Steve Newman, inferring in the *Island* poems and implying in
Songs of Innocence a dialogic play of what the title-page of the combined
Songs calls 'Contrary States' (Newman 2007, 145).

As Phillips has documented, the changes Blake made to the texts of
these three songs when transferring them to *Songs of Innocence* were
relatively minor. But the claims Phillips makes for the influence of *An
Island in the Moon* are on a larger scale. The manuscript is, he writes,
'the matrix of the *Songs*. Composed of parody and satire, street cries
and nursery rhymes, dramatic personae and ironic point of view, it
contains the essential elements that formed the basis of Blake's conception' (Phillips 2000, 1). One thing to note about Phillips' description
of *An Island in the Moon* here is its implication that the social, urban
engagement that we perceive most readily in later *Experience* poems
such as 'London' also framed certain lyrics of *Innocence* in their earliest
incarnation.

In the early to mid-1780s, when *Poetical Sketches* and *An Island in the
Moon* were produced, Blake was living, as he did for most of his life,
in London. Having completed a seven-year engraving apprenticeship
with James Basire in 1779, Blake was active as a professional engraver,
largely engaged in inscribing onto sheets of copper designs made by
other artists. Still, by the middle of 1784, when he was composing

An Island in the Moon, it seemed that 'every citizen with a project or a little stock in trade [could] seek his fortune as one of the "skilful and able"' (Erdman 1977, 90). Both personally and nationally, this time held the promise of prosperity (see also Bentley 2001, 78).

Key to the publication of *Poetical Sketches* and a satiric impetus of *An Island in the Moon* was Blake's involvement from 1782 to perhaps 1785 with Harriet Mathew, her husband the Reverend Anthony Stephen Mathew, and their circle, especially as it met in Harriet's salons or 'conversaziones' at 27 Rathbone Place, their home. Harriet Mathew was a generous patron, especially of musicians and artists. Her conversaziones were frequented by many such (see G 46–7 and Bentley 1958), including, according to the recollections of the artist and antiquarian John Thomas Smith, one 'William Blake, the artist, to whom she [...] had been truly kind. There I have often heard him read and sing several of his poems. He was listened to by the company with profound silence, and allowed by most of the visitors to possess original and extraordinary merit' (*BR* 30). It is possible that one of the poems sung by Blake at these gatherings was to become a song of *Innocence.*

With the Mathew salon, we see Blake participating in the informal intellectual life of his day – a point that is worth emphasising because it has rather been Blake's isolation (and allegedly, willed isolationism) that has been stressed by certain later critics, influenced by the fact that with illuminated books like *Songs of Innocence and of Experience,* Blake was, atypically for the time, not only the author, but also the printer and publisher of his works. Undoubtedly a participant in contemporary intellectual and artistic circles, though, Blake tended not to be received as an equal. His position in the hierarchy is suggested by the politics of the puff (the advertisement) written for *Poetical Sketches* by Anthony Mathew. In common with other labouring-class writers – the 'Thresher Poet', Stephen Duck, of the 1730s, the milkmaid Ann Yearsley and ploughman Robert Burns of the 1780s, and indeed the 'Peasant Poet' John Clare of the 1830s – Blake, as a working engraver, was introduced into the literary marketplace by means of an authorising apology. As Mathew writes, acknowledging in Blake a lack of the formal schooling so bucked against by the 'School Boy' of *Songs:*

■ The following sketches were the production of untutored youth [...] [H]is talents having been wholly directed to the attainment of excellence in his profession, he has been deprived of the leisure requisite to such a revisal of these sheets, as might have rendered them less unfit to meet the public eye.

> Conscious of the irregularities and defects to be found in almost every page, his friends have still believed that they possessed a poetic originality, which merited some respite from oblivion. These their opinions remain, however, to be now reproved or confirmed by a less partial public. □
>
> (*BR* 29)

It is not clear what Mathew perceived the volume's 'irregularities and defects' to be: certainly the volume as printed contained many typographical errors; varying and idiosyncratic metrical patterns that were to be found by Malkin 'to leave harmony unregarded' (*BR* 572); and subject matter, in 'Edward the Third', that seems to criticise English imperialism. What is clearer, albeit in its obfuscation, is Mathews' euphemism: distracted by training for his 'profession', Blake might as well be a middle-class clergyman as a labouring-class engraver (Bentley 2001, 76). Certainly authorising peritext, or framing, like this, which proliferates in eighteenth-century publications, is dispensed with by Blake in his independent printing and publishing of *Songs*. Yet the tenor of Mathew's remarks continued to mark the collection epitextually: his critical idiom and mingling of praise ('poetic originality') with blame ('irregularities and defects') are to be found in the contemporary reception of *Songs* likewise, as Chapter 2 surveys.

Songs of Experience and the Manuscript Notebook

We have seen that Blake's accumulation of poems for *Songs of Innocence* began over five years before the book's first publication in 1789. By 1791, Blake had started work on a companion volume, *Songs of Experience*, the majority of whose poems he drafted by hand over the next two years in a notebook, originally a sketchbook belonging to his younger brother Robert.

Since printing *Songs of Innocence*, Blake had been busy: producing numerous engravings and book illustrations for commercial publishers, including for Erasmus Darwin's *Botanic Garden* (1791) and Mary Wollstonecraft's *Original Stories from Real Life* (1791), and printing further illuminated books, *The Book of Thel* (1789), and *The Marriage of Heaven and Hell* (c. 1790), the first of the so-called 'prophetic books'. The fiery energy of revolution was burning just beyond English shores, in France, although in the early 1790s it seemed 'still in England [to be] damned and frozen by cold abstractions and proclamations of "Thou shalt not"' (Erdman 1977, 250).

If *An Island in the Moon* may be regarded as the matrix of *Songs*, then the notebook – held now by the British Library in London and accessible online – is the creative hub of a lot more besides.[3] Jostling together on its pages; drafted, revised, sometimes erased and written over; are passages of text and designs that were to be worked by Blake into numerous subsequent collections, including small drawings which would become the emblem book *For Children: The Gates of Paradise* (1793); illustrations of John Milton's *Paradise Lost*; prose passages about the contemporary art market and artistic vision (published by later editors as *Public Address* and *A Vision of the Last Judgment*); passages of a heterodox religious poem (posthumously stitched together and known as *The Everlasting Gospel*); vituperative personal and political epigrams; and some fifty poems, eighteen of which were to find a place in *Songs of Experience*.[4] The notebook also contains a 'Motto to the Songs of Innocence & of Experience':

■ The Good are attracted by Mens perceptions
And Think not for themselves
Till Experience teaches them to catch
And to cage the Fairies & Elves

And then the Knave begins to snarl
And the Hypocrite to howl
And all his good Friends shew their private ends
And the Eagle is known from the Owl. □

(E499)

This motto marks the first time the conflated title of *Songs* was used, although it was not to be printed within the collection.

The Notebook is fascinating for the hints it gives of autobiography: 'I say I shant live five years | And if I live one it will be a Wonder,' Blake writes in 1793, perhaps expressing a fear for his personal safety as counter-revolutionary controls took root in Britain, and any criticism of its government, monarchy, or national church was discountenanced and indeed punished (see Phillips 2000, 112, and Phillips, 1994). It has also proved fascinating as a kind of puzzle, an enigma: a scene of multiple compositional traces that a series of scholars and editors, including Dante Gabriel Rossetti, John Sampson, Geoffrey Keynes, David Erdman, and Michael Phillips have attempted to order and decode. Finally, like *Poetical Sketches* and *An Island in the Moon* only more so, the Notebook shows the multiple bursts of vision, perhaps the faltering stops and starts of *re*vision, that went into the making of *Songs*.

From 1787 (Robert had died, aged twenty-four, that year), following on from a few pages of his brother's drawings, Blake filled the right-hand pages ('rectos') and some of the facing pages ('versos') of the notebook with designs, primarily the emblems for *The Gates of Paradise*. He then flipped the book over and continued to use it, initially for poems, filling up every scrap of space with remarkable economy, and adding new materials until at least 1818 (Erdman and Moore 1973, 1). The notebook is not always a primary site of composition: some poems (for example drafts of 'The Clod & the Pebble' and 'Holy Thursday') are written continuously in the same ink or pencil, with minimal crossings out, signalling the likelihood that they were fair copies, that is, transcriptions of drafts that had been made elsewhere, whether on scraps of paper or in Blake's head (Erdman and Moore 1973, 8). Even fair copy poems such as 'London', though, could be extensively altered, with words, lines, or whole stanzas struck out, adjusted, or added. These poems may not have germinated on the page, but it was here that they were coaxed to near fruition. Take this draft of stanzas at once foreign and familiar:

■ I wander thro each dirty street
Near where the dirty Thames does flow
And see in every face I meet
Marks of weakness marks of woe

In every cry of every man
In every voice of every child
In every voice in every ban
The german forged links I hear. □

(N109)

Details of punctuation and capital letters aside, four peculiarities here might trip the eye or ear. Three of these are adjusted on the notebook page. 'German forged links' becomes 'mind-forgd manacles', metamorphosing what David Erdman sees as a precise historical and national reference to the counter-revolutionary activities of the Germans into a more complex, penetrating indictment of the way in which Londoners are not simply oppressed from without but internalise their repression, conforming themselves to a position of slavery (socio-economic, political, and imaginative) (Erdman 1977, 277). More subtly, patterns of repetition are realigned when 'every voice of every child' becomes 'every Infant's cry of fear', and the poem's narrator 'mark[s]' rather than 'see[s]' the Londoners' distress, rendering his point of view curiously projective (so perhaps unreliable) as well as prophetic (see Glen 1983, 211–12).

Discriminating the different shades of ink and nib-widths that mark 'London' in its entirety, Phillips suggests in *The Creation of the Songs* that Blake revisited the notebook version of the poem a total of five times. But one final change to the lines cited above waited to be realised in *Songs of Experience* itself, when the repeated adjective 'dirty' was replaced by the more resonant 'charter'd'. This was a word that Blake had used previously in the notebook, describing London's 'chartered streams' in the poem 'Thames'. 'Tho born on the cheating banks of the Thames', the poem's speaker imagines that the 'blasts of fear' that he endures in his own country might be mitigated or transformed by the freedoms achieved in post-revolutionary America: 'The Ohio shall wash his stains from me I I was born a slave but I long to be free' (N.113; see also Phillips 2000, 44–7). 'From this point in the *Manuscript Notebook*,' suggests Phillips, 'the politics of the winter of 1792 and spring of 1793 become a noticeable force in the making of *Songs of Experience*' (Phillips 2000, 47). The substitution of 'cheating' by 'chartered' in the published version of the poem (Erdman 1977, 276–7) provides a more subtle sense of the ambiguities of Britain's supposed liberties, perhaps picking up on Thomas Paine's critique of royal charters in his *Rights of Man* (see Chapters 6 and 7).

The changes Blake made to 'London' suggest an accretion of complexity. More is gained than is lost, it seems, when the text of the poem is transferred from the seedbed of the notebook to the plot of *Experience*. And yet there are casualties: texts revised into palimpsests are mined for their uppermost layer only, and entire lyrics such as 'Thames' are passed over. Once engraved on the copper-plates of an illuminated book, by contrast the texts (if not the order) of Blake's poems tended to be fixed – a matter of Blake's choice rather than of material necessity (see Viscomi 1993, 91, 373). Editors have tended historically to favour the texts given in *Songs of Experience* as Blake's most fully realised effort, relegating not only the substance of Blake's revisions but also the very fact that he revised at all to textual end-notes.[5] For this reason the notebook discloses a fascinating prehistory, tempering *Songs of Experience* with variant readings. It also situates the precursor poems of *Experience* as part of an untidy network of texts and images that Blake was to use, re-use, and redraft elsewhere, exhibiting an open-endedness that poststructuralist and postmodernist critics claim to see in the illuminated *Songs* also (see Chapter 8).

While drafting poems in the notebook, Blake himself acted as an editor, drawing a vertical line in pencil through those poems he considered placing together in a collection. On the same page as a draft of 'The Fly', the last of the drafts used in *Songs of Experience*, he even made a note of poems he considered engraving 'On 1 plate' of copper: 'O lapwing &c', 'An answer to the Parson', 'Experiment', 'Riches', 'If you trap &c' (N.101). As it happens, these poems were neither grouped on the same plate nor included in *Experience* at all, but as Phillips notes:

> ■ this memorandum [...] offers our only glimpse in the creation of the *Songs* into the process of Blake arranging word and image on copper, and is all the more valuable for being a negative example. This is an experiment in arrangement and design that failed. As such, it suggests that as much trial and error took place at this stage in production as the writing of the poems in the *Manuscript Notebook* themselves disclose. □
>
> (Phillips 2000, 86)

Songs as Illuminated Book

To arrive only now at *Songs of Innocence and of Experience* as it was composed, collected, engraved on plates of copper, hand-printed, and coloured as an illuminated book might seem belated. Once you have seen one of Blake's books, perhaps online using the Blake Archive, in a library consulting a facsimile, or if you are lucky, turning the pages of an original – white-gloved for most of us now, and watched by hawk-eyed custodians – there is no turning back. Witness the dynamism of the title-pages, whose hand-cut lettering winds out into ribbons, unfolds into leaf, or in the case of *Experience*, 'spreads like a bar across the page' (Damon 1924, 284), or puzzle over the curiously meek-looking tiger posed beneath the savage grandeur of Blake's verse: such illuminations are part of *Songs'* complexity. Not only the illustrations included in *Songs*, but also their colouring, and the form of their letters as Blake disposed them on the page, amplify and enrich Blake's poetry in a way that influences the interpretations and experiences of all those who read the books that issued from his press. Indeed, as we shall see in the next few chapters, reports by Blake's contemporaries and near-contemporaries of his illuminated books show that they are intrigued as much (and often more) by the pictures that accompany his poems and the ornamentation that embellishes them as by the texts themselves. Yet even to call these pictures 'illustrations' or to suggest they merely 'accompany' Blake's poetry is to suggest a subordination of image to text that seems inadequate to describe the illuminated books (especially as Blake's style from the mid-1790s became more pictorial, an issue that we touch on below). Instead we might adopt a term introduced in the mid-twentieth century by the critic Jean Hagstrum, 'composite art', which is glossed by Northrop Frye as a 'radical form of mixed art' which must be read as a unity (quoted by Mitchell 1978, 3&n.). (We subject this topic to further scrutiny in Chapter 8.) But why is the way in which Blake produced *Songs* so significant? Just what is an illuminated book in any case? And why is it worth thinking about and looking at *Songs* not just in typographic editions (by Keynes, Erdman, or Stevenson, say) but as composite art, as text and image combined?

Our emphasis so far in this chapter has been textual. We have seen that Blake ventured both to write poetry and to have it published before he came to print *Songs of Innocence* – the first illuminated part of *Songs* – in 1789. Where *An Island in the Moon* remained unpublished, in manuscript, *Poetical Sketches* was privately printed for Blake in conventional letterpress. Neither text was illustrated. The illuminated *Innocence* therefore represents a marked departure from these methods. It makes sense, though, in the context of Blake's wider practices at the time. Nowadays we think of Blake primarily as a poet, but in his lifetime he was more widely known as a visual artist, or perhaps more precisely because he was a professional engraver, as an artisan, 'a worker in a skilled trade, a craftsperson' (*OED*). Blake made his living not through the sale of poetry, or even of illuminated books such as *Songs*, but through commercial book illustration, when he was employed by publishers to provide designs to accompany other people's texts, sometimes simply engraving drawings by other artists, sometimes conceiving as well as engraving the designs himself, and sometimes producing drawings that went on to be engraved by neater and more fashionable contemporaries. Another substantial source of income was the commissions he received from a small number of patrons including Thomas Butts (1757–1845) and John Linnell (1792–1882) for his own paintings, drawings, and engravings, the subjects of which included the Bible and poetry by Milton and Dante. In this guide we focus on responses to *Songs* – but it is worth noting in passing that the most mainstream and widely accessible responses to Blake's works during his lifetime were not to the illuminated books at all. Instead, critics picked up in reviews (with various degrees of antipathy) on the drawings Blake made to illustrate Robert Blair's poem *The Grave* (1808) and the small exhibition he mounted of his paintings in 1809, with an accompanying 'Descriptive Catalogue'.[6]

The normal practice with illustrated books like *The Grave* was to handle the printing of texts and images separately. Texts were printed from casts of lead type laid in a wooden press by a printer, each regularly-formed letter at a time. Letters and punctuation marks were raised up and out of the lead in what is called 'relief'. Raised surfaces were then

see what Viscomi calls 'Blake's relaxed attitude to the *Songs*', whereby each copy of an illuminated book as he issues it is complete, whether or not it contains all the plates included in other copies (Viscomi 1993, 273, 268). In the case of another poem, 'A Divine Image', the consequences of Blake's conditional attitude towards completeness were more far-reaching. Blake drafted 'A Divine Image', which like 'The Human Abstract' in *Experience* answers 'The Divine Image' of *Innocence*, alongside other poems in his notebook in 1791–3. However, for some unknown reason he chose to include it in only one copy of *Songs*, produced in 1795. As a final twist to the tale, this copy of *Songs* was only located in 1980: before this date 'A Divine Image' tended not to be reproduced by editors as part of the collection.

A thornier issue for modern critics has been the order of poems in *Songs*, which for the most part was different in every copy until about 1818 – although the final seven copies of the book were ordered exactly alike (Viscomi 1993, 273). While Blake himself wrote out a list, headed 'The Order in which the Songs of Innocence & of Experience ought to be pages & placed', this corresponds to only one copy of the book printed in 1821 (Viscomi, 335–6).[8] The planned order that Blake in fact observed in the last seven copies was that of his own copy of *Songs*, a book he printed in 1795 but kept near at hand until 1819 when he sold it to John Linnell (Viscomi, 273, 311). It is this planned order that tends to be observed by modern editors of the collection. Critical debate about the meaning and possible motivations of the different orderings of *Songs of Innocence and of Experience* has been vigorous. Did Blake intend each copy of *Songs* to be unique, or were differences before 1818 simply the result of accident – of a working printer putting together sheets of paper in the order that they came to his hand? Was the relative fixity after 1818 an effort at standardisation, or simply a handy reminder at a time when Blake had no copies of *Songs* left in stock, even his own, and when printing sessions were less frequent and spaced at longer intervals? Such debate around Blake's conception of *Songs* as a book is explored further in Chapter 8.

One final example of *Songs'* flexibility deserves consideration: the question of which poems belong in which part of the collection. For before 1818, the boundaries between *Innocence* and *Experience* were curiously permeable. In 1789, 'The Little Girl Lost', 'The Little Girl Found', 'The School Boy', and 'The Ancient Bard' appeared in *Songs of Innocence*. By 1795, when *Innocence* and *Experience* were first printed together as the joint *Songs*, the 'Little Girl' poems had migrated to *Experience*, perhaps to balance up the number of pages contained in each part of the collection. The movement of 'The School Boy' was more 'erratic', as it bounced from *Innocence* to *Experience* in 1795, back to *Innocence*, then again to *Experience* in 1818. 'The Voice of the Ancient Bard' remained in *Innocence* until 1818, when it moved to *Experience* for good (Viscomi 1993, 273–4). These migrations involve us in problems of interpretation, whether intended by Blake or no: for how we understand the tone and meaning of individual poems in *Songs* tends to be influenced by the part of the collection in which they fall. For example, 'The Voice of the Ancient Bard' might seem to present 'an older and wiser version of the figure we have followed from carefree piping to prophetic indignation, from growth into and out of innocence'. This narrative is facilitated by the poem's inclusion in the *Experience* part of the joint *Songs*: but how would it have been interpreted before 1818 when it fell in *Songs of Innocence*, not least as the book might have been issued as a stand-alone volume (see Leader 1981, 190–1)?

Having emphasised not only the flexibility but also the proliferation of copies of *Innocence*, *Experience*, and the joint *Songs*, virtually all of which differ one from the other if only in colouring, it remains to make an important qualification. For more typically with books at the time – books that were printed in letterpress – far more copies, generally hundreds, would be produced within a single edition or print-run (and these copies, of course, would be virtually identical, homogenised by the mechanical means of their reproduction). Simply put: if we think of *Songs* as a printed book, then Blake printed very few of them indeed. This small number of copies is more comprehensible when we remember that from the mid-1790s, Blake's style of printing became more pictorial: and in fact, asserts Viscomi, 'when compared to the press runs of original prints of Gainsborough, Barry, [and] Stubbs', the number of illuminated books Blake produced is 'considerable' (Viscomi 1993, 338). Nonetheless, the fact remains that there were not many copies of *Songs of Innocence and of Experience* to go around. This could not but severely delimit the extent of Blake's audience – and condition the extent and quality of critical responses to *Songs*, likewise.

CHAPTER TWO

Blake's Contemporaries on *Songs*: Simplicity, Madness, Genius, and Swedenborgianism

The individuals whose reactions to Blake we consider in this chapter were writing before any editions of his poetry besides his own illuminated books were available. This is therefore a story of partial, if sometimes remarkably acute, interpretations, of snatched porings-over borrowed books, of preconceived ideas about genius, and madness, articulated. There is no agreed script. Benjamin Heath Malkin launched a nuanced critique of *Songs'* simplicity in *A Father's Memoirs of His Child* (1806) but made his mark primarily by bequeathing accessible transcriptions of some of Blake's texts to his readers, to do with, what they would. Henry Crabb Robinson transmuted Blake's apparent madness into a form of Romantic genius in an 1811 essay for the magazine *Vaterländisches Museum*, but his efforts, which were to be replicated to some degree by anti-materialist commentators in the early nineteenth century, were felt mainly more diffusely, as writers such as William Hazlitt, William Wordsworth, and Charles Lamb responded in their own ways, usually in private correspondence, to those parts of the *Songs'* poetry he made available to them. An important line of mystical commentary, sympathetic to the truth-claims of Blake's visions, was set in train in by Charles Augustus Tulk, a disciple of the unorthodox theologian Emanuel Swedenborg, who lent Samuel Taylor Coleridge his own copy of *Songs* in 1818 and who may have authored the blazing defence of Blake's myth-making imagination in the *London University Magazine* in 1830 (touched on in Chapter 3). Tulk was to hand the Swedenborgian baton to James John Garth Wilkinson, with whose early Victorian edition of *Songs of Innocence and of Experience* (1839) we end the next chapter.

The present chapter begins by ranging beyond Blake's production of the *Songs* as we described it in Chapter 1 to examine the books' dissemination, sale, and audience. We next discuss responses to *Songs of Innocence and of Experience* composed during Blake's lifetime (1757–1827), focusing on key writings by Malkin, Crabb Robinson, and Coleridge, and taking in scattered remarks by William Hazlitt, William Wordsworth, and Charles Lamb along the way. We also comment briefly on James Montgomery's printing of *Innocence*'s 'The Chimney-Sweeper' in a politically-orientated anthology of 1824. In the course of our discussion, we pause to define critical issues and terms – simplicity, enthusiasm, madness, genius, mysticism, Swedenborgianism (all terms in our index) – that recur in criticism of *Songs of Innocence and of Experience* through the ages.

Even though, as in the previous chapter, we attempt to be even-handed, the unprogrammatic quality of these early responses to Blake, in addition to the chronological proximity of critics' priorities to Blake's own, leads us to dwell for longer on individual responses than we do in later chapters. We also attempt, as lines of inheritance are clearer in this early period, to comment objectively on the actual historical influence of individual interventions, as well as to signal when we find interpretations of *Songs* particularly prescient or appealing. Malkin and Crabb Robinson thus emerge as perhaps unexpected heroes, even when compared to the astuteness (and nowadays, fame) of Coleridge or Hazlitt.

EARLY OWNERS, DISSEMINATION, AND SALE

Within Blake's lifetime, the few who acquired *Songs*, usually at less than its advertised price, tended to be friends, patrons, or fellow artists (a list is assembled by G. E. Bentley, Jr, in *Blake Books* (1977) and its *Supplement*).[1] Blake knew some of these customers in advance, whilst others were introduced to him by personal connection (John Linnell, Blake's patron, for instance, fostered a late sale of *Songs* to the collector James Vine in 1821) (Viscomi 1993, 334–5). Unusually for the time, when intermediary booksellers handled sales, Blake tended to make personal contact with those who bought books from him.[2] However, there are some indications that in the 1790s he brought, or tried to bring, his cottage productions onto the high street, writing a 'Prospectus' of 1793, addressed 'To the Public' and advertising *Songs*, perhaps as a flyer, 'prepared to accompany display copies at [Joseph] Johnson's and other friendly booksellers' (Davies 1999, 218–19). Johnson (1738–1809), a publisher and bookseller, was an important figure in literary London, around whom orbited writers and political radicals such as William Godwin, Mary Wollstonecraft, and Thomas Paine. He is known to have commissioned commercial engraving work from Blake, although whether he actually did display or sell copies of *Songs* at his London shop remains uncertain. At stake here would be the suggestion that Blake sought the isolation he found.

The earliest readers of *Songs of Innocence and of Experience* were in any case not only those known to have owned a copy. It was common at the time to share and show off books, displaying them to visitors, lending and borrowing them, and reading – and like Blake at Harriet Mathews' salon, even singing – parts of them aloud (see Chapter 1). Indeed it was not only Blake who sang or recited the *Songs*. One of Linnell's 'most vivid recollections of those days was of hearing Crabb Robinson recite Blake's poem "The Tiger"' at the home of Eliza Aders. 'It was a most impressive performance,' relates Linnell's biographer Alfred T. Story, 'and Linnell, catching the spirit of it, used to recite the poem as he had heard it done with great effect' (*BR* 395). It is by such indirect means that some of the most famous of Blake's early readers gained access to his work. Coleridge, for example, was lent a copy of *Songs of Innocence and of Experience* by Tulk; Hazlitt heard poems including 'The Chimney Sweeper' read aloud (again by Crabb Robinson); and William and Dorothy Wordsworth came across 'Holy Thursday', 'Laughing Song', and 'The Tyger' most probably as they were printed by Malkin in *A Father's Memoirs of His Child* (1806), copying them into one of their Grasmere notebooks (*BR* 336, 309, 571n.). The texts of Blake's *Songs* were made available in other ways too. 'Holy Thursday' from *Songs of Innocence*, perhaps gleaned from Malkin, was included by Ann and Jane Taylor in the hustle and bustle of their miscellaneous children's book *City Scenes; or, A Peep into London* (1818). 'The Chimney Sweeper' from *Innocence* appeared in an anthology called *The Chimney-Sweeper's Friend* compiled by James Montgomery, whose avowedly political aim was 'to satisfy the most supercilious, obdurate, and prejudiced' that employing children to sweep chimneys was 'inhuman, unnecessary, and altogether unjustifiable' (Montgomery 1824, vi).[3] As these examples indicate, the contemporary audience of Blake's *Songs* – or of some of their texts, at least – was more various and more numerous than simply totting up the number of illuminated books Blake printed can suggest. It remains to examine the substance of the most significant early responses.

BENJAMIN HEATH MALKIN, *A FATHER'S MEMOIRS OF HIS CHILD* (1806)

Benjamin Heath Malkin (1769–1842), a schoolmaster, historian, and writer, first met Blake in the autumn of 1805. His interest in Blake's artistry had been roused by the illustrations Blake had designed for

Robert Blair's poem *The Grave*, then in production. But Malkin soon interested himself in Blake's poetry too: he owned a copy of *Songs of Innocence*, which he gifted to a friend, Thomas Johnes, in 1805, and had clearly also read *Poetical Sketches* and *Songs of Experience* by the time he came to write the critical essay on Blake prefixed to *A Father's Memoirs of His Child* (1806). The *Memoirs* as a whole were intended to commemorate the short life and prodigious talents of Malkin's eldest son Thomas, who had died aged six in 1802. Malkin asked Blake to design and engrave a frontispiece portrait of his son, and Blake also contributed a brief, eulogistic assessment of Thomas's drawings, which showed, he thought, the same 'firm, determinate outline, struck at once' that was fundamental to his own theory and practice of art (E693). Yet overshadowing the body of the book in its bulk and importance to later critics is a forty-eight-page 'Introduction' which focuses on Blake's life and early works, and prints in full *Innocence*'s 'Laughing Song', 'Holy Thursday', and 'The Divine Image', *Experience*'s 'The Tyger', and two poems from *Poetical Sketches* ('How sweet I roamed' and 'Song' ['I love the jocund dance']).

Malkin's essay constitutes the earliest known published response to *Songs*. It is gratifyingly full and remarkably sympathetic both to Blake's beliefs and his works. It is also unusual amongst early responses in treating Blake as a poet as well as an engraver, and in locating Blake's poetry as part of tradition, and an august tradition at that – more typically, Blake's poetry was imagined to be *sui generis*, that is, to be one of kind, without precedent. Despite his lack of formal education, Blake, writes Malkin:

■ has made several irregular and unfinished attempts at poetry. He has dared to venture on the ancient simplicity; and feeling it in his own character and manners, has succeeded better than those, who have only seen it through a glass. His genius in this line assimilates more with the bold and careless freedom, peculiar to our writers at the latter end of the sixteenth, and former part of the seventeenth century, than with the polished phraseology, and just, but subdued thought of the eighteenth. □

(*BR* 565)

Malkin proceeds to unpack his scholarly survey in his remarks on particular poems. In the 'Fairy Glee' of 'Laughing Song' he discerns 'the style of thought' of the sixteenth-century poet and dramatist Ben Jonson, whose manner he also marks in the playfulness of 'How sweet I roamed' (*BR* 566, 569). In the thunderous thanksgivings of 'Holy Thursday' – a poem that he thinks 'expresses with majesty and pathos, the feelings of a benevolent mind, on being present at a sublime display of national munificence and charity' – he hears echoes of the Book of Revelation and Milton's *Paradise Lost* (1667) (*BR* 567). 'The Divine Image', he suggests, is influenced by the poetry of Shakespeare, which Blake read in his youth, as well as by 'the devotional pieces of the Hebrew bards' (*BR* 569, 567). Here Malkin was most probably thinking of the Biblical books of Job, the Psalms, and The Song of Solomon. Inspired writings like these were the reference point of Blake's 'ancient simplicity' mentioned above. Malkin also traced Orientalist inflections in 'The Tyger'. Again recalling Hebrew writers, the poem 'wears that garb of grandeur, which the idea of creation communicates to the mind of the higher order'. Its topic and imagery, furthermore, are 'of almost oriental feature and complection' (*BR* 570).

These influences might seem miscellaneous, and to be sure Malkin's aim is to give his readers 'contrast[ing]' examples of Blake's verse. Yet his criticism also isolates a common thread uniting Blakian lyric, Elizabethan song, and Hebrew sublimity: simplicity. Malkin marks, for example, the 'ancient simplicity' and 'simple language' of the Hebrew prophet-poets (*BR* 564, 567), the 'simple and pastoral gaiety' of 'I love the jocund dance', one of the poems he cites from *Poetical Sketches* (*BR* 570), and the 'simplicity and sentiment' of 'The Divine Image' (*BR* 568). Simplicity might seem like a pejorative term, and to an extent it is: Malkin's description of Blake's verse as 'irregular' and 'unfinished', 'bold and careless' (565) chimes ineluctably with Anthony Stephen Mathew's view, enlightened yet stinting, of 'irregularities and defects' in the *Poetical Sketches*. Likewise, Malkin's championing of Blake as 'untutored proficient' recalls Mathews' patronising advancement of Blake's 'untutored youth' (*BR* 565; see Chapter 1). Yet the space of Malkin's essay (and his critical intelligence) permits him more fully to develop the aesthetic on which he calls. Simplicity in his hands becomes a term of praise. It is the hallmark of the gifted individual like Blake or, for that matter, Malkin's son Thomas whose genius was natural, and whose talents were innate more than they were acquired. Simplicity was also of course held by contemporaries to be a quality of poetry like William Wordsworth's that broke, as Malkin suggests Blake's did, with the 'polished phraseology' of eighteenth-century verse. Crucial to Malkin's appraisal of Blake, though, is the association of the *Songs*' simplicity with that of the inspired Hebrew bard, who according to Malkin thinks with 'purity' and expresses himself in 'unaffected terms' (*BR* 567–8).

It is in the context of the alliance between Blake's *Songs* and Hebrew simplicity that Malkin broaches a potentially tricky issue: those formal

and stylistic choices made by Blake that might have seemed distaste-
ful to the educated, eighteenth-century ear. Here Malkin faces two
problems: first, *Songs'* unorthodox (and potentially blasphemous) use
of personification and figurative language, and second, the poems'
irregular metre. Malkin and his contemporaries had inherited from
Samuel Johnson the maxim that in devotional poetry, 'the sanctity
of the matter rejects the ornaments of figurative diction' (*BR* 567; see
Johnson 2009, III.310, also I.49–50). In this light, Malkin is aware that
Blake's figurative treatment of divine ideas in 'The Tyger' and 'The
Divine Image' needs to be handled with care. Thus Blake's rendering of 'the idea of creation' as a tiger is 'justified' because '[o]ur bard'
(note the sustained, implied Hebrew connection in the word 'bard')
has 'brought the topic he descants on from warmer latitudes than his
own' (*BR* 570). Equally, in 'The Divine Image' it is appropriate to treat
mercy and benevolence poetically because, Malkin claims, 'they are
in unison with the mild spirit of poetry' (*BR* 568). On the subject of
rhythm and metre, Malkin admits that *Songs* lacks 'the mechanical
prettinesses of cadence and epithet' that one might find in the work
of eighteenth-century religious poets such as Isaac Watts (1674–1748)
and Edmund Waller (1606–87).[4] But here the reasons for his careful
alliance of Blake with the Hebrew bards become clear. For in common
with Biblical scholars such as Robert Lowth, Malkin believed that
the Hebrew poets, writing in the heat of divine inspiration, were not
the neatest of versifiers either. How better to vindicate Blake against
charges of poetic indecorum than to associate him with the most ven-
erable of prior examples?

Malkin builds on this association in his discussion of 'The Divine
Image'. The politics of this poem, incidentally, are not his concern,
overtly at least. Malkin does not comment on the poem's equation
of 'God our Father' with 'the human form divine', or its urging that
'all must love the human form, | In Heathen, Turk, or Jew!' (E12–13)
(although one could read this omission as Malkin's tacit acknowledge-
ment of the poem's unorthodoxy). Instead, Malkin focuses on his
readers' possible objection to the poem's marriage of content and form,
its rendering of the Godhead and Christian virtues in the popular ballad stanza. Segueing from his discussion of Hebrew prophecy, Malkin
writes as follows:

■ Words and numbers present themselves unbidden, when the soul is
inspired by sentiment, elevated by enthusiasm, or ravished by devotion. I
leave it to the reader to determine, whether the following stanzas have any
tendency to vindicate this species of poetry; and whether their simplicity

and sentiment at all make amends for their inartificial and unassuming construction. □

(*BR* 568)

Malkin may leave the question hanging, but his own positive answer is implied. Throughout his essay, he deploys the term 'simplicity' as part of an unorthodox aesthetic armoury, allegiant to natural genius and the irregular, unaffected form of Hebrew poetry. Most straightforwardly, we see that Malkin aims to promote the prestige of Blake's *Songs*, by placing them in the same company as Biblical writings and the works of luminaries such as Shakespeare, Milton, and Jonson.

When Malkin expands beyond his commentary on *Songs* to tackle Blake's reputation more broadly, the religious bias of his discussion of simplicity is cast into relief. Malkin is concerned in particular to explicate and qualify his readers' understanding of Blake's religious 'enthusiasm', which to prejudiced contemporaries might have looked like mere insanity. 'Enthusiasm' is a term that continues to crop up in discussions of *Songs* over the centuries. At the time, it was 'associated with a wide spectrum of religious and political views', including 'belief in free grace, in freedom from the moral law (antinomianism), in special spiritual insight, in divine personal favour or salvation, in direct spiritual communication, in ecstatic experience, and in emotional rather than rational religious or political impulses'. Enthusiasm had political connotations too, being associated in the 1790s with 'social and political subversion' (McCalman 1999, 498). To hail enthusiasm as madness therefore might be to defuse it as a threat – and equally, to embrace it as Blake did in others of his writings as the 'All in All!' might be dangerous (E645). As the avowed aim of Malkin's essay was to widen the constituency of the *Songs*' readers, he needed to broach Blake's enthusiasm delicately. Blake's 'merit', he writes, 'ought to be more conspicuous' but has been hampered by 'opinions and habits of an eccentric kind' (*BR* 561). In particular:

■ Enthusiastic and high flown notions on the subject of religion have hitherto, as they usually do, prevented the general reception, as a son of taste and of the muses. The sceptic and the rational believer, uniting their forces against the visionary, pursue and scare a warm and brilliant imagination, with the hue and cry of madness. [...] By them, in short, has he been stigmatised as an engraver, who might do tolerable well, if he was not mad. □

(*BR* 564–5)

Here we see insult added to injury, as disparagement of Blake's trade is compounded by suspicions of his sanity – and indeed accusations of madness were to haunt responses to Blake's *Songs*. The writer and collector William Beckford, for example, was to write in his copy of Malkin's *Memoirs*, impugning even the messenger:

■ Some splendid Specimens from that Treasury of Nonsense – Mr Blake the mad draughtsman's poetical compositions –
    Tiger, Tiger burning bright
    In the forest of the night – &c
Surely the receiver & Disseminator of such trash is as bad as the Thief who seems to have stolen them from the walls of bedlam. □
                  (*BR* 571fn.)

Diagnosing what he implies would be a misguided and unreflecting response to Blake's 'high flown notions', Malkin does not so much vindicate his enthusiasm as secularise and so recuperate it. Thus he characterises Blake as a 'visionary' with 'a warm and brilliant imagination', whose poetry cannot be divined by 'the test of cold calculation and mathematical proof' (*BR* 564–5). The enthusiasm Malkin recuperates is poetical rather than religious – although having raised enthusiasm's spectre, he leaves hanging the possibility that the religious and even the political ideas to be found in Blake's *Songs* might be subversive.[5] Where Malkin's own sympathies lay in this regard is difficult to decide, although he is said to have 'shared' Blake's interest in 'radical politics' (*BR* 223&fn.).

Malkin's commendation of Blake's *Songs* came at a time when, as Malkin notes, 'the public have hitherto had no opportunity of passing sentence on [...] a collection, circulated only among the author's friends, and richly embellished by his pencil' (*BR* 565). The inclusion of poems from *Songs of Innocence and of Experience* in *A Father's Memoirs of His Child* undoubtedly changed this, swelling the early audience of Blake's *Songs* if only relatively modestly. In the decade following its publication, *Memoirs* sold fairly slowly at a rate of about 45 copies a year (Bentley 1977, 285), but the ripples of its influence carried Blake's poems a little further. It appears to be thanks to Malkin's reprinting of 'Holy Thursday', for example, that the poem was included in miscellanies for children such as Priscilla Wakefield's *Perambulations in London* (1809, 1814), and Jane and Ann Taylor's *City Scenes* (1818–45). However, reviewers of the *Memoirs* tended not to share Malkin's positive assessment of Blake's poetry. The most positive note was sounded by the *Annual Review* of 1807, which found Blake's poems 'certainly not devoid of merit' (see Bentley 1975, 44–6).

HENRY CRABB ROBINSON, 'WILLIAM BLAKE: ARTIST, POET, AND RELIGIOUS MYSTIC' (1811), DIARY, AND *REMINISCENCES* (1852)

Another sympathetic contemporary reader of Blake's *Songs* was Henry Crabb Robinson (1777–1867), diarist, writer, and lawyer. Crabb Robinson was a student of German Romantic philosophy and psychology, and interested himself particularly in Blake's thought and mind. 'Shall I call him Artist or Genius – or Mystic – or Madman?' he was to write upon his first meeting with Blake on 10 December 1825; 'Probably he is all' (*BR* 420). The Blake who emerges from Crabb Robinson's pencil was not influenced by Jonson and Shakespeare, but by Plato, Spinoza, mystical writers such as Emanuel Swedenborg and Jakob Boehme, and an eccentric take on Christianity. In his efforts to reconcile these influences, Crabb Robinson became the first in a long line of critics to attempt to treat Blake's thought as a system. By identifying Blake's madness as inextricable from, indeed necessary to, his genius, he also bequeathed to subsequent critics a way of coming to terms with some of the idiosyncrasies of Blake's vision.[6]

Crabb Robinson was a participant in and astute observer of the intellectual life of his day both in Britain and on the continent. Between 1811 and 1867 he recorded his experiences in a diary that extended to thirty-three handwritten volumes. This diary is a fascinating document, vividly relaying Crabb Robinson's conversations with Blake, Wordsworth, and Coleridge, among numerous others. Vincent Newey has called it 'the bedrock of future knowledge' of Blake because of the incorporation of relevant passages into Alexander Gilchrist's landmark *Life of Blake* (1863), which we examine in Chapter 4 (*ODNB*). Crabb Robinson himself was to edit his diary down into the four-volume *Reminiscences*, published by Thomas Sadler in 1869, two years after Robinson's death. Yet if the wider influence of Crabb Robinson's writings about Blake was not felt until later in the nineteenth century, his efforts to promote the reputation of Blake and of *Songs* were steady and not without success even during Blake's lifetime.

We begin our consideration of Crabb Robinson's writings with his essay 'William Blake: Artist, Poet, and Religious Mystic', translated into German and published, in 1811, in the magazine *Vaterländisches Museum*. This account (about whose contemporary influence little is known, and which was not reprinted until the twentieth century) (D 17; see also Junod 2012) 'poses the issues that were to crop up over and over again in the first half of the nineteenth century', as Anthony J. Wittreich notes: 'Blake's genius and/or madness, his mysticism, his religious orthodoxy, the wild irregularity of the lyric poems and the "obscurity" of the prophecies' (prophecies here meaning Blake's illuminated books *Europe* (1793) and *America* (1794), of whose difficulty Crabb Robinson confesses his 'inability to give a sufficient account') (*BR* 602; Wittreich 1970, 52). The essay also comments directly on *Songs of Innocence and of Experience*, printing parts of the 'Introduction' and 'Holy Thursday' from *Songs of Innocence*, and 'The Tyger' and 'The Garden of Love' from *Experience*, in order 'to make our author as well known as possible' (*BR* 601). In 1826 Crabb Robinson was to acquire his own copy of *Songs*, buying it directly from Blake's own hands. When working up his essay in 1810, though, he had to rely on the copy belonging to Elizabeth Iremonger (1789–1813) ('a Unitarian [...] a sort of free-thinker'), as well as on Malkin's *Memoirs* – the publication that had inspired Crabb Robinson to write about Blake in the first place (*BR* 298&fn., 296).

Most of Crabb Robinson's essay is concerned with Blake's visual art, including his designs for Blair's *Grave* (1808) and for Edward Young's *Night Thoughts* (1797), as well as with the 'Descriptive Catalogue' that Blake produced to accompany his 1809 exhibition of paintings. Turning eventually to *Songs*, a 'remarkable little book of poems [...] which is only to be met with in the hands of collectors', Crabb Robinson admits:

> ■ It is not easy to form an overall opinion of the text, since the poems deserve every praise and every censure. Some are childlike songs of the greatest beauty and simplicity; these are the *Songs of Innocence*, many of which, nevertheless, are extremely childish. The *Songs of Experience*, on the other hand, are metaphysical riddles and mystical allegories. Among them are poetic pictures of the highest beauty and sublimity and again poetical fancies which can scarcely be understood even by the initiated. □
> (*BR* 601)

Having cited the title of the collection in full – 'Songs of Innocence and of Experience, shewing the two contrary states of the human soul' – Crabb Robinson is the first to imply a contrary relationship between its two books. The poems of *Songs of Innocence* are simple and intelligible, even too straightforward; those of *Songs of Experience* are sublime, mystical, and sometimes obscure. Yet Crabb Robinson does not fall into the sharp binarism of later critics: Blake's talents remain 'many-sided', and each part of *Songs* has both merits and defects (*BR* 601). His comments on the poems he transcribes are sparing: 'Introduction' and 'Holy Thursday' from *Innocence* are 'joyous and delicious songs'; 'The Tyger' is 'inspired and original'; and 'The Garden of Love' is an 'allegorical' poem that, unlike others in *Experience*, Crabb

Robinson feels able to decode (*BR* 601–2). Thus unencumbered by detailed commentary, Blake's poems are left to speak for themselves (albeit in German).[7]

While the 1811 essay tends to parade Blake as a 'character' who 'will never produce complete and immortal work' (*BR* 603), Crabb Robinson's diary, in the detailed record it keeps of their conversations in 1825–7, shows him crediting Blake's ideas to a much greater degree. Blake seems to have said nothing directly about *Songs*, so we must pay the diary only scant attention here – even though it is packed with suggestive remarks. Take Blake's view of 'the Divinity of Jesus Christ': 'He is the only God – [...] And so am I and so are you' (*BR* 421), which bears comparison to the God represented in 'The Divine Image' as dwelling in 'the human form' (ll. 17, 20, E13). Or take Blake's comment on the commonality and innateness of imagination: 'Of the faculty of Vision he spoke as One he had had from early infancy – He thinks all men partake of it – but it is lost by not being cultiv[ate]d' (*BR* 428). Again we see Malkin's 'untutored proficient', and of course the clear-eyed wisdom of childhood attested to throughout *Songs of Innocence and of Experience*. It was to Crabb Robinson that Blake 'spoke of his horror of Money', of 'his turning pale when money had been offerd him', as it was necessarily in the sale of *Songs* (*BR* 435). It was Crabb Robinson, too, who smoothed off some of Blake's rough edges, glossing over his economic hardship later in life and masking the working engraver as a gentleman. 'There is a natural sweetness & gentility ab^t Blake which are delightful', he writes in his diary, and again in a letter to Dorothy Wordsworth, 'there is something so delightful about the Man – tho' in great poverty, he is so perfect a gentleman with such genuine dignity & independence' (*BR* 425, 438). Blake's natural gentility was to become a common theme of Victorian criticism. Yet while it may capture Blake's temperament, to critics writing in the wake of David Erdman's *Prophet Against Empire* (1954) this view also seems to euphemise Blake's class and disavow his radicalism.

Revising material from his diary for the *Reminiscences* of 1852, Crabb Robinson confessed of the section on Blake that he had not attempted 'to reduce to order, or make consistent the wild & strange rhapsodies utterd by this insane man of genius, thinking it better to put down what I find as it occurs'. This was justifiable because Blake did not suffer from 'mere madness', but from 'Monomania' (*BR*, 692), denoting 'an idée fixe, a single pathological preoccupation in an otherwise sound mind' (Goldstein 1987, 155–6). Above all, Blake was a 'Verüngluckter Genie' (*sic*), a failed genius, or more precisely, a genius who has fallen on hard

times ('unglück' connotes both unhappiness and bad luck; 'ver' suggests these have befallen a person without his agency) (*BR*, 693).[8] In his
account of Blake's state of mind, Crabb Robinson might seem scathing.
He nonetheless gives Blake's words and ideas more credit than would
early biographers such as Cunningham and Gilchrist. Moreover, in his
self-confessed failure 'to reduce to order, or make consistent' the various aspects of Blake's thought, Crabb Robinson manages to preserve its
vitality in a way that the later, more confident system-building of W. B.
Yeats, Edwin Ellis, and Northrop Frye might not.

CRABB ROBINSON'S COAT-TAILS: WILLIAM HAZLITT, WILLIAM WORDSWORTH, CHARLES LAMB, AND JAMES MONTGOMERY

In addition to the substance of its remarks about Blake, Crabb Robinson's
diary also reveals much of his attempts to widen the readership of
Blake's *Songs*, by showing, lending, and reading aloud its poems to
friends and acquaintances. In the absence of his own personal copy of
the book, Crabb Robinson made handwritten transcriptions of some of
its poems and passages from *America* and *Europe*, gathered from books
owned by his friends (*BR* 296–8). Thus when the essayist and critic
William Hazlitt (1778–1830) paid him a visit in March 1811, Crabb
Robinson was able 'to read him some of the Poems' as well as showing
off his copy of Blake's illustrations for *Night Thoughts*. Although Hazlitt
thought little of the illustrations:

■ He was much struck with [the Poems] & expressed himself with his
usual strength & singularity[.] [']They are beautiful,['] he said, [']& only
too deep for the vulgar[;] he has no sense of the ludicrous & as to a God
a worm crawling in a privy is as worthy an obj[ect] as any other, all being
to him indifferent[.] So to Blake the Chimney Sweeper &c[.] He is ruined
by vain struggles to get rid of what presses on his brain – he attempts
impossibles['] – I added – [']he is like a man who lifts a burthen too heavy
for him; he bears it an instant, it then falls on & crushes him[.'] W. H.
preferred the Chimney Sweeper. □

(*BR* 309)

Hazlitt's appreciation of Blake's poetry suggests to Duncan Wu that 'as
in much else, he was ahead of his time' (Wu 2008, 137). His antipathies
characteristically reveal more of his opinions than does his fondness.
Hazlitt is astute, for example, to say that for Blake 'a worm crawling
in a privy is as worthy an object as any other', as the clods, pebbles,

and flies given voice by *Songs of Innocence and of Experience* vouchsafe (although that said, these objects seem not 'indifferent' but as singular and determinate as Hazlitt's own opinions). His suggestion that Blake's poems are 'too deep for the vulgar', furthermore, echoes the Miltonic proclamation of Blake's 1809 'Descriptive Catalogue': 'Fit audience find tho' few' (E527). Hazlitt's word 'vulgar' here may seem ambivalent, poised between class criticism and a more generally diffused want of taste ('vulgarity' in one of Hazlitt's essays signifies both 'a low origin' and 'an innate meanness of disposition'; in Blake's writings it tends to mean the latter) (Hazlitt 1821, 375). But it is noteworthy that Hazlitt writes against the grain in suggesting that *Songs* might not be childish and simple in the pejorative sense, but profound. Hazlitt is less sympathetic to Blake in his remark that 'he has no sense of the ludicrous', and that in 'The Chimney Sweeper' he is 'ruined by vain struggles to get rid of what presses on his brain': in this, Blake appears less a thinking artist than a malfunctioning automaton. Perhaps Hazlitt's response to *Songs* is not, then, as avant garde as Wu would have us believe.

Crabb Robinson again had his manuscript copies of certain *Songs* at hand in May 1812, when he took a walk across the fields to Hampstead Heath with the poet William Wordsworth (1770–1850) – although Wordsworth, of course, had already come across some of Blake's poems in the 'Introduction' to Malkin's *Memoirs*. In his diary, Crabb Robinson notes:

■ I read W. some of Blake's poems he was pleased with Some of them and consid[ere]d B as hav[in]g the elements of poetry – a thousand times more than either Byron or Scott. □

(*BR* 312)[9]

Later in life, his account of Wordsworth's words was more colourful: 'There is no doubt that this man is mad, but there is something in this madness which I enjoy more than the Sense of W: Sc: or Lord B:' This is quite some reversal of hierarchy: George Gordon Lord Byron and Walter Scott were among the bestselling writers of the day (which may fuel Wordsworth's disparagement). Sensing 'an affinity' between Blake and Wordsworth, Crabb Robinson did his best to engineer their meeting, although he did not succeed (*BR* 436, 438).[10]

Another contemporary writer to whom Crabb Robinson introduced Blake's works – certainly the paintings Blake exhibited in 1809, and perhaps also *Songs* – was the essayist and children's book author Charles Lamb (1775–1834) (*BR* 299, 395). As with Hazlitt and certainly Wordsworth, Lamb's comments about *Songs* are sparse and on occasion negligent (for example, he apparently called Blake 'a "mad Wordsworth"') (*BR* 313).

And yet the later Victorian poet A. C. Swinburne, himself the author of a critical essay about Blake, was to hail Lamb as '[t]he one man of genius alive during any part of Blake's own life who has ever spoken of this poet with anything like a rational admiration' (S 8). The spur for Swinburne's remark is a letter that Lamb wrote in May 1824 to the Quaker poet Bernard Barton, which was to be excerpted in Allan Cunningham's influential chapter on Blake in *Lives of the Most Eminent British Painters, Sculptors, and Architects* (1830). Blake, Lamb tells Barton, is 'a most extraordinary man, if he be still living':

■ His poems have been sold hitherto only in Manuscript. I never read them, but a friend at my desire procured the Sweep Song. There is one to a Tiger, which I have heard recited, beginning

> Tiger Tiger burning bright
> Thro' the deserts of the night –

which is glorious. But alas! I have not the Book, for the man is flown, whither I know not, to Hades, or a Mad House – but I must look upon him as one of the most extraordinary persons of the age. □

(*BR* 394)

The occasion of Barton's writing is the appearance of Blake's 'The Chimney Sweeper' from *Songs of Innocence* in James Montgomery's *The Chimney-Sweeper's Friend, and Climbing-Boy's Album* (1824), hailed by Judith Plotz as 'a philanthropic work of literary activism', and 'the first extended literary response to child labor' (Plotz 2000, 95). Montgomery initially sent out a request for original contributions, to 'upwards of twenty of the favourite poets of the day', including Wordsworth and Scott, who both declined his invitation (Montgomery 1824, viii). Lamb declined also, having 'batter'd my brains [...] for a few verses' (cited by Plotz 2000, 98), but communicated instead a poem from what Montgomery terms 'a very rare and curious little work', 'BLAKE's *Songs of Innocence*' (Montgomery 1824, 343, 344). Lamb was to call Blake's 'Chimney Sweeper' 'the flower' of Montgomery's collection (cited by Plotz 2000, 98). Yet he introduces a telling revision, renaming Blake's 'Tom Dacre', 'Tom Toddy'. In this way, argues Plotz, 'a bitter name gives way to a sweet one':

■ 'Dacre' carries the bitter implications of 'acrid' and 'darker' and the associated ideas of the bitter taste of soot, the bitter lot of the child, the darkness of the night in which the sweeps rise, the darkness of their filthy skins and the darkness of their fate. The alliterating 'Tom Toddy' suggests the comfort of a hot drink [...] and, especially, the charm of a toddler. [...] From all accounts, however, young sweeps did not toddle; rather they staggered and shuffled because of the weight of their soot bags and the deformities of their knees. 'Dacre' is a name suggesting the environmental conditions; 'Toddles' is a name attaching to the child in and of himself. □

For Plotz, '[t]he changed name indicates that Lamb prefers to contemplate the untouched ideal atemporal essence of the child rather than', like Blake, 'concentrating on determining circumstances' (Plotz 2000, 98). But her interpretation neglects a popular meaning of 'toddy' both then and now: an alcoholic drink, 'a beverage composed of whisky or other spirituous liquor with hot water and sugar' – and Lamb himself was no stranger to a jar (*OED*). Arguably, therefore, Lamb's renaming of Blake's Tom does maintain a reference to 'environmental conditions': to intoxication, whether of the sweeps or others, or perhaps simply to comfort or to counterpoison – as in Lamb's 1822 essay 'The Praise of Chimney-Sweepers' where the climbing boys sip the warm, non-alcoholic tea-like 'sassafras' (a drink that Lamb himself declines as indigestible) as a 'sweet lenitive' to the 'bitter' lot that has been accorded to them (Lamb 1987, 'The Praise of Chimney-Sweepers', 125).

However we interpret Lamb's 'Tom Toddy', his admiration for Blake must surely be celebrated, not just as a sign of what Barton called his 'critical taste & penetration' (*BR* 507), but as testimony to the radical political valence of *Songs of Innocence*. If this is wishful thinking, it is identified as such not just by modern critics, but also by Blake's very contemporaries. Nonetheless, Blake was not widely enough known to have been sent one of Montgomery's letters, and Lamb feels justified in issuing forth one of his poems without consulting Blake himself, in ignorance even of whether he is alive or dead.

SAMUEL TAYLOR COLERIDGE, *LETTERS* (1818)

The poet and philosopher Samuel Taylor Coleridge (1772–1834) did not own a copy of *Songs of Innocence and of Experience*, but as we have seen, was lent one by Charles Augustus Tulk, a friend, whose appreciation of Blake was to continue to make itself felt into the 1840s. In February 1818, while *Songs* stopped with him at Highgate, Coleridge twice made mention of Blake in his letters. First, writing to Henry Francis Cary (1772–1844), a translator, Coleridge made glancing reference to Blake's mysticism. Second, in a letter that accompanied his return of the volume to Tulk, Coleridge anatomised his responses to each of its poems in turn. Both of these letters are coloured by Coleridge's belief that Blake was a Swedenborgian, that is, a believer in the teachings of the unorthodox theologian, scientist, and mystic Emanuel Swedenborg (1688–1772).

To mention Swedenborg in connection to Blake – and for that matter, to Coleridge also – is rather to open a can of worms, although it is important that we do so: as we explain in Chapter 3, the first letterpress and facsimile editions of *Songs of Innocence and of Experience* were produced by Swedenborgians in the early Victorian period, and it was a Swedenborgian version of Blake that travelled over the Atlantic to inform Transcendentalist responses in the 1840s (Dent and Whittaker 2002, 25). Furthermore, Coleridge's assessment of Blake makes best sense in a Swedenborgian context, even though the reaction of each to Swedenborg's writings (which Blake read and annotated in the 1780s, and Coleridge in the decade following 1818) was ambivalent. The Swedenborgian Church founded in 1787 was riven by sectarian squabbles (certain Swedenborgians made peace with the Established Church whilst others remained fiercely independent), and Swedenborg's fundamental belief in the reality of the immaterial world might be interpreted variously as compatible with or running counter to Christianity, or simply as ridiculous – for example, Swedenborg claimed to have seen and conversed with angels. Certainly, for many the term 'Swedenborgian' was a slur, which may account for Coleridge's reluctance ever to make his sympathies known in public (Jackson 2004, 5). For his part, Blake is known (though probably not by Coleridge) to have attended, with Catherine, the First General Conference of the New Jerusalem Church (a Swedenborgian organisation) in April 1789, and his annotations to Swedenborg's 1788 work *Divine Love and Divine Wisdom* are broadly sympathetic. However, in the illuminated book *A Marriage of Heaven and Hell* (1790), Swedenborg's writings represent only a partial truth that must be superseded in order to ascend to a higher level of spiritual enlightenment, and in Blake's final explicit engagement with Swedenborg, the marginalia to *Divine Providence* (also 1790), he indignantly denounces Swedenborg's predestinarianism (see Rix 2007, 49). It is safest to say that Coleridge's belief, in 1818, that Blake was a Swedenborgian was exactly that, an assumption predicated on his knowledge of Tulk's own involvement with the Swedenborg Society, a London-based group that translated, published, and promoted Swedenborg's works (Tulk had co-founded the Society in 1810).

In his initial mention of Blake to Cary, Coleridge greets him as:

■ a Genius – and I apprehend, a Swedenborgian – certainly, a mystic emphatically. You perhaps smile at my calling another Poet, a Mystic; but verily I am in the very mire of common-place common-sense compared with Mr Blake, apo- or rather ana-calyptic Poet, and Painter! □

(*BR* 336)

Anchoring this judgement and Coleridge's assessment of *Songs* as a whole is not simply an assertion that Blake is a mystic, but a question of whether Blake is the right or the wrong kind of mystic, a question that implicates Coleridge's own wary self-representations. For Coleridge knew that he too might be called a mystic – and further, that this term most commonly had the pejorative sense of an obscure, confused, and irrational spiritual belief (akin to the religious enthusiasm that, Malkin observed, might seem proximate to madness) (Jackson 2004, 5). He and Blake were most often linked, as Deborah Dorfman notes, because they were both 'reputed to be mystical, obscure, and unstable' (D 19). Coleridge himself upheld a philosophical mysticism, 'a disciplined spec-ulative form of thought aimed at the vision of God' (Hedley 2003, 282), but plainly found Blake's mysticism some distance from this ('I am in the very mire of common-place common-sense compared with Mr Blake'). As poet and painter Blake is, in Coleridge's pun on Greek pre-fixes, an 'ana-calyptic' rather than an 'apo-calyptic' artist: 'apo-' means 'off', and 'calypse' 'to cover'; 'ana-' means 'back', 'again', or 'renew' (*OED*). Blake's prophetic visions thus do not reveal previously hidden truths, but return any glimmer of truth to obscurity. Still Coleridge does not write Blake off. In the next letter about Blake he continues to puzzle at *Songs* – and at no point equates Blake's beliefs with madness.

The evaluation of *Songs of Innocence and of Experience* that Coleridge sends to Tulk is scrupulous if summary, as he grades each poem in accordance with the degree of pleasure it gave him. *Songs of Innocence* finds particular favour: 'The Divine Image', 'Night', and above all 'The Little Black Boy' give Coleridge pleasure 'in the highest degree'. In *Songs of Experience*, 'Nurses Song', 'My Pretty Rose Tree', 'Ah! Sun-flower', and 'The Lilly' please Coleridge likewise. But not all of Coleridge's remarks show the 'Loves and Sympathies' that he says predominate in his assessment. 'The Blossom', 'The Voice of the Ancient Bard', and both 'Chimney Sweeper' poems leave him 'perplexed', with 'no opin-ion'. 'To Tirzah' and 'A Poison Tree' please him but perplex him still (*BR* 337). Four parts of *Songs* provoke Coleridge to more extended com-mentary, which focuses on Blake's representation of the natural world and material reality, and their relation to the divine.

Let us begin with Coleridge's most straightforward objection (straight-forward at least by Coleridgean standards; this is virtuosic stuff). 'Infant Joy' is overall a poem that pleases him, but he takes exception to its tenth line, 'Thou dost smile'. 'For a Babe two days old does, cannot *smile*,' writes Coleridge, 'and innocence and the very truth of Nature must go together. Infancy is too holy a thing to be ornamented' (*BR* 337). Coleridge seems to rehearse the same objection made by Samuel Johnson to the use of figurative language in devotional poetry, except that for him, it is childhood rather than the Godhead that should be rendered faithfully. Babies, Coleridge believes, cannot smile at two days old, and it is grossly indecorous that Blake's poem imagines they would. *Songs* again offend Coleridge's conception of what is natural, real, and representable in their title-page and 'following emblem' (presumably the frontispiece of *Songs of Innocence*), which, he thinks, indulge in a 'despotism of symbols [...] and occasionally, irregular unmodified Lines of the Inanimate' (*BR* 336). Again in line with Johnson, it seems, for whom 'immateriality' should be kept 'out of sight' (Johnson 2009, I.184), Coleridge thinks Blake confuses spirit with matter, bodying forth in engraved outline spiritual ideas that in his view are unrepresentable (perhaps the acquisition of knowledge by Adam and Eve, perhaps the moment of the piper's inspiration, perhaps unfurling letters and squiggled embellishments that are in a radical way without meaning or referent).

Likewise indecorous, but now because it represents reality too faithfully, is 'A Little Girl Lost', in which a naked youth and maiden disport themselves fearless of moral censure. Coleridge would have had 'A Little Girl Lost' 'omitted' from *Songs*, '– not for the want of innocence in the poem, but for the too probable want of it in many readers' (*BR* 337). His final, most complex and convoluted objection is to 'The Little Vagabond', a poem that contrasts the coldness of the Christian church to the warmth of the alehouse. If the church were more like the alehouse, Blake's poem slyly suggests, then people would spend more time there:

■ And God like a father rejoicing to see,
His children as pleasant and happy as he:
Would have no more quarrel with the Devil or the Barrel
But kiss him & give him both drink and apparel. □

(ll. 13–16, E26)

For Coleridge, 'The Little Vagabond' falls into a Swedenborgian error of renouncing an abstract God ('the abysmal Aseity') in favour of an embodied, all too human Christ ('the Love of the eternal *Person*'), aspects of the Godhead that Coleridge thinks are and should be indivisible. What is worse, 'Scholars of Em. Sw[edenborg]' thereby tempt '*weak* minds to sink this Love itself into *good nature*' – here the grubby, drunken conviviality of the alehouse, which Coleridge persists in thinking is upheld by Blake himself as a positive alternative to the church (and persists in thinking could not be so). Nonetheless Coleridge admires the '*audacity*' of the poem:

■ I disapprove the mood of mind in this wild poem so much less than I do the servile, blind-worm, wrap-rascal Scurf-coat of FEAR of the *modern Saints* (whose whole Being is a Lie, to themselves as well as to their Brethren). □

(*BR* 337–8)

Rather like Wordsworth electing the madness of a Blake over the sanity of a Scott, Coleridge celebrates Blake's poetry even though it offends Christian virtues. Yet he seems to miss a trick here when he identifies Blake with the poem's speaker, and does not observe the potential irony that 'in "The Little Vagabond" the two alternatives, Church and Ale-house, merge – the ossifying with the stupefying', as Deborah Dorfman puts it (D 22). By Dorfman's reading, the ale-house is not an alternative to the church, but its counterpart. Perhaps Coleridge's mistake, then, is too credulously to read Blake as a Swedenborgian – and too hastily to separate out the spiritual from the basely material.

With Coleridge's criticism of Blake comes the sense of a brilliant mind momentarily arrested. For all his and Blake's differences in opinion; for all the double-tongued dissonance of his commentary, split between the pursuit of pleasure and censure; Coleridge did at least treat Blake as a thinker, and a mystical thinker at that: alive, in these brief, unpublished forays, to *Songs of Innocence and of Experience* intellectually as well as affectively. In this he stands singular among contemporary critics.

CHAPTER THREE

Reviving Blake in the 1820s and 1830s: Obituaries, Biographies, and the First New Editions

'The words of a dead man, | Are modified in the guts of the living,' writes W. H. Auden: and it was on Sunday 12 August 1827 – prompted proleptically by fond negligence such as Charles Lamb's – that Blake, like Auden's Yeats, 'became his admirers' (Auden 1969, 141). Blake had been ill with shivering fits and 'a cold in [his] stomach' intermittently since 1825 (E777, 75; *SP* 434–4). But he had kept on working until his last days, primarily on visual art such as his designs inspired by Dante's *Divine Comedy*. In April 1827 Blake had been commissioned by Thomas Griffiths Wainewright (1794–1847), artist, art critic and, later, reputed poisoner, to print what would be for him the final copy of *Songs of Innocence and of Experience*, a particularly opulent edition coloured richly in watercolour and liquified gold (E784; Viscomi 1993, 352–3, 365).

This chapter charts Blake's immediately posthumous reputation and the fortunes of *Songs* from the late Romantic to the early Victorian period. The prevailing mood of this span of years is one of calm, lull, and indifference – spiked by obituaries (1827–8), influential early biographies (1828, 1830), and the first new editions of *Songs* (1830, 1839, 1843). A decisive bequest of this early criticism is a stark binarism that continues to affect thinking about Blake's life and writings to the present day, arguably for the worse. Treatments of Blake's life isolate on the one hand the truth-claims he made for his visions, a source of both cheap amusement and alarm, and on the other, the normalising influence of his deathbed piety, his natural gentility even in poverty, his harmonious home-life with Catherine, and even his domestic (and domesticised) printing. Blake's writings are also divided into two, this time mainly diachronically rather than more synchronically, as with his state of mind. First comes more intelligible early work such as *Songs of Innocence and of Experience*, to be followed by the relative obscurity of the later 'prophetic books' – longer, usually illuminated poems such as *The Marriage of Heaven and Hell* (1790), *Visions of the Daughters of Albion* (1793), *America a Prophecy* (1793), *Vala: or, The Four Zoas* (c. 1796–1807), *Milton a Poem* (c. 1804–11), and *Jerusalem: The Emanation of The Giant Albion* (1804–c. 1820). Assessments of *Songs* were also themselves sometimes marked by schism, as *Experience* was drawn away from *Innocence* into the ambit of Blake's later, more disturbing and less rationally intelligible works. In this chapter we see Allan Cunningham and John James Garth Wilkinson distrustful of the 'prophetic books' to the point where they wilfully refuse to engage with him, an attitude that was also to a large extent adopted by Alexander Gilchrist, as we explain in Chapter 4.

We begin the present chapter with a mention of the first magazine obituaries, before examining early biographies by John Thomas Smith in 1828 and Cunningham in 1830. Cunningham's *Lives of the Most Eminent British Painters, Sculptors, and Architects* sold well and was highly influential, not least on Gilchrist. However, it also had its detractors, notably the sensitive, acute, and anonymous author, perhaps Tulk, of the article 'The Inventions of William Blake, Poet and Painter' (1830), which we also touch on in this chapter section. The chapter concludes by discussing the first re-publications of *Songs*, notably by the Swedenborgian Wilkinson in 1839.

MAGAZINE OBITUARIES AND JOHN THOMAS SMITH, *NOLLEKENS AND HIS TIMES* (1828)

In the years immediately following Blake's death, 'there was more printed praise of him than might have been expected' (*BR* 465). Informed, anonymous obituaries appeared in the *Literary Gazette* and *The Literary Chronicle and Weekly Review* in the autumn of 1827. In 1827–8 five further magazines followed suit, reprinting material from the earlier obituaries with only minor variations (*BR* 467fn.). Taken together, these obituaries tend not to mention *Songs* or any other illuminated book – offering yet more evidence of their limited availability, as well as the greater satisfactions afforded by titillating biographical anecdote. *The Literary Chronicle* (1 September 1827), for example, is distracted from making any serious assessment of Blake's life or works by 'the singularity of his opinions' and 'his pretended knowledge of the world of spirits' (Bentley 1975, 168). This is manifest, the obituarist thinks, in the visionary sketches of historical personages and other beings that Blake drew in 1819 for the astrologer, painter, and art teacher John Varley (1778–1842), the so-called (and much derided)

'Visionary Heads', of which the best known is 'Ghost of a Flea' (see further, Bentley 2001, 379). Blake's alleged madness and the truth-claims he made for his visions ('This World Is a World of Imagination & Vision I see Every thing I paint In This World, but Every body does not see alike') were to continue to trouble commentators, including Cunningham and Gilchrist (E702).

A more elegiac obituary in the *Literary Gazette* (18 August 1827) iso-lates a different theme, emphasising Blake's moral worth, quietism, and 'Contentedness', and reproaching its readers for their neglect of the artist during his lifetime. Blake '[d]ied as he lived! piously cheer-ful! talking calmly, and finally resigning himself to his eternal rest, like an infant to its sleep'(Bentley 1975, 165–6). Blake's quiet resig-nation to his lot and poverty were to be rehearsed by a generation of Victorian critics, even though, as Frederick Tatham (1805–78) reminds us, Blake was sufficiently well off 'in the early part of his life' – when he was composing *Songs*, that is – to afford 'comforts' as well as 'neces-saries' (*BR* 677). Tatham was an artist associated with the 'Ancients' (see Chapter 4), and Blake's friend in later years. He completed a man-uscript biography of Blake perhaps in 1831, although this lay undiscov-ered until 1864 (Wittreich 1970, 195).

A much fuller and more thoroughly researched account of Blake's life than appeared in the obituaries was given by the 'honest, prosaic' John Thomas Smith (1766–1833) in 1828 (G 342). Smith was an engraver, painter, and historian, and also keeper of prints at the British Museum. He had known Blake personally for over forty years, and like him had benefited from the patronage of Harriet and Anthony Stephen Mathew (who sponsored the publication of Blake's *Poetical Sketches* in 1783). Smith's biography of Blake appears as the final chapter in an anecdo-tal, sometimes gossipy two-volume compendium of artists' lives called *Nollekens and His Times: comprehending a Life of that Celebrated Sculptor; and memoirs of several Contemporary Artists, from the time of Roubiliac, Hogarth and Reynolds, to that of Fuseli, Flaxman, and Blake* (1828). Blake's 'origi-nality' (*BR* 607) and the collectability of his visual art and illuminated books are such that Smith devotes to them a relatively lengthy chapter, longer even than the space he allows to the now-celebrated painter Thomas Gainsborough, or the 'inimitable' sculptor and draughtsman John Flaxman (Smith 1828, ii.439). Blake's name is also, of course, highlighted in the full title of Smith's work.

Smith's primary interest in *Nollekens and His Times* is in Blake as an artist, and he comments at length on Blake's technique of illuminated printing and methods of colouring. Smith also testifies to the artistry of Catherine Blake: not only did she aid her husband in printing, but she also 'became a draughtswoman' in her own right, producing 'draw-ings equally original, and, in some respects, interesting' – although virtually no evidence of these productions survives (*BR* 608). Smith includes in his chapter letters written by Blake and numerous anec-dotes furnished by contemporaries. What he says of the content of Blake's works, however, is mediated: descriptions of *Songs of Experience*, *America*, and *Europe* are supplied by a fellow historian and librarian, Richard Thomson, and Smith himself must rely on a collector, William Upcott, for 'sight of some of Blake's works' (*BR* 618). Indeed, a refrain throughout Smith's chapter is the scarcity of Blake's works, to which their desirability is in inverse proportion. The 'most interesting speci-mens' of Blake's art 'are now extremely rare,' he writes, 'and rendered invaluable by his death' (*BR* 618). Furthermore, the very neglect of Blake becomes a selling point. It was only 'the uninitiated eye' that was 'incapable of selecting the beauties' of Blake's works; to appreci-ate them, therefore, would be to prove one's own connoisseurship and taste (*BR* 617, 626). Smith here is writing specifically for 'the collector' (*BR* 626), and although he trusts that 'a time will come when Blake's finest works will be as much sought after and treasured up [...] as those of Michel Angelo are at present', they will be confined as treasure to 'the portfolios of men of mind' (*BR* 616).

In Thomson's plate-by-plate description of *Songs of Experience*, the designs take precedence over the poetry. For instance, Thomson notes:

■ *A Poison Tree*. Four Stanzas. The tree stretches up on the right side of the page; and beneath, a dead body killed by its influence. □

'The poetry of these songs', Thomson concludes summarily:

■ is wild, irregular, and highly mystical, but of no great degree of elegance or excellence, and their prevailing feature is a tone of complaint of the misery of mankind. □

Thomson's partial eye nonetheless reminds readers of subsequent typo-graphic editions, of what they do not see. Thomson marks in 'London', for instance, the 'figure of the old man [...] whose position appears to have been a favourite one' with Blake; it appears again, he notes, in *America* and, by implication, in the 'Death's Door' design Blake contrib-uted to Blair's *Grave* (*BR* 618–19). This is the first recorded recognition of iconographic analogues recurring within the wider corpus of Blake's works, a recognition that was to prove fertile for deconstructionist crit-ics of *Songs* writing in the late twentieth century (see Chapter 8).

Smith's own voice comes to the fore in the information he excavates about Blake's life: his involvement with the Mathews' salon (with which Blake fell out of favour due to his 'unbending deportment' or 'manly firmness of opinion') (*BR* 606); the sponsorship of patrons such as William Hayley and Linnell; his bitter falling out with the engraver and publisher Robert Cromek, who refused to trust Blake to engrave his own designs for Blair's *Grave*, shuffling the commission on instead to the more fashionable Luigi Schiavonetti. Smith also suggests Blake's musical ability. As we saw in Chapter 1, he witnessed Blake 'read and sing several of his poems' at the Mathews' intellectual gatherings in the late 1780s, one of which just may have been destined for *Songs of Innocence*. In *Nollekens and his Times*, Smith expands:

■ Much about this time, Blake wrote many other songs, to which he also composed tunes. These he would occasionally sing to his friends; and though, according to his confession, he was entirely unacquainted with the science of music, his ear was so good, that his tunes were sometimes most singularly beautiful, and were noted down by musical professors. □

(*BR* 606)

Following Blake's example, readers of *Songs* have over the years continued to set its lyrics to music (no records survive of Blake's own settings). Among the most notorious attempts is that of the American Beat poet Allen Ginsberg, whose recording *Songs of Innocence and Experience by William Blake, tuned by Allen Ginsberg* was released by MGM Records in 1970.

ALLAN CUNNINGHAM, *LIVES* (1830)

Smith's account was mined by the Scottish poet Allan Cunningham in the preparation of his own biography of Blake, which appeared in the six-volume *Lives of the Most Eminent British Painters, Sculptors, and Architects* in 1830. Unlike Smith, Cunningham seems not to have been personally acquainted with Blake,[1] although they had appeared together in print: Cunningham's poem 'The Orphan Child' was contained along with Blake's 'Chimney Sweeper' in Montgomery's 1824 collection, *The Chimney-Sweeper's Friend*. Cunningham was, furthermore, prone to exaggeration (or as Bentley puts it, he was 'a first-rate storyteller') (*BR* 627). The shorter chapter in the first edition of *Lives* paints Blake in 'Jekyll and Hyde' monochrome as a kind of lunatic whose madness was only absolved by the piety of his death (Dent and Whittaker 2002, 149). It also tends – heedless of Malkin's warnings – to disparage Blake's poetry as 'rude', that is, discordant, unskilled, unrefined (this last with class connotations). 'The Chimney Sweeper' of *Innocence*, for instance, is, like earlier effusions from *Poetical Sketches*, 'rude enough truly', if also 'not without pathos' (*BR* 629, 634). That said, Cunningham is always more positive about the 'original and natural' *Songs of Innocence and of Experience* than he is about Blake's other poetry (*BR* 633). He, moreover, added passages to the second edition of *Lives* (also published in 1830) that mitigated the scorn for Blake's poetry carried over from their predecessor. Blake's 'claims to the distinction of a poet', Cunningham now feels able to conclude, 'were not slight' (*BR* 660). It is easy to cavil; Cunningham's praise here is faint indeed: but the fact remains that Cunningham's life of Blake 'was more important than any other publication in keeping Blake's name alive until 1863. The series of which it formed a part [the *Family Library*] was enormously popular from its first publication [...], and the demand for it was steady on both sides of the Atlantic for over sixty years' (*BR* 627).

A significant merit of Cunningham's biography, in its expanded second edition at least, is that unlike Smith's, it commented as much on Blake's poetry as on his visual art. It is also impressive in the sheer amount of the *Songs*' poetry that it made available. Cunningham may glean most of the texts of Blake's poems from Malkin's *Memoirs*; he may even make 'unauthorized' alterations 'in almost every line' of verse that he transcribes (D 107); but he still goes further than either Malkin or Smith in the extent of his quotation, reprinting 'Introduction', 'The Chimney Sweeper', 'Holy Thursday', 'Laughing Song', and 'The Lamb' from *Innocence*, and 'The Tyger' from *Experience*, as well as others of Blake's writings. Furthermore, while Cunningham recounts with relish his exposure to Blakeana by private collectors – 'He closed the book, and taking out a small panel from a private drawer, said, "this is the last which I shall show you; but it is the greatest curiosity of all"' – he laments the confinement of Blake's works to 'the sketch-book and the cabinet' (*BR* 650, 637). If Blake's poems 'are as wild and mystical as the poetry of his Urizen, they are as well in manuscript', he states; 'if they are as natural and touching as many of his songs of Innocence, a judicious selection might be safely published' (*BR* 660).

While Cunningham treats Blake's poetry at greater length than Smith, he shares with the previous biographer the recognition that Blake's art was composite, was poetry and picture combined. Indeed, Cunningham gives first priority in *Songs* to its images: it is every pictured scene that 'has its poetical accompaniment, curiously interwoven with the group or the landscape' (*BR* 634). He furthermore follows Smith in asserting that the achievements of Blake's composite art were aural as well as visual: 'as he drew the figure', Cunningham imagines, Blake 'meditated the song which was to accompany it, and the music to which the work was to be sung, was the offspring too of the same moment' (*BR* 633). More recently critics have been sceptical of the dislocations they perceive between the musical piping, lyrical wording, and final writing of Blake's *Innocence* piper. Cunningham, though, entertains the possibility that pictorial line, word, and melody might have come to Blake at once.

Most vivid in Cunningham's life of Blake are those scenes supposedly revelatory of the artist's character whose details Cunningham either embroiders or invents: mad Blake on the Sussex sea-shore, visionary Blake conjuring spirits to his rooms, and Blake becalmed on his deathbed, welcoming death with joy ('I glory [...] in dying, and have no grief but in leaving you, Katherine') (*BR* 639–40, 648–61, 654–5). The deathbed scene (BR 654–5) was for many the focal point of Cunningham's biography, inspiring Felicia Hemans, Bernard Barton, and Dante Gabriel Rossetti to poetical effusion (see Dorfman 1969, 29–30, 61). Also influential was Cunningham's attribution to Blake of a kind of schizophrenia, first manifest, he suggests, while Blake was staying under William Hayley's patronage in Felpham, Sussex, in 1800. Summoning for his readers 'the true two-fold image of the author's mind', Cunningham writes:

■ During the day he was a man of sagacity and sense, who handled his graver wisely, and conversed in a wholesome and pleasant manner: in the evening, when he had done his prescribed task, he gave a loose to his imagination. [...] [A]t the close of the day away went Blake to the sea shore to indulge in his own thoughts and
'High converse with the dead to hold' □

(*BR* 639–40)[2]

Such a dichotomy was to 'reappea[r] in the biographical approaches of Wilkinson, Gilchrist, and, through Gilchrist, almost every writer after him' (D 32). Yet its content in Cunningham's biography seems to shift. Initially, one might presume that Blake's daylight work comprises the engravings he made for commercial publishers or respectable patrons such as Hayley and Linnell, and his darkling indulgences, self-guided work like the illuminated books. Plainly, Blake's best work, for Cunningham, is 'managed and directed' by what Colin Trodd calls, with appropriate scepticism, 'the superior organizational relations inherent in any proper patronal relationship' (Trodd 2012, 42). Some pages later, however, when Cunningham delineates his prejudices more plainly, his terms seem to shift: *Songs of Innocence and of Experience*, Blake's emblem book *For Children: The Gates of Paradise* (1793), and his illustrations of the Book of Job (1821, 1823–6) comprise 'his best and most intelligible works'; longer prophetic poems such as *Europe, America, The Book of Urizen*, and especially *Jerusalem*, on the other hand, are 'unmeaning, mystical, and extravagant' (*BR* 656). This disparaging treatment of what we now call Blake's 'prophetic books' would continue until the saving efforts of Swinburne's commentary in his 1868 *Critical Essay* (see Chapter 4). *Songs*, by contrast, makes sense, conforming itself to its audience (or as Trodd puts it, 'the rationalizing and worldly practices of [...] academic culture') rather as Blake conformed himself to his patrons.

Cunningham's biography had its detractors, most notably a rousing, anonymously authored article, 'The inventions of William Blake, painter and poet', published in the *London University Magazine* in 1830 (the author is said to be Coleridge's friend Tulk).[3] The article has large targets in view: so inured are the English to 'works of the mind', and so attached, like Cunningham, to 'natural knowledge', that their country, 'in the eyes of the thinking world, seems fast sinking into a lethargy, appearing as if the *Poison Tree* had poured the soporific distillation over its body, which now lies under it almost dead and lifeless' (Bentley 1975, 201). The anti-material philosophy of works by Coleridge, Flaxman, and Blake – including *Songs of Innocence and of Experience* and the *Book of Thel* (1789), a fascinatingly left-field choice for the time – augur, for this author, no less than 'a national political renaissance' (Bentley 1975, 200; D 44). According to the *London University Magazine* article, then, Cunningham did not further Blake's cause. But for others, he did, and for some, this was cause for concern. Cunningham's very inclusion of a biography of Blake in *Lives of the Most Eminent British Painters, Sculptors, and Architects* after all implied praise, however equivocal. In April 1834, the *Edinburgh Review* found that 'Mr Cunningham's partialities in favour of some artists [...] [are] a little shown even in the selection [...]. Blake, the able, but alas! insane author of some very striking and original designs, could scarcely be considered a painter' (let alone, we infer, a poet) (*BR* 510).

Most reactions to Cunningham's biography were more positive, more credulous, even if the Blake they perceived was inimical to some of the poet's staunchest admirers. The publication of the *Lives* 'provoked a spate of comment upon Blake in the spring of 1830' (*BR* 503f.), and stimulated 'the first known North American interest in Blake', five paragraphs in the *Philadelphia Casket* for May 1830 'illustrating Blake's eccentricity from his visions' (*BR* 530). Undeniably, Cunningham converted many to the cause of Blake's verse, however malignly he influenced their assessments of his sanity. These included the Rossetti brothers, Gabriel and William, whose attention, 'after reading

Cunningham's memoir, [...] was fixed upon Blake'. It was from this point that they 'began looking out for [Blake's] work whenever [they] could' (W. M. Rossetti 1906, ii.302).

REPUBLISHING *SONGS*: PIRATE PRODUCTIONS (C. 1831–40), JOHN JAMES GARTH WILKINSON (1839), AND CHARLES AUGUSTUS TULK (1843)

So far we have charted the reprinting or reiteration of *Songs of Innocence and of Experience* piece-meal, in criticism, miscellanies, commonplace books, and obituaries, and even in song. We have tried to give a sense of how very difficult it was for contemporary readers and early enthusiasts to gain sight of the illuminated book, even the bare verses, whose accessibility we now take for granted. The irony, oft-observed, is that Blake's desire for his works to reach an appreciative public was thwarted by his means of cottage production – however principled, in its defiance of the homogeneity of mechanical reproduction, that might have been. The audience for illuminated books like *Songs* only began to grow once they were reinscribed in a medium and by a means of production arguably antipathetic to their author. This did not happen wholesale until 1863 in the second volume of the *Life of William Blake*, although this was soon superseded by William Michael Rossetti's *The Poetical Works of William Blake, Lyrical and Miscellaneous*, published in the Aldine Edition of the British Poets series in 1874. This was the edition of Blake's texts most consulted until the early twentieth century (see Chapter 5). However, there were numerous, significant attempts to make *Songs* more widely available along the way, beginning in the decades immediately following Blake's death.

Our first, intriguing example comes with a clutch of copies that are at once Blake's and not Blake's. In Chapter 1, we examined the means by which Blake, working together with Catherine, produced some 32 copies of *Innocence*, 13 of *Experience*, and 16 of the joint *Songs* over the course of his lifetime. The same dates recur on the title-pages of all copies of *Innocence*, *Experience*, and the joint *Songs* (1789 and 1794) because Blake always printed them from the same copper plates. However, hypothesising from contextual information and other factors, such as the dates watermarked on the paper Blake used or techniques of colouring and framing, scholars have recognised that illuminated books were reprinted at intervals over time. Furthermore, the production of illuminated books did not cease with Blake's death in 1827. Not only were certain 'authentically printed' copies coloured by unknown hands after Blake's death, but Blake's copper plates were also re-used, perhaps by Catherine and certainly by Tatham, to produce some eleven 'posthumously printed copies' between 1831–2 and perhaps 1838 or 1840, '[a] few' of which 'have passed as Blake's work' – that is, were in effect fakes or even forgeries (Viscomi 1993, 367). Tatham had inherited the Blakes' effects from Catherine when she followed her husband to the grave in October 1831.

Yet it was only with the editorial intervention of John James Garth Wilkinson in 1839 that *Songs of Innocence and of Experience* was made available to reach a (slightly) larger audience. Wilkinson (1812–99) was a Swedenborgian writer and medic. His friend Tulk, generous as he had been with Coleridge, lent Wilkinson his own copy of *Songs of Innocence and of Experience* in 1838 (C. J. Wilkinson 1911, 25). The offspring of Wilkinson's perusal was what he called his 'Republication' of *Songs* in 1839 under the auspices of the London-based publishers William Pickering and W. Newbery (J. J. G. Wilkinson 1839, xxi). Although Wilkinson called it a republication, 'he of course knew', writes Frederick H. Evans in 1912:

■ that the only previous publication, if it could be called so, was in the home-engraved and coloured copies prepared entirely by Blake's and his wife's hands, and sold privately to patrons; the issue under notice was therefore practically the first public edition. □

(Evans 1912, 20)

Wilkinson's edition contained all the poems from *Songs of Innocence and of Experience* in the order in which they appeared in Tulk's copy (excepting, in the edition's first printing, 'The Little Vagabond', the poem that had so vexed Coleridge's attempt to read the collection in the light of Swedenborgian ideas) (see Chapter 2). In a nod to what was then Blake's most well-known work, Wilkinson also appended a poem by Blake dedicating his designs for Blair's *Grave* 'To the Queen'. Preceding the poems was a lengthy introduction, in which Wilkinson 'laboured to present Blake's poems within a Swedenborgian framework' (Rix 2007, 117). 'If the Volume gives one impulse to the New Spiritualism which is now dawning of the world', he writes:

■ if it leads one reader to think, that all Reality for [Blake], in the long run, lies out of the limits of Space and Time; and that Spirits, and not bodies, and still less garments, are men [...] it will have done its work in its little day; and we shall be abundantly satisfied. □

(J. J. G. Wilkinson 1839, xxi)

When he came to read Wilkinson's 'very curious' preface in 1848, Henry Crabb Robinson was more admiring of his critical efforts than he had been of Cunningham's. 'Wilkinson develops his Swedenborgianism most inoffensively,' he judged, 'and his love of Blake is delightful' (Robinson 1938, II.675, 767). Yet Wilkinson's presentation of *Songs of Innocence and of Experience* as an essentially Swedenborgian text disavows the ambivalence of Blake's own reaction to Swedenborg, which we discussed in Chapter 2. Swinburne, certainly, confessed himself 'surprised [...] to find the most eminent disciple of Swedenborg', that is, Wilkinson, 'a convert to the worship of Blake. (Blake being so very heretical a Swedenborgian[)]' (Swinburne 1959–62, I.295). Furthermore, to suggest that Wilkinson 'love[d]' Blake tells only part of the story, for he disliked Blake's prophetic books, particularly their artwork, and his antipathy inflected his response to *Experience* and even *Innocence*.

A source of tension in Wilkinson's preface, and central to his ambivalent reaction to *Songs*, is what he frames as the problem of Blake's 'Ego-theism', a kind of self-fixated iconoclasm that, as it was manifest in his books, threatened the very reason and integrity of their audience-members (who remain in Wilkinson's rendition essentially iconophobic, that is, 'fear[ful] of an art where representation aspires to a condition beyond the direct articulation of natural objects') (Trodd 2012, 104). This is something that Wilkinson thinks Blake, in his prophetic books especially, had in common with Percy Bysshe Shelley:

■ From the opposite extremes of Christianity and Materialism, they both seem, at length, to have converged towards Pantheism, or natural-spiritualism; and it is probable, that a somewhat similar self-intelligence, or Ego-theism, possessed them both. They agreed in mistaking the forms of Truth, for the Truth itself; and, consequently, drew the materials of their works, from the ages of type and shadow which preceded the Christian Revelation. □

(J. J. G. Wilkinson 1839, xviii–xix)

This is the 'first comparison' between Blake and Shelley (1792–1822), and was to be reinscribed by Swinburne and the poet James Thomson later in the nineteenth century, although they emphasised their politics as Wilkinson had not (D 50–1; see Thomson 1896b, 317–18; and S 17, 136, 234). Indeed, politics are beyond the purchase of Wilkinson's 'Preface', as of all writing about Blake at this time. Blake's 'natural-spiritualism' is, above all, for Wilkinson a site of incoherence and of hubris. His works force their readers 'to peer into compositions which proclaim a capacity to actively make worlds rather than represent the world' (Trodd 2012, 103). For Gabriel Rossetti and Swinburne, however, this was part of their appeal, as we shall examine in Chapter 4.

Relative to his assessment of Blake's prophetic books, Wilkinson's attitude to *Songs* is largely positive: his edition 'contains nearly all that is excellent in Blake's Poetry'. But he reserves his more confident praise for *Songs of Innocence*: Blake 'here transcended Self, and escaped from the isolation which Self involves; and [...] his expanding affections embraced universal Man [...] [M]any of these delicious Lays, belong to the ERA as well as to the Author'. *Songs of Experience*, by contrast, consists 'of darker themes', vexed as it is by 'the dark becloudment which rolled and billowed over Blake in his later days' (J. J. G. Wilkinson 1839, xx). Such breadth of brush-stroke establishes an important opposition between the two books, *Innocence* and *Experience*, which persists to the present day. The themes of *Experience* may be 'darker':

■ but they, too, are well and wonderfully sung; and ought to be preserved, because, in contrastive connexion with the *Songs of Innocence*, they do convey a powerful impression of 'THE TWO CONTRARY STATES OF THE HUMAN SOUL'. □

(J. J. G. Wilkinson 1839, xx–xxi).

In this way Wilkinson utilises the sub-title of Blake's 1794 collection to inscribe a contrary relationship between its two books. *Innocence* may be heavenly, and *Experience* hellish, if you like: but both seem necessary to what in the manner of Blake's *Marriage of Heaven and Hell* we might cast as a dialectic of 'progression' (E34).

This is at least how Wilkinson's preface attempts to resolve itself. Yet there is a worm at the heart of the fruitful contrariness he identifies, a negative energy Wilkinson has tried to cast out, although its residue remains. It is worth emphasising at this point that in his edition of *Songs*, Wilkinson strips away its illuminations and images and disciplines its hand-drawn lettering into type. The artist Samuel Palmer (1805–81), noting the absence, called Wilkinson's *Songs* 'that edition without designs' (Palmer 1972, 245). Edward Quillinan (1791–1851), a poet, lamented that 'some trivial verses' seemed 'well in [the] illustrated book, but somewhat weak for unadorned publication' (Bottrall 1970, 53). The most obvious explanation for Wilkinson's editorial decision would seem to be cost, rendering the publication of *Songs* affordable to him and his subscribers, and accessible, at its initial publication at least, to readers of more modest means, although prices soon rose. However, what Wilkinson has to say about Blake's art suggests he was motivated also by taste and spiritual scruple. There is something about

Blake's artwork, even the illuminated *Songs*, which he finds deeply disturbing. The 'Illustrations to the Songs of Innocence' may be 'exquisite' (and we should note the omission of *Experience* here), but 'even in these, his noblest Works':

■ [Blake prefers] seeing Truth under the loose garments of Typical, or even Mythologic Representation, rather than in the Divine-Human Embodiment of Christianity. And accordingly, his Imagination, self-divorced from a Reason which might have elevated and chastened it, and necessarily spurning the Scientific daylight and material Realism of the nineteenth century, found a home in the ruins of Ancient and consummated Churches; and imbued itself with the superficial obscurity and ghastliness, far more than with the inward grandeur of primeval Times. □

(J. J. G. Wilkinson 1839, xvi–xvii)

Wilkinson seems unable to decide whether the illuminated *Songs* show 'sane self-possession', as he initially asserts, or a free-wheeling, unchastened imagination that gives 'free vent to the hell' within its author (J. J. G. Wilkinson 1839, xvi–ii). Writing, 'painful[ly]' of Blake's prophetic books and 'a host of unpublished drawings', Wilkinson has the impression that 'we are looking down into the hells of the ancient people' (J. J. G. Wilkinson 1839, xviii). And commenting, in his correspondence, on some of Blake's 'Designs', Wilkinson writes, 'I almost wish I had not seen them. The designs are disorder rendered palpable and powerful, and give me strongly the impression of their being the work of a madman' (C. J. Wilkinson 1911, 30; see further, Trodd 2012, 101–2). Wilkinson fights to hold this disturbance at bay from his typographical *Songs*. He feels 'puzzled what to say', he writes, 'of the man who was compounded of such heterogeneous materials as to be able at one time to write the 'Songs of Innocence' and at another 'The Visions of the Daughters of Albion' (C. J. Wilkinson 1911, 30). And yet his praise is never unadulterated. The *Songs* text remains unruly, marred by 'an utter want of elaboration' (perhaps Christian or Swedenborgian unorthodoxy; perhaps the open-endedness that some readers savour), 'and even, in many cases, [...] an inattention to the ordinary rules of grammar' (J. J. G. Wilkinson 1839, xx). Wilkinson took it upon him to amend these, correcting 'errors in tense, agreement, and principal parts', and changing or supplying punctuation (D 109).

With Wilkinson we have another example of a critic writing before the merit of Blake's writings had been generally accepted. Not only Wilkinson's relative antipathy to *Songs of Experience* but also the idiosyncrasy of his edition's Swedenborgian framing are therefore instructive. His antipathy is instructive because even though it draws stark distinctions between the *Songs'* two books we may not want to observe (see Chapter 1's account of *Songs'* variable ordering) and he cannot quite either, it identifies in Blake's bipartite collection a negative case in ineluctable dialogue with a positive one. His Swedenborgianism is instructive because it helps us appreciate anew how the reputation of *Songs* was in these early years maintained on the fringe of acceptability. Though this fringe was growing. Despite the bias of his 'Preface', Wilkinson's edition of *Songs* was far-reaching in its influence. It carried Blake's poetry over the Atlantic to American Transcendentalists such as Elizabeth Peabody, who gave a copy of Wilkinson's *Songs* to William Emerson in 1842 (Elliott 2009, 211). However, there remained but few copies to go around. In 1863, Gilchrist recalls that only '[a] very limited impression was taken off, and the reprint soon became almost as scarce as the costly and beautiful original' (G 122). The next edition of *Songs* after Wilkinson's was issued by Tulk in 1843, and had even less of an impact. '[S]paced as in the Original, in order that any who chose, might copy in the paintings with which the original is adorned', only twelve copies were printed (handwritten note, in Wilkinson c. 1843). It waited until the 1860s for Blake's poetry to become more widely accessible.

CHAPTER FOUR

Enshrining Blake in the 1860s and 1870s: Pre-Raphaelitism, Aestheticism, and Counter-Attack

In this chapter we witness the explosion of interest in Blake in the mid-Victorian period, and consider two of its crowning critical achievements at length. First, the two-volume *Life of William Blake: 'Pictor Ignotus'* published in 1863. Largely written by Alexander Gilchrist, and augmented after his death in 1861 by his wife Anne, and Dante Gabriel and William Michael Rossetti, the *Life of William Blake* is perhaps the most decisive positive intervention in the reception history of *Songs of Innocence and Experience* there has ever been. Combining biography with a selection from Blake's writings – and privileging Blake's *Songs* and his euphonic designs for the Biblical Book of Job (1821, 1823–6) over all his other work – the *Life* has consistently been hailed as seminal, landmark, monumental. The second key publication we discuss is Algernon Charles Swinburne's *William Blake: A Critical Essay* (1868). This is not a biography or textual edition but a critical monograph – a poem of praise in prose. As well as vindicating the 'prophetic books' from their alleged obscurity, Swinburne presents *Songs* as party to Blake's deliberate and quite sane rebellion against the moral law.

As we have illustrated in the previous chapter, mid-Victorian criticism of Blake did not come out of nowhere. Furthermore, it was not confined to the writings of Gilchrist and Swinburne, as we explain below. In the first part of the chapter, we nuance our account of Gilchrist's *Life* by examining the sometimes conflicting views of his collaborator, Gabriel Rossetti. In the second, we address writings by James Thomson and James Smetham, contextualising Swinburne's *Critical Essay* as one among several responses to Gilchrist's *Life*. Thomson's writing about Blake notably sustains the thread of mystical criticism we saw beginning with Swedenborgianism; the co-ordinates of his commentary are therefore different from those of the Rossetti brothers, Smetham, and even Swinburne, who were bound together by personal association and a shared sense of belonging to a 'Culture of the Opposition' (mysticism being outlawed even from this). Indeed, even admitting Swinburne's iconoclasm, he seems to have used Blake rather as Smetham and the Rossetti brothers did, 'to reinforce the solidarity of a coterie position' (Dorfman 1969, 168). This at least was the perception of a phalanx of hostile critics who in writing against the Rossettis and Swinburne in particular also wrote against Blake. We discuss essays by three of these hostile critics – Oswald Crawfurd, Coventry Patmore, and Henry G. Hewlett – in the closing section of the chapter.

ALEXANDER GILCHRIST, *THE LIFE OF WILLIAM BLAKE: 'PICTOR IGNOTUS'*, EDITED BY ANNE GILCHRIST, WITH THE ASSISTANCE OF D. G. AND W. M. ROSSETTI (1863)

Collecting his diary notes early in 1852, Henry Crabb Robinson returns us to the calm, lull, and indifference we suggested characterised early Victorian attitudes to Blake. He observes:

> ■ since Blake's death Linnell has not found the market I took for granted he would seek for Blake's works. Wilkinson printed a small edition of his poems including the 'Songs of Innocence & Experience' a few years ago. And Monckton Milnes talks of printing an edition. I have a few coloured engravings, but B[lake] is still an object of interest exclusively to men of imaginative taste & psychological curiosity. I doubt much whether these Memoirs will be of any use of this small class. □
>
> (D 63)

Three years later, in 1855, things began to change. The young art critic and life-writer Alexander Gilchrist (1828–61), began work on a biography of Blake, his interest having been sparked by seeing some of Blake's designs in London the previous year (D 1). Also in 1855, Dante Gabriel Rossetti (1828–82), the painter, poet, and founder member of the Pre-Raphaelite Brotherhood, turned over to Gilchrist 'the most famous purchase of his life (besides his wombat)', Blake's notebook, which he had acquired in 1847 (D 59, 63). As we said in Chapter 1, this notebook contained the seeds of *Songs of Experience*, among numerous other writings and designs. A gathering interest in Blake is also suggested by the decision of the Irish poet William Allingham (1824–89) to include four poems from the 'celestial-infantine' *Songs* in his anthology, *Nightingale Valley* (Allingham 1860, ix). But the crowning achievement of the period came with the publication in 1863 of Gilchrist's *The Life of William Blake: 'Pictor Ignotus'* – its Latin subtitle, meaning 'unknown painter', taken from a poem by Robert Browning. From the first publication of two thousand copies of the opulently illustrated, two-volume *Life*, Blake, writes G. E. Bentley, has 'been part of [the English] literary heritage. After 1863, all references to the poet are traceable, directly or indirectly, to Gilchrist's biography' (Bentley 1975, 220, 269).

Of course, the authorship of the *Life* was not Gilchrist's alone. Upon his premature death from scarlet fever in 1861, several hands joined to complete his work. Gabriel Rossetti added a chapter 'Supplementary' to the first volume of the *Life*, as well as compiling and editing some of Blake's writings for the second, to which his brother William (1829–1919), civil servant, essayist, and lynchpin of the Pre-Raphaelite movement, also contributed an important 'Annotated Catalogue'. The artist Samuel Palmer contributed a description of Blake's designs for *The Marriage of Heaven and Hell* to the biography, as well as a memorial letter. Furthermore, Anne Gilchrist (1828–85), Gilchrist's wife, seems to have acted as the *Life*'s largely unacknowledged general editor, as Shirley Dent has recently reminded us. Anne herself downplays her role, in the 'Preface' she wrote for the first edition of the *Life*: drowning out her efforts by the thanks she gives to Linnell, Palmer, and the Rossetti brothers, and subordinating all to the guiding plan of 'my dear husband', whose name is the only one to appear on the volumes' title-pages (G xv). Yet, in a letter to the *Reader* in 1867, William Michael Rossetti writes of the *Life* that 'Mrs Gilchrist has edited it, and (if I may be permitted to say so) very efficiently' (a not unequivocal endorsement) (Dent 2007, 35). Especially in view of the 'Memoir of Alexander Gilchrist' that Anne appended to the second edition of the *Life* in 1880, the work becomes as much a shrine to the departed Alexander as a memorial of William Blake. In view of the differing critical emphases of its several contributors, moreover, and especially as essays by James Smetham and Frederic Shields were added to its expanded second edition, the *Life of William Blake* may appear more mélange than monument, 'more a chamber of rival Blake emanations than a settled biography' (Trodd 2012, 51).

Before we come to these critical differences, however, we had best begin by establishing Gilchrist's own views, both of Blake himself and of *Songs of Innocence and of Experience*. Gilchrist was responsible for researching and writing a large part of the first, biographical volume of the *Life*, drawing on the recollections of those few of Blake's friends who were still alive, and reading those accounts of Blake that were then available. His account of Blake's visions, for example, is clearly influenced by Cunningham, and his account of the simplicity of poems from *Songs*, by Malkin. Crabb Robinson's recollections made their way into the *Life* as well, although Gilchrist's overarching emphasis was on Blake the man rather than his works or even his conversation. Indeed, reading Gilchrist's account, one might almost believe that Blake was quite the model of Victorian respectability, his 'outrageous[ness]' in 'words' domesticated and defused by his happy home-life, prolific work-rate ('he was constitutionally [...] industrious'), frugality ('he was never, amid all his poverty, in debt'), and innate 'gentlemanliness' (G 327, 15, 330, 325).[1]

The essential conservatism of Gilchrist's biography, as well as what Laurence Housman was to call its 'domestic fondling' ('not seemly done in public over a man of [Blake's] greatness', he thinks) has been attributed to his choice of primary sources (D 59; Housman 1893, xxvi). These numbered not only John Linnell, the upright landscapist, but also the Ancients, an association of young London artists, notably its members Palmer and George Richmond (1809–96). Actually reading Blake's writings was a task that Gilchrist deferred until the final stages of his project, and died before completing (D 69). A late chapter of the *Life*, 'Hampstead: and youthful disciples, 1825–27', puts Palmer's fond reminiscences of Blake centre stage. Indeed, Gilchrist's Blake is in many ways 'a fleshing out' of the 'man without a mask; his aim single, his path straightforwards, and his wants few' sketched in the memorial letter by Palmer, which is cited by Gilchrist at length (D 70).

One thread of Palmer's commentary that deserves to be singled out is his suggestion of *Songs*' 'pastoral sweetness' (G 321), for talk of Blake's pastoralism – or to borrow a more apt phrase from the Victorian art critic John Ruskin, his art's truth to nature – is woven throughout the two volumes of the *Life*, binding together its contrary pulls towards Blake's art and poetry on the one hand, and his biography and temperament on the other. Traversing the fields to Hampstead to visit Linnell and his family, or rambling with Palmer, for whom '[t]o walk with [Blake] in the country was to perceive the soul of beauty through the forms of matter', Gilchrist's Blake moves against a more rural backdrop than theretofore (G 319). Gilchrist observes pastoral modes glimmering in *Songs of Innocence* too: in the 'little pastoral, entitled *The Shepherd*', or in the book's designs, 'poeticized domestic scenes' whose landscapes are 'given in pastoral and symbolic hints' (G 75, 77). His extended account of reading *Songs of Innocence and of Experience* as an illuminated book – bursting rhapsodically from the midst of more humdrum details of the book's material composition – calls on the pastoral likewise:

■ the effect was as that of an angelic voice singing to oaten pipe, such as Arcadians tell of; or, as if a spiritual magician were summoning before human eyes, and through a human medium, images and scenes of divine loveliness; and in the pauses of the strain, we seem to catch the rustling of angelic wings. The Golden Age independent of Space or Time, object of vague sighs and dreams from many generations of struggling humanity – an Eden such as childhood sees, is brought nearer than ever poet brought it before. For this poet was in assured possession of the Golden Age, within the chambers of his own mind. As we read, fugitive glimpses open, clear as brief, of our buried childhood, of an unseen world present, past, to come; we are endowed with new spiritual sight, with unwonted intuitions, bright visitants from finer realms of thought, which ever elude us, ever hover near. □

(G 72–3)

Wilkinson's Blake at his best 'transcended Self' (see Chapter 3); Gilchrist's dissolves into magical worlds both ideally rural ('Arcadian') and prelapsarian ('Eden'). Yet for Gilchrist, Blake's passage to these transpersonal states is conducted, paradoxically, by 'the chambers of his own mind'. Rather than reducing this to Wilkinson's 'Ego-theism', we might alternatively discern in the essentially human medium of Gilchrist's Blake-as-spiritual-magician what Gabriel Rossetti, in his defence of viewing a subject from within rather than without, would call an 'inner standing-point' (cited by McGann 2003, xxv–vi). 'Thy soul I know not from thy body, nor | Thee from myself, neither our love from God' writes Rossetti in his sonnet 'Heart's Hope' (1871) (ll. 7–8; see McGann 2012, 99). Gilchrist's encounter with 'these weird Songs', to use his words, seems to enable in him a similar state, if not merging and if not quite so bodily, then flitting, fleetingly, from human to divine, from personal psychological ('our own buried childhood') to collective unconscious ('vague sighs and dreams from many generations of struggling humanity'), from past to present to future.

Gilchrist was writing at a time when '[a]lmost anything acting to make Blake's art more natural helped its cultural assimilation' (Trodd 2012, 180). And albeit that what is natural for Pre-Raphaelitism may be (less assimilably) what is felt or imagined as much as what is seen, the truth of Blake's art to nature is advanced yet further by Gabriel Rossetti than it is by Gilchrist. In the 'Supplementary' chapter he contributed to the first volume of the *Life*, Rossetti comments directly on

Songs in connection to his remarks on Blake's 'system of colour, in which tints laid on side by side, each in its utmost force, are made by masterly treatment to produce a startling and novel effect of truth':

■ In Blake's colouring of landscape, a subtle and exquisite reality forms quite as strong an element as does ideal grandeur; [*as when*] we find him dealing with the pastoral sweetness of drinking cattle at a stream [*in 'The Clod and the Pebble'*] [...] For pure realism, too, [...] let us turn to the dingy London street, all snow-clad and smoke-spotted, through which the little black chimney-sweep wends his way in the *Songs of Experience*. □
(G 392–3)

We have read much of Blake's inner vision; it is startling, therefore, to read of his realism. But such realism is no mere empiricism: not only is it married with the 'ideal', a product of 'memory and genius' which Rossetti warily concedes might 'almost' stand in the place of 'immediate consultation with nature', but it is also not a microscopic, prying rendition of 'all' that is present in a scene. Instead, Blake's realism bears a sense of natural plenitude – a Keatsian rather than a Wordsworthian naturalism, if you like. Indeed so plenitudinous are Blake's natural scenes that Rossetti, moving on, one suspects, from *Songs* to later works (perhaps *Urizen*), suggests that '[e]ven a present-ment of the most abstract truths of natural science', such as 'some old skeleton folded together in the dark bowels of earth or rock', shows us 'in figurative yet not wholly unreal shapes and hues, the mingling of organic substances, the gradual development and perpetual transfu-sion of life' (G 393). This really is a milestone in the critical reception history of Blake's works, for Rossetti allows that Blake's art might cre-ate life, rather than being a direct reproduction of it (see further, W. M. Rossetti 1874, xcv, ciii–civ, and S 5, 85).

Gabriel Rossetti, as we mentioned in Chapter 3, had been interested in Blake since reading Cunningham's biography of him at some point in early adulthood. It is true that Blake, unlike Keats and Shelley, Byron and Wordsworth, had not been included in the 'list of Immortals' agreed and countersigned by the founding members of the Pre-Raphaelite brother-hood in 1848 (Armstrong 2012, 15–16). But if Blake was not a group interest, Rossetti's keenness continued undiminished. Although William Holman Hunt and John Everett Millais did not share in his enthusiasm, his siblings William and Christina, as well as Swinburne, did.[2] Having acquired Blake's notebook in 1847, Rossetti had been 'stimulated' in his own, more broadly Pre-Raphaelite anti-academicism by its ejaculatory epigrams disparaging 'Correggio, Titian, Rubens, Rembrandt, Reynolds, and Gainsborough' (D 60–1). He composed a brief 'aesthetic-moralist' 'Epitaph' on Blake in 1849 (D 61–2), and a sonnet, 'William Blake', in 1880. Moreover, as Jerome McGann has argued, Rossetti's innovation of the so-called 'double work of art', art of usually discrete textual and visual elements in dialogue, is profoundly influenced by the composite art of Blake's illuminated books (McGann 1998, 123–40). Blake appeared to Rossetti to be a Pre-Raphaelite *avant la lettre*: Blake's teenage copying of the Gothic monuments in Westminister Abbey, well documented by Malkin and Gilchrist after him, foreshadowing Pre-Raphaelite medievalism; his determinately drawn outlines anticipating early Pre-Raphaelite drawing techniques (Cruise 2012, 47–61); his 'prismatic' colouring so like that of 'a whole new section of the English school', that is, the Pre-Raphaelites (G 392); his interpolation of text and image blending the literary and artistic in a way that presaged the mixed-media experiments and literary-artistic influences of the Brotherhood. Scholars are used to thinking of the *Life* as Gilchrist's, and sometimes we adopt this shorthand designation in our guide. But looking back on the *Life* in 1907, the poet and scholar Arthur Symons judged Rossetti's contributions far superior. He writes, 'It is to D. G. Rossetti that we owe the recovery, if not also the discovery, of Blake' (Symons 1907, 67). It is, then, all the more surprising that when Rossetti comes to write about the texts of *Songs* in the second volume of the *Life*, his comments are ambivalent, for all his felt affinities to Blake's art.

Before coming to Gabriel Rossetti's estimation of the *Songs* text, however, we should return to Gilchrist, for whom *Songs of Innocence and of Experience* is Blake's highest achievement, outstripped only by *Inventions to the Book of Job*. The 'tender loveliness' of the poems from *Songs of Innocence* especially 'will hardly appear in Blake's subsequent writing', claims Gilchrist. 'Darker phases of feeling, more sombre colours, profounder meanings, ruder eloquence, characterize the *Songs of Experience* of five years later' (G 76). Yet *Experience* remains the necessary 'complement' to *Innocence*:

■ The first series, quite in keeping with its name, had been of far the more heavenly temper. The second, produced during an interval of another five years, bears internal evidence of later origin, though in the same rank as to poetic excellence. As the title fitly shadows, it is a grander, sterner caliber, of gloomier wisdom. Strongly contrasted, but harmonious phases of poetic thought are presented by the two series. □

(G 118)

It is striking that Gilchrist allows *Experience* to be equal in poetical merit to *Innocence*: here he departs, for example, from Cunningham and Wilkinson (as well as from Rossetti, as we shall see). Gilchrist is not prone to assimilate *Experience* to the prophecies; its writing is 'more lucid', 'freer from mysticism and abstractions' (G 118). 'Blake never again sang to like angelic tunes; nor even with the same approach to technical accuracy. His poetry was the blossom of youth and early manhood' (G 121). To the Prophetic Books, Gilchrist, along with the Rossetti brothers, turns a blind eye, an omission that Anne laments in her 'Preface' (G xiv).

In his equal valuing of *Innocence* and *Experience*, Gilchrist describes the paired poems of the collection as having a typological relationship, allowing that 'The Tyger' of *Experience* is 'an antitype' to 'The Lamb' of *Innocence*, rather as the types of the Old Testament shadow forth or prefigure the anti-types of the New (G 74). The implications of this remark perhaps outstrip the conservatism of Gilchrist's biographical agenda: for while *Innocence* offers 'simple *affirmations*', *Experience* consists of 'earnest, impassioned arguments [...] on the loftiest themes of existence' (G 121). Hence more troublesome arguments realise the potential of more pious affirmations, intimating, for example, that 'The Human Abstract's' assertion, 'Pity would be no more | If we did not make somebody Poor,' is more manifest in its truth, while still dependent on 'The Divine Image's' avocation, 'To Mercy Pity Peace and Love | All pray in their distress: | And to these virtues of delight | Return their thankfulness' (ll. 1–2, E27; ll. 1–4, E12).

Whilst in the first volume of the *Life* Gilchrist champions *Experience* alongside *Innocence*, in the second, a contradiction emerges: for not only does Gabriel Rossetti, the volume's editor, favour *Innocence* over *Experience*; he also criticises *Experience* poems both explicitly and implicitly for their lack of finish. Weighing up, in a head-note, the relative merits of the two books, he suggests:

■ The first series is incomparably the more beautiful of the two, being indeed almost flawless in essential respects; while in the second series, the five years intervening between the two had proved sufficient for obscurity and the darker mental phases of Blake's writings to set in and greatly mar its poetic value. [...] [T]here can be no comparison between the first *Chimney Sweeper*, which touches with such perfect simplicity the true pathetic chord of its subject, and the second, tinged merely with the common-places of social discontent. [...]

As the purpose of these republications from Blake is hardly furthered by including anything of inferior value, I confess that it occurred to me at first to omit any pieces which seemed really chargeable with triviality and incompleteness, and therefore likely to obstruct appreciation with many readers; but I was unwilling, on mature reflection, to dismember the work as Blake wrote it, particularly as the second section would have thus come to bear no proportion in bulk to the first. □

(A. Gilchrist 1863, ii.25)

Not only Rossetti but also the artistic movement of which he was a founder member had united with Blake in their reaction against the idealising, generalising aesthetic propagated by Joshua Reynolds (1723–92), the first President of the Royal Academy of Arts: 'general nature' rather than 'particular customs and habits' lives forever, thinks Reynolds; 'the general effect and power of the whole' must 'take possession of the mind', 'suspend[ing] the consideration of the subordinate and particular beauties or defects' (Reynolds 1997, iv.73, xi.192). For Rossetti, however, ironically in common with Reynolds, it is precisely the defects, as he sees it, of the *Songs'* poetry that give him pause. Flawed, marred, and incomplete, *Songs of Experience* threatens to infiltrate and disturb his own editorial judgement. His initial, violent impulse to 'dismember' Blake's corpus seems prompted by the incoherent assemblage that is *Songs* itself. Working more discreetly – adopting Cunningham's bowdlerised version of 'The Tiger' ('What immortal hand or eye | Framed thy fearful symmetry', rather than Blake's more daring, 'What immortal hand or eye | Could frame thy fearful symmetry', for example); adding a second 'Cradle Song' from the notebook to *Songs of Experience*; generally 'shaking up [...] Blake's rhymes' and tidying his grammar and punctuation (H. H. Gilchrist 1887, 94) – Rossetti is able to knit together what Blake had left disjointed (see D 121). 'Social discontent', moreover, seems a blot too ugly to countenance. The art of Rossetti's Blake is removed from the social. His brother William was to agree in the 'Prefatory Memoir' he wrote for *The Poetical Works of William Blake, Lyrical and Miscellaneous* (1874): 'Blake almost totally ignores actual life and its evolution, and the passions and interactions of men as elicited by the wear and tear of real society.' Instead, Blake focuses on 'the large range of primordial emotion, from the utter innocence and happy unconscious instinct of infancy, up to the fervours of the prophet' (W. M. Rossetti 1874, cxi–cxii).

If for Gabriel Rossetti the 'incompleteness' of poems from *Songs* was a cause for concern, for Gilchrist as for Malkin, the 'bold and careless freedom' of the *'unfinished'* lyrics of *Innocence* at least could not be bettered. Flaws, by Gilchrist's aesthetics, became a sign of vitality, as 'The most deceptively perfect wax-model is no substitute for the living flower' (G 73). Endorsing Malkin's avowal of the *Songs'* 'ancient simplicity',

Gilchrist proceeds to recommend Blake's childlikeness (G 73). Of the
Innocence poem 'Spring', for instance ('Little boy | Full of Joy. | Little girl
| Sweet and small, | Cock does crow | So do you [...] | Little lamb | Here
I am, | Come and lick | My white neck. | Let me pull | Your soft wool'),
Gilchrist writes:

> ■ From addressing the child, the poet, by a transition not infrequent with
> him, passes out of himself into the child's person, showing a chame-
> leon sympathy with childlike feelings. Can we not see the little three-
> year-old prattler stroking the white lamb, her feelings made articulate
> for her? – Even more remarkable is the poem entitled *The Lamb*, sweet
> hymn of tender infantine sentiment appropriate to that perennial image
> of meekness [...]. In *The Lamb*, the poet again changes person to that of
> a child. □

> (ll. 10–15, 19–24, E15; G 74)

James Thomson was also to suggest Blake's identification with children, although for him this was unconscious, even transmigratory:

> ■ The adult cannot sing like a child; but Blake in these Songs does so: he
> did not *act* the infantine, for he *was* infantine, by a regeneration as real while
> as mysterious as ever purest saint experienced in the religious life. □

> (Thomson 1896a, 252)

Gilchrist is nowhere so mystical, but his consideration of 'The Lamb's'
'chameleon sympathy', together with his description of the illuminated *Songs*, represent Blake as curiously shape-shifting. Crucially,
furthermore, it is exactly that lack of finish disdained by Rossetti that
gives Gilchrist's imagination the licence to soar. Coming down from
his song-hopped rhapsody, Gilchrist writes:

> ■ True, there are palpable irregularities, metrical licence, lapse of gram-
> mar, and even of orthography; but often the sweetest melody, most daring
> eloquence of rhythm, and, what is more, appropriate rhythm. [...] [W]ould
> finish have bettered their bold and careless freedom? □

> (G 73)

Shirley Dent and Jason Whittaker render the sense here well, noting
how 'Gilchrist distinguishes his work from Aesthetic formalism. It does
not detract from the "spiritual sight" of Blake's works that the aesthetic
and formal details are imperfect. Gilchrist is an epiphanic critic, celebrating the fullness of the experience between spectator and creator'
(Dent and Whittaker 2002, 33).

Gilchrist, then, unlike Rossetti, celebrates the imaginative potential of Blake's *Songs* as unfinished artwork. Yet there is a stumbling block here. To appreciate works like *Songs*, Gilchrist writes:

> ■ [one] needs to be *read* in Blake, to have familiarized oneself with his unsophisticated, archaic, yet spiritual 'manner' – a style *sui generis* as no other artist's ever was, – to be able to sympathize with, or even understand, the equally individual strain of thought, of which it is the vehicle. And one almost must be *born* with a sympathy for it. He neither wrote nor drew for the many, hardly for work'y-day men at all, rather for children and angels; himself 'a divine child', whose playthings were sun, moon, and stars, the heavens and the earth. In an era of academies, associations, and combined efforts, we have in him a solitary, self-taught, and as an artist, *semi*-taught Dreamer. □
>
> (G 3)

His style without precedent, 'himself "a divine child"', Gilchrist's Blake appeared verily to the *Quarterly Review* (1865) 'to have lived apart from chronology' (quoted by D 85). Eschewing 'academies' in the manner of the Pre-Raphaelites, he also eschews 'associations, and combined efforts'. He seems not so much to take up a position in the field of culture as to absent himself from it. The composite artwork of *Songs* is removed from culture too, and indeed from social life: 'workaday', we should note, signifies not working-class but 'ordinary humdrum everyday life' (*OED*). It is true that, ironically, Gilchrist's biography ends up rendering such life in exhaustive detail; true, too, that it is from the interstices of quotidian detail that Gilchrist's rhapsodic description of the illuminated *Songs* leaps forth. There could never be anything so determinate as a bridge built between life and art, it seems; the epiphany depends on a gap. Yet for some, for most, this gap cannot be traversed – not just, Gilchrist seems to say, because only a scanty band would be capable of doing so, but because if the composite dimension of Blake's rare, hand-made books were to have been removed, the gap would never have opened up in the first place. Such is the price of veneration, here of those same hand-made books that we ourselves have tended to glorify in this guide.

LEGACIES OF GILCHRIST'S *LIFE*: WRITINGS BY JAMES THOMSON (1866, 1879), ALGERNON CHARLES SWINBURNE (1868), AND JAMES SMETHAM (1868)

Such was the *Life*'s labour of recovery that in a sense all accounts of Blake that follow are its legacies. However, in this section we offer a streamlined account of the writings, predominantly from the late

1860s, of three key critics, all of whom hailed Blake as a genius, and all of whose work takes off from an explicit engagement with the *Life*. Albeit in different ways, all three critics also position Blake outside the critical establishment and so conspire to ensure his continuing marginalisation: Thomson positions Blake within a mystical tradition and Swinburne within an Aestheticist one; Smetham, most curiously, makes Blake the idol of a religion of art and casts his admirers as disciples.

James Thomson, 'The Poems of William Blake' (1866) and 'A Strange Book' (1879)

James Thomson (sometimes spelled Thompson) (1834–82) was a poet and satirist, and is best known today for his long visionary poem 'The City of Dreadful Night' (1874). He wrote about Blake twice at relative length among numerous other pieces of journalism, although affinities to Blake's writings have also been traced in his poetic output (see Harper 1953; Dent and Whittaker 2002, 53–4, and Chapter 9 below). 'The Poems of William Blake', the better-known essay of the Blakean pair, was written in 1864 and published in the *National Reformer* in 1866 (Thomson 1896b, 321). 'A Strange Book', longer but less interested in Blake, was published in the *Liberal* in 1879. Both were reprinted in the posthumous *Biographical and Critical Studies* (1896). In 'The Poems of William Blake', Thomson recommended that 'all good readers' consult Gilchrist's and the Rossettis' *Life*, and in some measure William Rossetti repaid the compliment in his 'Prefatory Memoir' (1874), when he quoted a passage from Thomson's essay with admiration (W. M. Rossetti 1874, cxix). Thomson's later essay, 'A Strange Book', brings criticism by Swinburne as well as the Rossettis into play. But despite these textual links Thomson was a relative outsider; unlike Swinburne and Smetham, not an intimate of the Pre-Raphaelite Rossettis. Furthermore, as Thomson's primary focus is Blake's mysticism (reiterated by Swinburne but turned to Aestheticist ends), he returns us to that vein of Swedenborgian criticism of Blake that we last mentioned in the previous chapter in connection to Wilkinson. Indeed, Wilkinson is an important reference point for Thomson, not least as Thomson first encountered Blake's poetry in Wilkinson's 1839 edition of *Songs* (Thomson 1896a, 240).

However idiosyncratic in its mysticism, 'The Poems of William Blake' shows Thomson to be ahead of his time. Just one year after the publication of the *Life*, and a full four before the appearance of Swinburne's

Critical Essay, he announces a commitment to examining the more obscure parts of Blake's writings that we are more used to attributing to his Aestheticist successor (see Thomson 1896a, 258). What is at stake for Thomson, however, is not primarily a full elucidation of Blake's writings – indeed, at the time of writing 'The Poems of William Blake' he had not read the prophetic books, the *Life*'s 'Selections' having been too meagre to enable him 'to form a settled opinion' (Thomson 1896a, 257–8). More pertinent, for him, is a mystical tradition at large, of which Blake's works, Thomson writes, are the 'early effects' rather than the 'efficient cause'. In writing about mysticism Thomson is unhindered by Blake's immediate historical context, and so it matters little that Blake 'was scarcely listened to at all' in his lifetime (Thomson 1896a, 241). The mysticism of which he writes:

■ is by no means strict in its theology, being Swedenborgian in one man and Pantheistic in another, while in the East it has readily assimilated Buddhism and Brahmanism and Mohammedanism. Its supreme tendency is to remain or to become again childlike, its supreme aspiration is not virtue, but innocence or guilelessness: so that we may say with truth of those whom it possesses, that the longer they live the younger they grow, as if 'passing out to God by the gate of birth, not death.' □

(Thomson 1896a, 262)

It is in the context of this larger, mystical progression-by-regression that Thomson reflects on the childlikeness of *Songs* and the unconscious, even transmigratory identification with the child speaker that he observes in the 'holy and tender and beautiful babe-lullabies' of Blake's *Innocence* in particular (Thomson 1896a, 253; cited above). In *Experience,* as one might expect from the biographical analogy, Blake grows up, if not – for Thomson wishes to preserve the essential innocence of the entire, favoured collection – to full maturity:

■ the singer is an older child, and even a youth, but not yet a man. The experience is that of a sensitive and thoughtful boy, troubled by the first perceptions of evil where he has believed all good, thinking the whole world cruel and false since some playmate-friend has turned unkind, seeing life all desolate and blank since some coveted object has disappointed in the possession. □

(254)

It is not in the 'early maturity' of *Poetical Sketches,* but in the 'second childhood and boyhood and youth' of *Songs of Innocence and of Experience* that Blake 'was withdrawn from common life into mysticism' (which for

Thomson is a compliment). In this work, as in 'Auguries of Innocence' (c. 1800–4), Blake's achievement is but one part of a wider mystical resurrection:

■ [a seed] of much which is now half-consciously struggling towards organic perfection, and which in two or three generations may be crowned with foliage and blossoms and fruit as the Tree of Life for one epoch. □
(260–1)

Thomson's comments on Blake's works in both of his essays do not stoop to particulars (although we should note that allusions in 'The City of Dreadful Night' attest conversely to his attentiveness). What Thomson does give us, though, is a genealogy of mystical thinkers. 'A Strange Book' traces a line 'from the most ancient Indian gymno-sophists to the Hebrew prophets and poets, to Christian apostles, as Paul and John, to Plato and Plotinus, to Mohammed and the Sufis, to early and mediaeval Christian eremites and saints [...], to George Fox and his Quakers [...], to Behmen and Law, to Swedenborg and Blake, to Shelley' (Thomson 1896b, 326). 'The Poems of William Blake' forges links between 'Elizabethan works', Cowper and Burns, Shelley, Robert Browning, and Ralph Waldo Emerson, who 'stands closest of all in relation to Blake, his verse as well as his essays and lectures being little else than the expression of [...] mystical sim-plicity' (Thomson 1896a, 267). Like Gabriel Rossetti in his chapter 'Supplementary' to the *Life*, Thomson makes extensive connections between Blake and Wilkinson, not only as editor of *Songs*, but also as the author of the poetry collection 'Improvisations of the Spirit' (1857).

Interesting in the links it makes between Blake and nineteenth-century writers both British and North American, Thomson's mystical genealogy is also tacitly oppositional. For where Gilchrist suggested that Blake was so extraordinary that he stood alone, Thomson insists that he had his fellows, albeit on the margin that was mysticism.

Algernon Charles Swinburne, *William Blake: A Critical Essay* (1868)

William Blake: A Critical Essay, by the poet and literary reviewer Algernon Charles Swinburne (1837–1909), was the most influential response to the *Life*. For many indeed *A Critical Essay* outshone the work that was both its precursor and its provocation. 'One cannot read this book and not love Blake,' writes the symbolist poet and scholar Arthur Symons (1865–1945), in his own critical biography, *William Blake* (1907):

■ No one has done so much to vindicate Blake's sanity of imagination as this poet who is no mystic, and who does not naturally love a mystic. [...] [W]hat Swinburne has done is to set the man of genius in his own place as a maker, a poet; he has challenged the world to accept Blake, not for his doctrine, not as either prophet or visionary, but as the writer of great poems and the artist of great designs. □

(Symons 1907, 84, 85)

Less popular than the Gilchrists' and Rossetti brothers' *Life* (Swinburne himself called it 'the most unlucky and despised of all my brain-children' (quoted by Rooksby 1997, 161)), the *Critical Essay* is nonetheless the more glorious critical achievement: the first critical monograph about Blake's writings; the first vindication of his 'prophetic books'; the first attempt, after Henry Crabb Robinson's more scattergun if vital effort in the 1820s, to understand his philosophy. *William Blake: A Critical Essay* was also the occasion for Swinburne's first enunciation of the Aestheticist motto, 'art for art's sake' – the first time, indeed, that this motto had been expressed in English in the context of contemporary art, although for Swinburne it is at the same time a statement about William Blake (Prettejohn 2007, 37).

Swinburne's interest in Blake had been sparked when Gabriel Rossetti showed him the manuscript notebook in late 1859 (Rooksby 1997, 60). In 1862, when Anne Gilchrist was checking proofs of the *Life* in consultation with the Rossettis, he determined to begin work on 'a distinct small commentary of a running kind' on Blake's works, particularly the prophecies (Swinburne 1959–62, I.60). After some delay and considerable enlargement in scope and ambition this was finally published as *William Blake: A Critical Essay* early in 1868 (79). By this time Swinburne had become notorious, thanks to the furore surrounding his shocking, dazzling collection *Poems and Ballads*, published, withdrawn from sale, then issued again in 1866 (*ODNB*). His friends anticipated that this would fuel public interest in *A Critical Essay*. But Swinburne's reputation could work the other way too. To the reviewer Oswald Crawfurd, writing in 1874, it seemed that he 'employ[ed] Blake and his opinions as a sort of stalking-horse in his own onslaught upon the proprieties. [...] Blake [...] comes out of Mr. Swinburne's crucible with the attributes and aspect of a satyr!' (Crawfurd 1874, 490; see further, Paley 1974).

A Critical Essay runs to over three hundred pages in length, and is divided into three sections: 'Life and Designs', 'Lyrical Pieces' (which includes his comments on 'art for art's sake' as well as on *Songs*), and, most capaciously, 'The Prophetic Books'. It is at once a 'review' of Gilchrist's *Life* (S iii); a detailed commentary, affective and critical, on Blake's ideas and writings; and an occasion for Swinburne to develop his own aesthetic ideas and practice. Urgent, ardent, and uncompromising, Swinburne's essay is not a balanced critical assessment – and it is not designed to be. Everywhere there is a 'fierce rushing' akin to that which Blake describes in his poem *America*; poet talks about poet 'in bursts of Bacchic energy, pushing at the limits of interpretation' (E56; Dent and Whittaker 2002, 34).

For closer comment, let us take first Swinburne's reaction to the *Life*, before proceeding to his remarks on *Songs*, and finally his presentation of Blake as an exemplum of the Aestheticist artist. Swinburne's criticism of Gilchrist was oblique but would have been obvious enough, such was his precursor's success. The main bone of Swinburne's contention is Gilchrist's neglect of Blake's prophetic books, and by extension, the neglect of the Rossetti brothers also (Swinburne 1959–62, I.60). '[C]ritics who attempt to judge [Blake] piecemeal do not in effect judge him at all', Swinburne writes. 'If the "Songs" be so good, are not those who praise them bound to examine and try what merit may be latent in the "Prophecies"?' (S 106). Swinburne's celebration of Blake's prophetic books, especially *A Marriage of Heaven and Hell*, sets him apart from the other critics whose views we have read so far in these pages. Granted, he may halt at the face of *Jerusalem*: 'Seriously, one cannot imagine that people will ever read through this vast poem with pleasure enough to warrant them in having patience with it' (S 276). His readings may be impressionistic at times – or better, felt rather than thought. But Swinburne's broader praise remains intact: 'Let all readers and all critics [...] know and remember [...] that in these strangest of all written books there is purpose as well as power, meaning as well as mystery' (S 185–6).

Such is Swinburne's perseverance in the face of difficulty that we may wonder what he makes of the simpler *Songs*. And the answer is that his assessment of the collection again contrasts with that of previous critics. Swinburne's praise of *Songs of Innocence and of Experience* is qualified; he reads it in light of the later prophetic books and in many ways as an adjunct to them:

■ What was written for children can hardly offend men; and the obscurities and audacities of the prophet would here have been clearly out of place. It is indeed some relief to a neophyte serving in the outer courts of such an intricate and cloudy temple, to come upon this little side-chapel set about with the simplest wreaths and smelling of the fields rather than incense, where all the singing is done by clear children's voices to the briefest and least complex tunes. Not at first without a sense of release does the human mind get quit for a little of the clouds of Urizen, the fires of Orc, and all the Titanic apparatus of prophecy. □

(S 114)

Songs *of* innocence are not simply songs *for* innocence, of course, and after dipping in to praise and elucidate 'Night', 'The Little Black Boy', 'Introduction', 'The Chimney Sweeper', and 'Infant Joy', Swinburne seems to recognise this. He also discovers his contentious view of the superiority of *Experience* to *Innocence*, which, unlike Thomson, Gilchrist, and Wilkinson before him, he does not trace to Blake's biography:

■ Against all articulate authority we do however class several of the *Songs of Experience* higher for the great qualities of verse than anything in the earlier division of these poems. If the *Songs of Innocence* have the shape and smell of leaves or buds, these have in them the light and sound of fire or the sea. Entering among them, a fresher savour and a larger breath strikes one upon the lips and forehead. In the first part we are shown who they are who have or who deserve the gift of spiritual sight: in the second, what things there are for them to see when that gift has been given. Innocence, the quality of beasts and children, has the keenest eyes; and such eyes alone can discern and interpret the actual mysteries of experience. □

(S 116)

At first sight a subordination of *Innocence* to *Experience*, this in fact suggests something more nuanced. *Experience* does not succeed and supersede *Innocence* as maturity usurps immaturity. For *Experience* can be interpreted only by 'Innocence, the quality of beasts and children'. We might here – in keeping with Swinburne's holistic method – recall a note that Blake made in the manuscript of his poem *The Four Zoas*: 'Innocence dwells with Wisdom but never with Ignorance' (E697). Swinburne seems either to echo or to pre-empt this when, earlier in *A Critical Essay*, he describes 'the wise innocence of children' (S 27). Furthermore, and again like Blake, he does not always align childhood utterances with 'purity and goodness' (D 125). In 'Infant Joy', for example, Swinburne finds a 'little bodily melody of soulless and painless laughter' (S 116).

The 'wise innocence' Swinburne defends, then, is not coterminous with purity and goodness, and indeed this identification might restrict its potential. Such is the implication of Swinburne's reading of the

'Motto to the Songs of Innocence & of Experience', which he is bringing into print from Blake's notebook for the first time:

■ The Good are attracted by Mens perceptions
And Think not for themselves
Till Experience teaches them to catch
And to cage the Fairies & Elves □

(ll. 1–4, E499)

Swinburne interprets this verse ironically, from the point of view of 'The
Good' whose innocence has been restricted or perverted to the point
that even 'Experience' is viewed with suspicion. He writes, contrarily:

■ Experience must do the work of innocence as soon as conscience
begins to take the place of instinct, reflection of perception; but the moment
experience begins upon this work, men raise against her the conventional
clamour of envy and stupidity. She teaches how to entrap and retain such
fugitive delights as children and animals enjoy without seeking to catch or
cage them; but this teaching the world calls sin. □

(S 124–5)

Swinburne's identification of experience with sin (or more precisely
with freedom from the restraints of moral law), and his own predilec-
tion for both, means that despite his vindication of 'wise innocence',
he seems 'much more personally engaged' when writing about *Songs
of Experience* (D 131). Like the Milton of Blake's *Marriage of Heaven and
Hell*, he is 'of the Devils party', but Swinburne knows it (pl. 5, E35). In
his commentary on *Experience*, sometimes he is touched by the music
of its verse: the 'glory of metre' and 'sonorous beauty of lyrical work'
in 'Earth's Answer'; the 'fervent beauty and vigour of music' in 'The
Tyger' (S 119). But he is also concerned to explicate the poems' meaning (and here one may sense a dig at earlier criticism):

■ It is pleasant enough to commend and to enjoy the palpable excellence
of Blake's work; but another thing is simply and thoroughly requisite – to
understand what the workman was after. □

(S 127)

At the heart of Blake's creed, Swinburne thinks, is what he calls Blake's
'antinomian mysticism', which he defines as follows:

■ as long as a man believes all things he may do any thing; scepticism
(not sin) is alone damnable, being the one thing purely barren and

negative; do what you will with your body, as long as you refuse it leave
to disprove or deny the life eternally inherent in your soul. □

(S 96)

'First get well hold of the mystic,' he writes of *Songs*, 'and you will then
at once get a better view and comprehension of the painter and poet'
(S 127). Hence his invocation of 'To Tirzah', the poem in which Blake
'set[s] forth his spiritual creed' most 'clearly and earnestly' (S 121):

■ Thou Mother of my Mortal part,
With cruelty didst mould my Heart,
And with false self-decieving tears
Didst bind my Nostrils Eyes & Ears. □

(ll. 9–12, E30)[3]

'[T]hus those who live in subjection to the senses would in their turn
bring the senses into subjection', writes Swinburne; 'unable to see
beyond the body, they find it worth while to refuse the body its right to
freedom' (S 125). He also summons 'Earth's Answer':

■ Prison'd on watry shore
Starry Jealousy does keep my den
Cold and hoar
Weeping o'er
I hear the father of the ancient men. □

(ll. 6–10, E18)

'Thus,' Swinburne enlightens us:

■ in the poet's mind, Nature and Religion are the two fetters of life, one
on the right wrist, the other on the left; an obscure material force on this
hand, and on that a mournful imperious law: the law of divine jealousy,
the government of a God who weeps over his creature and subject with
unprofitable tears, and rules by forbidding and dividing: the 'Urizen' of the
'Prophetic Books'. □

(S 118–19)

William Blake: A Critical Essay has been called 'a creative misread-
ing', more about Swinburne himself than about his putative subject.
And to be sure, Swinburne 'played down the significance of Blake's
Christianity and developed some odd parallels with de Sade' (*ODNB*).[4]
But provocatively, and we think convincingly, Swinburne also cast
Blake as a rebel (S 3), and a literal as well as Gilchrist's ideal repub-
lican (S 17, 223–5; see G 349). His theorisation of the relationship in

Blake's wider writings between the body and soul, imagination and reason, and man and God, seem likewise to be spot on. Most appositely, Swinburne also put Blake in the company of Shelley and the American poet Walt Whitman (1819–92). He writes:

■ The points of contact and sides of likeness between William Blake and Walt Whitman are so many and so grave, as to afford some ground of reason to those who preach the transition of souls or transfusion of spirits. The great American is not a more passionate preacher of sexual or political freedom than the English artist. To each the imperishable form of a possible and universal Republic is [...] requisite and adorable. □
(S 300–1)

Whitman's verse furthermore seems to Swinburne to be less esoteric, more natural and accessible, than Blake's:

■ Whitman has seldom struck a note of thought and speech so just and so profound as Blake has now and then touched upon; but his work is generally more frank and fresh, smelling of sweeter air, and readier to expound or expose its message, than this of the prophetic books. □
(S 303)

Swinburne's paralleling of Blake and Whitman was to be reiterated and extended in a rich and wonderful review of *A Critical Essay* that was published in *The Fortnightly Review* in 1868 by the North American social reformer and ethical critic Moncure Daniel Conway (1832–1907) (see Conway 1868, and Ferguson-Wagstaffe 2006).

Having marked the many justices of Swinburne's reading of Blake, we cannot leave *A Critical Essay* without comment on his Aestheticism, which for Symons, of course, was the point in all its pertinency ('Blake's mysticism can be studied elsewhere [...] but what Swinburne has done is to set the man of genius in his own place as a maker, a poet'). At the opening of the second part of the *Essay*, just before he comes to *Songs*, Swinburne makes the following assertion, which has come to have a life of its own quite apart from its original context in *William Blake: A Critical Essay*:

■ Art is not like fire or water, a good servant and a bad master; rather the reverse. She will help in nothing, of her own knowledge or freewill: upon terms of service you will get worse than nothing out of her. Handmaid of religion, exponent of duty, servant of fact, pioneer of morality, she cannot in any way become; she would be none of these things though you were to bray her in a mortar. [...] [I]f the artist does his work with an eye to [advantages of a sort you may call moral or spiritual] or for the sake of bringing about such improvements, he will too probably fail even of them. Art for art's sake first of all, and afterwards we may suppose all the rest shall be added to her (or if not she need hardly be overmuch concerned). □

(S 90–1)

'Or if not she need hardly be overmuch concerned': with this seeming afterthought Swinburne raises the stakes. This is more than antino-mianism, more than an assertion of the primacy of poetry over moral laws and social quietism: not only religion, duty, fact, and morality, but any direct opposition to them become, in art, negligible, dispen-sable. We should, however, remember here that Swinburne is making a point in relation to the concrete instance of Blake's practice as well as announcing a more carrying credo: it is Blake who 'had a faith of his own, made out of art for art's sake, and worked by means of art; and whatever made against this faith was as hateful to him as any heresy to any pietist' (S 101).[5] Such resistance to generalisation, to abstract theorisation, might give us pause. For Swinburne names in order to defame not merely religion, duty, fact, and morality, but art's role as handmaid, exponent, servant, pioneer; he attacks art as public policy, if you like, art as positivist assertor, art as instrument, rather than art's entanglement in religious, scientific, or moral processes per se. Elizabeth Prettejohn puts it well: for Swinburne, it 'is not that the work of art must be devoid of moral implications, but rather that it must not aim at, or deliver, a particular moral *result*' (Prettejohn 2007, 46). Whether this fits *Songs* is for us – for you – to decide. But surely it emphasises that part of Swinburne's critical project which finds the interpretation of Blake's works 'worth the trying' (S 4), even if they resist our attempts to settle them into any fixed form or message.

James Smetham, 'Essay on Blake' [1869] (1880)

From the flexible Swinburne to a third, important response to Gilchrist's *Life*: 'Essay on Blake' by the artist and writer James Smetham (1821–1889). Smetham's review essay was first published in *The London Quarterly Review* in January 1869, and reprinted in the *Life*'s second edition of 1880. It is transfixed by Blake's visual art, particularly, as Gabriel Rossetti had been, by its colouring. Responding synaestheti-cally to the illuminated *Innocence*, Smetham describes:

■ a sort of rainbow-coloured, innocent page, in which the thrilling music of the verse, and the gentle bedazzlement of the lines and colours so inter-mingle, that the mind hangs in a pleasant uncertainty as to whether it is a picture that is singing, or a song which has newly budded and blossomed into colour and form. □

(Smetham 1880, 331)

Of the bipartite *Songs, Innocence* is Smetham's particular favourite. He still praises *Experience*, but seems baffled by it: snatching quotations from its lyrics, borrowing testimonials of its merit from early nineteenth-century critics, re-stating the importance of looking at word and design together (339–43).

Of greater note than Smetham's comments on *Songs*, however, is the mood and message throughout his essay, of right worship. To a far greater extent than Gilchrist, the Rossetti brothers, or Swinburne, 'Smetham presented his readers with a full-fledged cult of beauty with Blake as its patron saint; there is no question that Blake is anything but a specialized taste' (D 169; see also Trodd 2012, 58–63). Blake 'stands, and must always stand, eminently alone', writes Smetham. 'The fountain of thought and knowledge to others, he could never be the head of a school. [...] He can never be popular in the ordinary sense of the word, write we never so many songs in his praise' (Smetham 1880, 351). However, Smetham's Blake can stand as 'cultural idol' for a select band of 'disciples or votaries' (Trodd 2012, 62). These Smetham imagines in the closing pages of his essay, gathering in a sort of Blakean cathedral:

■ If we might have our wish, we would select some accessible but far removed, quiet vale [...]. Here we would have built a strong, enduring, grey-stone, simple building of one long chamber, lighted from above. This chamber should be divided into niches. In each niche, and of the size of life, there should be done in fresco, in low tones of simple, deep colour, one of [Blake's] grand designs [from the *Book of Job*], inlaid in a broad gold flat, which should be incised in deep brown lines with the sub-signification of Blake's *Marginalia* [*the text included on each page of the Job designs*]. They should be executed by men well paid by the Government – men like G. F. Watts and D. G. Rossetti, and Madox Brown and Burne Jones, and W. B. Scott. At the inner end of this hall of power there should be a marble statue of Blake, by Woolner[.] □

(Smetham 1880, 350–1)

Smetham's vision is both iconic and iconoclastic: iconoclastic in that the artists he deploys all had a vexed relationship, whether still live or historical, with the Royal Academy, and iconic in that Blake's designs will be fixed, like saints or idols, in ornamented recesses, and a statue of Blake himself erected. In common with Thomson and Swinburne, then, Smetham conspires to present Blake as a niche interest (if you will forgive us the pun): Thomson, with his talk of mysticism; the infamous Swinburne, with his oppositional, elusive Aestheticist credo; Smetham, with his casting of those interested in Blake as disciples. Together with the association of Gilchrist's and the Rossetti brothers' *Life* with Pre-Raphaelitism, the scene was set for rebarbative reaction.

THE COUNTER-ATTACK: REVIEW ESSAYS BY OSWALD CRAWFURD (1874), COVENTRY PATMORE (1876), AND HENRY G. HEWLETT (1876)

By the 1870s it was impossible to extricate Blake's name from those of his Pre-Raphaelite and Aestheticist admirers. The Rossettis had cemented their role as recoverers of Blake's reputation when in 1874 William Rossetti edited *The Poetical Works of William Blake, Lyrical and Miscellaneous*, a handy octavo volume published by George Bell and Sons in the Aldine Edition of the British Poets series. William Rossetti's lengthy 'Prefatory Memoir' discusses Blake's art in terms familiar from his brother Gabriel's contributions to the *Life*. On the subject of Blake's writings, it agrees likewise that *Songs of Experience* is more 'faulty' a collection than its counterpart, *Songs of Innocence* (W. M. Rossetti 1874, cxiv–cxv; see also the first section of this chapter, above). However, Rossetti still much prefers the collection to Blake's prophetic books, at which he can take only 'a hasty and half-shuddering glance', excluding them, for the main part, from his edition (W. M. Rossetti 1874, cxxix).

A second important advancement of Blake's reputation in the early 1870s was again associated with the Pre-Raphaelites: the Burlington Fine Arts Club's *Exhibition of the Works of William Blake*, mounted in London in 1876 and curated by the poet and painter William Bell Scott (1811–90), an associate of the Rossettis. In addition to numerous of Blake's paintings, prints, and engravings, the exhibition also displayed samples of his written work and composite art, including several illuminated books. Two copies of *Songs of Innocence and of Experience* were exhibited in book-form, under glass. Pages of other copies were displayed as pictures in frames.[6] The Burlington Fine Arts Club was 'one of the most important private cultural institutions of the day', and the Blake exhibition kick-started 'the gradual emergence of Blake's pictorial work into the wider public world' (Trodd 2012, 156). Still, Scott's praise of Blake's 'genius' in his 'Introductory Remarks' to the exhibition catalogue was seen by certain critics to tie Blake's fortunes inextricably to his own and those of his associates (Scott 1876, 9). Exposed to Blake's works for the first time, some (especially those already biased against the Pre-Raphaelites) found the exhibition 'a disappointment' (D 183).

The reaction against these advancements by a clutch of reviewers writing in the 1870s was broadly rebarbative and regressive. For Oswald Crawfurd (1834–1909), writer, editor, and diplomatist, Coventry Patmore (1823–96), poet and essayist, and Henry Gay Hewlett (1832–97), civil servant, amateur poet, and essayist, Blake's reputation was inextricable from the reputation of his most notorious commentators, the Rossetti brothers and Swinburne. Patmore and Hewlett extended their attack to Blake's writings as well. These two, in particular, had no truck with the prophecies, finding any attempt to vindicate them or the values of mysticism or obscurity they seemed to exemplify wilfully perverse and even socially dangerous. *Songs* again finds correlative favour, relatively speaking, as it had with Gilchrist and critics before him. Where *Innocence* is found pleasingly 'childlike' by Crawfurd and tritely childish, even 'namby-pamby', by Hewlett, *Experience* (with the exception of some of its lyrics) seems to foreshadow the 'obscurity' that blasts the prophetic books (Crawfurd 1874, 484, 483; Hewlett 1876, 766, 770, 771).

The most lengthy and complex essay of the three is Hewlett's 'Imperfect Genius: William Blake', published in the *Contemporary Review* (October 1876). Blake's 'genius' seems 'imperfect' to Hewlett because, measured against criteria that 'have stood the test of time', Blake's capabilities fall far short, whatever the claims of his admirers (Hewlett 1876, 760). Works by canonical greats such as 'Homer, Phidias, Rafaelle, Shakespeare, Milton, Beethoven' manifest 'qualities of originality, fertility, equability, coherence, and articulateness' each of which Hewlett finds almost entirely lacking in Blake's writings (Hewlett 1876, 756). The inclusion of Raphael in this list is a knowing dig at the Pre-Raphaelites, who aspired to return art to its state before the advent of Raphael and his school. Turning to Blake's works, Hewlett discerns that although *Songs of Innocence* is not as derivative as *Poetical Sketches*, it savours strongly of Isaac Watts's *Divine and Moral Songs for Children*, as well as Shakespeare, Beaumont and Fletcher, and Pope (766). The 'antithetical' *Songs of Experience*, which in its answers to poems in *Innocence* seeks 'to disillusionize the minds of [Blake's] young disciples', is equally lacking in inventiveness (767). Here Blake is guilty of 'self-repetition', not only in going over the same ground as *Innocence*, but also in anticipating the prophetic books; 'this habit of riding an idea to death is among the most marked of Blake's characteristics' (Hewlett 1876, 768). In *Experience* are also 'the first striking indications of the new influence which henceforth dominated [Blake's] mind. [In] all his later verse [...] [f]orm is sacrificed to idea, the luxuries of grace and music to the urgent necessities of utterance and denunciation' (771).

Hewlett's knives are sharpest when he confronts (and names) Gilchrist, the Rossettis, and Swinburne, also invoking Scott and the young scholar and positive reviewer of the Aldine Blake, George Saintsbury, whose 'fervid zeal' in support of Blake was 'likely sooner or later to provoke reaction' (763). '[D]uring the last few years,' he writes:

> ■ claims [...] have been advanced on behalf of William Blake, and urged by a few of his advocates with such strenuous persistence as to secure his provisional apotheosis. Thanks to their exertions, we have already a small library of Blakeian literature, which threatens to become larger every year, and the limited circle within which his designs used to be known has recently been widened by the exhibition of them in collected form. The enthusiasm excited by his name is still confined to a comparatively select school, but what it lacks in breadth is made up in intensity. □
>
> (760)

Hewlett's criticism of Blake's admirers is cutting if contradictory. On the one hand, they succumb to 'the exquisite fascination of belonging to the esoteric circle of disciples, of being among the privileged few who have discovered an unrecognized treasure, and possess the secret of a charm denied to the multitude'. On the other hand, their 'worship of indefiniteness in art' has a spreading, socially disruptive potential: for it is 'those who find beauty in chaos, and have no scruple about upsetting social fabrics which they cannot rebuild' who will most favour the 'prophet of revolutionary ideas' that is William Blake (759).

CHAPTER FIVE

Blake and the Moderns:
Symbolism and Scholarship

For John Todhunter (1839–1916), lecturing on *Songs of Innocence and of Experience* to the female students of Dublin's Alexandra College in the early 1870s, William Blake, by virtue of his social and political utopianism, was emphatically 'a modern'. 'But unlike many of our modern men,' thinks Todhunter, 'the genius of Blake led him not in the direction of rationalism and materialism, but in that of spiritualism and mysticism' (Todhunter 1874, 14). Todhunter, a playwright and poet, uses the word 'modern' not to mean 'contemporary', but 'to describe Blake's *avant garde* qualities' (Fletcher 1974, 6). Far from being a coterie poet, Blake, 'quite a new discovery even for literary men', is for Todhunter a prophet of 'the universal brotherhood of democracy'. The endeavour of Todhunter's lectures is to make Blake's poetry accessible, immediate. He refers to Gilchrist's *Life*, but also recommends a separate edition of *Songs* (probably R. H. Shepherd's; see below) which may be had 'for a few shillings' (Todhunter 1872, 7). In all, Todhunter shows 'a discriminating enthusiasm at a moment when Blake's reputation was still equivocal' (Fletcher 1974, 5).

With the dawning of the twentieth century, there were indications that Blake's moment had arrived. *Songs* had begun its slow creep into the national cultural consciousness in the pages of general anthologies of verse; textual editions were proliferating and becoming increasingly accurate and scholarly. On 20 March 1926 the British Prime Minister Stanley Baldwin and others wrote to the editor of *The Times* soliciting subscriptions for a 'Centenary Memorial' of Blake to be erected in St Paul's Cathedral – quite an irony given that Blake was 'one of the most anti-ecclesiastical' of poets, as the North American academic Helen C. White observed in 1927 (White 1927, 7). 'To-day', the letter to *The Times* continues, '[Blake's] works command the highest prices in two hemispheres, while the verses for which he despaired of any readers now even appear in advertisements in our streets and are sung at national gatherings.'

Songs of Innocence and of Experience and the verses which open *Milton* – better known as the hymn 'Jerusalem' since being set to music by Hubert Parry in 1916 – seemed, then, to be assuming canonical status. But the reputation of Blake's prophetic books continued to lag behind. In this chapter we will see that Swinburne's efforts to recuperate Blake's later writings continued, first in the hands of Edwin Ellis and W. B. Yeats in the 1890s, and then with somewhat greater, albeit slow-burning, success by the efforts of S. Foster Damon and Geoffrey Keynes in the 1920s. Such an emphasis on the prophetic books meant that, in the hands of Ellis and Yeats in particular, *Songs* was interpreted almost exclusively – and sometimes awkwardly – in the light of Blake's later writings. One of the things that the abstruse, learned, and increasingly scholarly criticism we survey in this chapter reminds us is that the critics' Blake is not the same as the public's Blake, or at least that writers of this period tended to make Blake writerly: to make interpreting his works a task and challenge as well as a pleasure; to dive deep to retrieve allegorical meanings; to read widely in order to establish Blake's relation to tradition with authority. *Songs* was no longer simple – or if it was, this needed, for the most part, to be said in the most complex of ways.

Writers also saw in Blake's works their own aesthetic, reflected (or in the case of T. S. Eliot, distorted). Hence the Irish novelist and poet James Joyce (1882–1941), noting in his 1912 lecture on Blake how 'amazed' he was 'that the symbolic beings Los and Urizen and Vala and Tiriel and Enitharmon and the shades of Milton and Homer came from their ideal world to a poor London room, and no other incense greeted their coming than the smell of East Indian tea and eggs fried in lard' (Joyce 1959, 218). Hence Ellis and Yeats, imagining that Blake, like them, was an Irishman. The criticism we look at in this chapter also tends to situate Blake, even the Blake of *Songs*, as an oppositional figure, set in particular against what Joyce calls 'the hurried materialism now in vogue', and intent on joining the temporal and eternal worlds (220).[1]

The chapter is in four sections. It begins by giving an account of the complex 'Symbolic System' developed by Ellis and Yeats in *The Works of William Blake* (1893). It next compares Yeats's view that Blake's writings were cut off from living tradition with T. S. Eliot's criticism in *The Sacred Wood* (1920) of Blake's 'home-made' philosophy. While the opening of Eliot's essay countenances the possibility that Blake might be a powerful, self-made artist despite his position outside 'the Latin traditions', in the end it is Blake's isolation from tradition that prevents him from becoming 'a classic' (Eliot 1997a, 133–4). The final two chapter sections establish Damon's study of Blake's mysticism, *William Blake, His Philosophy and Symbols* (1924), and then Keynes's scholarly edition of *The Writings of William Blake* (1925) as the first sustained twentieth-century scholarship on Blake, portentous, respectively, of the later criticism of Northrop Frye and David Erdman we examine in Chapter 6.

THE SYMBOLIC SYSTEM: W. B. YEATS AND EDWIN ELLIS, *THE WORKS OF WILLIAM BLAKE, POETIC, SYMBOLIC, AND CRITICAL* (1893)

There is no getting away from the difficulty of Yeats and Ellis's *Works*, whose account of *Songs* opens by asserting that 'The "Songs of Innocence", like the book of "Vala", begin with Tharmas' (E-Y II.9). Nonetheless, we shall try. Flawed but compelling, Ellis and Yeats's three-volume *The Works of William Blake* (1893) is perhaps the least accessible of the critical responses to *Songs* we consider in this guide. Yet as the twentieth-century Blake scholar Kathleen Raine contends, it need not have been that way. Ellis and Yeats's symbolic language 'might be called "occult" or "esoteric", since it[s meaning] is hidden from all but initiates; yet it is so hidden only in so far as its terms are incomprehensible except in the light of knowledge of a certain kind. [...] There is a learning unknown to textual scholars and literary historians which is no less exact than theirs; and this learning of the imagination Yeats instantly recognized in Blake' (Raine 1986, 88, 87) (we discuss Raine's criticism in its own right in Chapter 6).

Let us begin by drawing some lines of connection between Ellis and Yeats's *Works* and the criticism we have already described, before putting their knowledge of Blake in context, and proceeding finally to their criticism of *Songs*. Such preparatory work will, hopefully, enable us to return to Tharmas better informed. Like Wilkinson (Chapter 3) and Thomson (Chapter 4), then, Ellis and Yeats are interested in Blake's mysticism, and make frequent and thoroughgoing mention of the writings of Swedenborg and Boehme, among numerous other sources. Like the Pre-Raphaelites (Chapter 4), they see Blake as the prophet for what Yeats, in his essay 'William Blake and the Imagination' (1897), would call 'the religion of art' (Yeats 1903c, 168). Like Swinburne, they prioritise the prophetic books, which they conceive of (in a characteristic wrenching of Blakean language) as the 'symbolic' books, above Blake's lyrical or, they say, 'literary' writings. For Ellis and Yeats, though, the 'symbolic' books, pre-eminent among which was Blake's unfinished, manuscript poem *Vala: Or The Four Zoas* (1797–c. 1810), were consistent, successful, and intelligible, as *Jerusalem*, for example, had not seemed to Swinburne. More than this: the 'symbolic' books cohered, they thought, into a greater whole: a 'Symbolic System' (E-Y I.viii, 233–420). In a final departure from previous critics, Ellis and Yeats categorised *Songs* wholesale as not 'literary' like *Poetical Sketches, An Island in the Moon*, and the manuscript notebook poems, but 'symbolic' – they categorised it, in short, as one of the prophetic books. *Songs of Innocence and of Experience*, they write:

■ contain more than one indication that the great mystical building was already planned. [...] [Blake] was going through a period of mental change, ceasing to be a poet who enjoyed mysticism, and becoming a mystic who enjoyed poetry. □

(E-Y I.22)

That said, as we shall explain, the book does not quite fit its category. Ellis seems to sense this when he writes, 'The symbolic element in the songs is slight, delicate, evanescent. Here, more even than elsewhere, the heavy tread of the interpreter is oppressive' (E-Y II.9).

William Butler Yeats (1865–1939), the poet, had first encountered Blake's verse in youth. When he was 'fifteen or sixteen', and 'in all things Pre-Raphaelite', his father had told him about Rossetti and Blake and given him their poetry to read (Yeats 1999, 114). Edwin John Ellis (1848–1916), a poet, illustrator, and '"mathematician with the mathematics left out" – his father was a great mathematician', also first heard of Blake in a Pre-Raphaelite context, picking up his passion in its painters' studios (Yeats 1999, 144). Ellis, a friend of Yeats's father, had been developing a numerological theory of *Jerusalem*, and Yeats, nearly twenty years Ellis's junior, was becoming increasingly interested in occultism, cabbalism, and practical magic, when in the spring of 1889 they pooled their talents and began work on their critical edition. After the publication of *The Works of William Blake* four years later, Ellis would go on to produce his own edition of *The Poetical Works of William Blake* (1906) and a biography, *The Real Blake* (1907). He also edited a facsimile edition of *Songs* (1893), which covers much of the same ground as the comments on the collection in *Works*, but is far more explicit. This has the benefit of clarity at the cost of suggestiveness.

Yeats's engagement with Blake was even more extensive and enduring: he edited an accessibly-introduced, more textually accurate, and reasonably-priced volume of Blake's early writings and selections from the prophecies for The Muses' Library series in 1893; he included two essays on Blake in his collection *Ideas of Good and Evil* (1903) – 'William Blake and his Illustrations to *The Divine Comedy*', and 'William Blake and the Imagination', first published respectively in the *Savoy* (July–September 1896) and the *Academy* (19 June 1897); and in the 1920s he wrote Blake into the sixteenth 'Phase' of his own elaborate myth, *A Vision* (1926; rev. 1937). But there are finer threads of Blake's influence than we have space to unpick here woven throughout Yeats's oeuvre, in his poetry as well as his prose – for example, his pairing of poems such as 'The Song of the Happy Shepherd' and 'The Sad Shepherd', which seems to Edward Larrissy to be patterned after *Songs* (Larrissy 2006, 2–4).[2]

The question of who wrote what in the *Works* has seemed important to settle not least as its quality is undeniably uneven. Its 'writing' was 'mainly Ellis's', Yeats later said, but its 'thinking [...] as much mine as his'. Volume 1 comprises a memoir of Blake's life written primarily by Ellis, and an account of the symbolic system written by Yeats. Volume 2, in which the comment on *Songs* appears, consists of explanations of Blake's poems written by Ellis but based on notes by Yeats; and Volume 3 contains the texts of Blake's works (note on flyleaf of Yeats's personal copy of E-Y, cited by Adams 1955, 47–8). '[W]hat Blake needed most in 1889 was a clean, complete, and accurate text,' writes Northrop Frye in his essay 'Yeats and the Language of Symbolism'. But unfortunately Ellis and Yeats were not the ones to give it to him: 'neither [...] knew much about editing, nor could they read Blake's handwriting with consistent accuracy' (Frye 1963, 231). Often erroneous, although including lithographs of varying quality of some of the prophecies at least, the *Works'* final volume is almost universally disparaged. The 'Memoir' in its initial volume has also met with ridicule, especially for its outrageous, unevidenced claim that Blake – like Ellis and Yeats – was an Irishman, son of the impecunious John O'Neil who, fleeing his debtors, had taken the name of his lower-born wife, Ellen Blake. William Blake's 'rebellious political enthusiasm' and 'reckless generosity in money matters' were both owing, apparently, to his 'wild O'Neil blood'. Furthermore, '[t]he very manner of Blake's writing has an Irish flavour, a lofty extravagance of invention and epithet, recalling the *Tain Bo Cuilane* and other old Irish epics' (E-Y I.2–3).

The 'Memoir' is also shaped by the interest of both Ellis and Yeats in practical magic, which inflects their treatment of Blake's visions especially. In attempts to prove the truth of what Blake saw, and thereby to demonstrate his sanity, the duo conducted 'curious experiments

[...] with persons who, on receiving a symbol, have the power of seeing and conversing with visionary forms raised by that symbol' (see, for example, E-Y I.96). Their pseudo-scientific experiments might seem dubious, but at stake for Ellis and Yeats were the origins and truth of the symbolic system they were mapping. Blake's visions, Ellis writes, 'suggested a vast symbolic myth to him, containing a whole language of names and personages'; they arose from 'an atmosphere of visionary matter always ready to permeate him, to which from time to time he was more or less open' (E-Y I.95–6).

Better received from *The Works of William Blake* have proved to be Yeats's essay 'The Necessity of Symbolism', printed mid-way through Volume 1, and the account in the *Works'* 'Preface' of the relationship in Blake's writings between nature and imagination. With Palmer, Gilchrist, and even to a degree the Rossetti brothers, we saw Blake's *Songs* in particular drawn into the ambit of pastoralism. Summing up '[t]he whole of Blake's teaching', Ellis and Yeats argue, by contrast, that for Blake 'Nature' has nothing to do with reality and seems only by a corrupted consciousness to belong to such:

■ Nature, he tells (or rather he reminds us), is merely a name for one form of mental existence. Art is another and a higher form. [...]

Nature, – or creation, – is a result of the shrinkage of consciousness, – originally clairvoyant, – under the rule of the five senses, and of argument and law. [...]

In Imagination only we find a Human Faculty that touches nature at one side, and spirit on the other. Imagination may be described as that which is sent bringing spirit to nature, entering into nature, and seemingly losing its spirit, that nature being revealed as symbol may lose the power to delude.

Imagination is thus the philosophic name of the Saviour, whose symbolic name is Christ, just as Nature is the philosophic name of Satan and Adam. [...]

Art and poetry, by constantly using symbolism, continually remind us that nature itself is a symbol. To remember this, is to be redeemed from nature's death and destruction. ☐

(E-Y I.xii–xiii)

These were the terms within which Ellis and Yeats read *Songs*, and like Swinburne, they found the collection's comment on nature and imagination encapsulated in 'To Tirzah'. 'The song may be looked on as an abbreviated form of all the Prophetic Books,' writes Ellis. 'Experience and sense – the female of mind – have closed in on the true intellect, until it seems as though man had a body distinct from his mind. But

Imagination enters the dark region, – Jesus dies, – and the chain is broken' (E-Y II.17).

'Two principal causes have hitherto kept the critics [...] from attaining a knowledge of what Blake meant,' write Ellis and Yeats in their volumes' 'Preface': 'The first is the solidity of the myth, and its wonderful coherence. The second is the variety of terms in which the sections of it are named' (E-Y I.viii). The 'master-key' to Blake's 'Symbolic System', they thought, was their realisation that for Blake 'Humanity' was fourfold, 'divided under the names of the Four Zoas in the myth' (E-Y I.ix) – that is, in Blake's poem *Vala*, Urizen, Luvah, Tharmas, and Urthona. 'Zoa' is commonly glossed as 'living creature' (see Damon 1924, 145). As we are approaching what the *Works* have to say about *Songs*, it may help to indicate that in certain of their guises, the Zoas are associated in turn with the occupations of ploughman (Urizen), weaver (Luvah), shepherd (Tharmas, who 'before the fall, minds the flocks of innocence') (E-Y I.280), and blacksmith (Urthona). However, they can take many guises and assume several names – W. H. Stevenson gives a helpful, condensed guide in *Blake: The Complete Poems* (Stevenson 2007, 297). It is probably best to think of the Zoas not as characters or gods, but as dynamic principles or bundles of attributes. Ellis and Yeats go into a good more detail than this, and their schematic manner of laying it out, in lists, diagrams, and fold-out charts, can give a sense of monolithic density and inflexibility. The irony is that the myth whose harmonics they seek to sound in Blake's writings is shifting and dynamic. As Yeats counsels:

■ It must always be remembered that when Blake speaks of any of these personages [the Zoas] he does not mean merely this or that particular attribute, but all the attributes in various degrees according to the point of view from which we choose to take the story. A perfect mystical symbol or fable can be read in any region of nature and thought – mineral, meteoric, religious, philosophical – it is all one. Things we have to give in *succession* in our explanatory prose are set forth *simultaneously* in Blake's verse. From this arises the greater part of the obscurity of the symbolic books. The surface is perpetually, as it were, giving way before one, and revealing another surface below it, and that again dissolves when we try to study it. □

(E-Y I.287)

And so we return to Tharmas, with whom '[t]he "Songs of Innocence", like the book of "Vala", begin':

■ But it is the innocent Tharmas whose face Vala blesses, whose flocks give her companionship and whose rivers grow reeds fitted for the pen that should write what 'every child may joy to hear'. He is now quite different from the 'false tongue' or 'sense of touch' to whom the spirit of Forgiveness and Imagination was sacrificed. The portion of 'Vala' which beings with Night IX., l. 384, shows the return of nature, now the 'sinless soul', to the state of innocence. □

(E-Y II.9)

Riffling through the pages of Volume 3 of the *Works* (or using Nelson Hilton's online concordance, or even relying on memory),[3] we may follow each reference in turn, both explicit (to *Vala*) and implied by quotation (of *Milton* and *Jerusalem*). However, we should bear in mind that in terms of Ellis and Yeats's symbolist approach, the golden threads of connection are already vibrating in unison. It is of no matter that the name Tharmas was not applied by Blake to an aspect of his myth until he began composing *Vala* in 1797. According to Ellis and Yeats, the chord struck at the beginning of *Songs'* first 'Introduction' works to unsettle our learned association of nature with innocence. Tharmas appears as one returned to innocence, or more properly, perhaps, as a figure who can be both innocent and not innocent. We tend to think in a linear fashion of innocence being followed by experience, but here their relationship is unsettled, defamiliarised.

Disconcertingly, and with the whiff of self-contradiction, Ellis and Yeats return us to linearity when they introduce *Experience*: 'In the Introduction the Bard speaks out more clearly. Many visions had been seen and some prophetic books written between the date when these songs were engraved (1794) and that of the previous collection (1789)' (E-Y II.12). Soon enough, though, we are returned to the Zoas, when the 'Earth' of the second *Song of Experience* speaks as 'Vala' and asserts that jealousy, darkness, and 'the state when "the masculine separates from the feminine, and both from man"' – a Blakean statement but not an actual quotation – still have power. 'This', Ellis writes gnomically, 'is "Experience"' (E-Y II.12).

Inevitably, subsequent critics have picked out blind spots in Ellis and Yeats's approach. Recently, for example, Nicholas M. Williams has remarked on the loss they incur by 'cutting Blake off from the stream of history and confining him to the purely mental world of mystical meaning'. Ellis and Yeats read 'The Little Black Boy', writes Williams, 'entirely in terms of the relations of the temporal and eternal worlds, with no reference to the colonial slave system' (Williams 2006, 10). As the *Works* puts it:

■ the 'Little Black Boy' [...] cannot be understood, unless it be taken as part of the general mystical manifesto that runs through all the work. In this poem Man's heart and imagination need, we are told, to be exercised for a while on the dark things of the five senses with their seemingly solid and opaque world around. Man is then the little black boy, taught by mother Nature underneath the tree that is the Vine in its good aspect, and becomes Mystery when Priesthood perverts this teaching. The mother, who is the 'vegetative happy,' – Mnetha herself, – points to the East while she teachers symbolism. The sun is the signal of Love, that paradoxically manifests itself by giving us a cloud, the dark body, to screen us from Himself. By death or by inspiration we shall presently be free of it, and then it will be seen that the white boy is also the inhabitant of a cloud as much as he who is outwardly dark. □

(E-Y ɪɪ.9–10)[4]

We might agree with Williams that Ellis and Yeats delimit their under-standing of darkness to 'the dark things of the five senses' (which is, in effect, skin colour-blind, as 'Man is [...] the little black boy'; Ellis and Yeats use the cloud as Swedenborg did to symbolise the physical body). Yet Williams's understanding, both of the black boy's darkness and of the proper subjects of critical enquiry, may be delimited also. Both contexts, the mystical and the political, seem implied by Blake's poem. Witness Damon's comment in *William Blake, His Philosophy and Symbols* (1924) that 'The Little Black Boy' was 'doubly inspired by the anti-slavery agitation of Blake's times, and by Isaac Watts's [religious poem] *Grace Shining and Nature Fainting*' (Damon 1924, 269) (and see also, Saree Makdisi's remarks on the poem, discussed in Chapter 9, below). Furthermore, to return to Williams's criticism of Ellis and Yeats, a neglect of the colonial politics of slavery and the slave trade was common to virtually all nineteenth-century writings on *Songs of Innocence and of Experience*. It is striking then that Williams might use Ellis and Yeats's omission to take a side-swipe at mysticism. For far from being concerned with the 'purely mental', mysticism, patterned after Swedenborg's idea of 'correspondences', articulated the rela-tionship between outer and inner, nature and spirit.[5] Margaret Rudd, a critic sympathetic to Yeats, sees an example of this in 'Laughing Song'. 'When the green woods laugh, with the voice of joy | And the dimpling stream runs laughing by', writes Blake (ll. 1–2, E11), seeming to Rudd to show 'the creatures of nature responding to the human mood' (Rudd 1953, 77). Yeats himself broached the subject in 'The Necessity of Symbolism', where he opposes mysticism to sci-entific positivism, and makes a finer distinction between mysticism and poetry:

■ A 'correspondence', for the very reason that it is implicit rather than explicit, says far more than a syllogism or scientific observation. The chief difference between the metaphors of poetry and the symbols of mysticism is that the latter are woven together into a complete system. □

(E-Y I.238)

Ellis and Yeats bequeathed to their readers (somewhat surprisingly, some may think) a sense that even the notoriously obscure prophetic books were both intelligible and coherent, and that their author was capable of systematic design. As *Works* was preceded by the writings of Wilkinson and Thomson, it was soon followed by further studies of Blake's mysticism, including Pierre Berger's *William Blake: mysticisme et poésie* (1907; trans. 1914 as *William Blake: Poet and Mystic*), and Helen C. White's *The Mysticism of William Blake* (1927). Yet, on the whole, people have tended not to read Ellis and Yeats's *Works* very sympathetically (paradigmatically, Bloom 1970), and their commentary on *Songs* has been widely and unjustly neglected. That said, this commentary is also enormously frustrating. For Ellis and Yeats, Blake's poems tell 'a continuous story'; they must be understood as a coherent 'whole instead of as a succession of unrelated fragments' (E-Y II.3). Yeats writes:

■ It is the charm of the mythic narrative that it cannot tell one thing without telling a hundred others. The symbols are an endlessly inter-marrying family. They give life to what, stated in general terms, appears only a cold truism, by hinting how the apparent simplicity of the statement is due to an artificial isolation of a fragment, which, in its natural place, is connected with all the infinity of truths by living fibres. □

(E-Y I.382–3)

However, what this approach can lose, in the *Works*, is the occasion, the instance. The metaphorical and rhythmical patterning of a particular lyric; the tale-within-the-tale which is the dialogue between *Innocence* and *Experience*: both are flattened by the juggernaut that is the symbolic system. Ellis and Yeats's opening remark linking *Songs of Innocence* to Tharmas, for example, conflates the 'Introduction' with 'The Shepherd'. Not until Joseph Wicksteed's *Blake's Innocence and Experience* (1928) and John Middleton Murry's *William Blake* (1933) did the *Songs'* texts begin to be read more sensitively. Wicksteed, for example, maintains that '[Blake] weaves his meaning over and under the surface of his song, and by tracking its course above and below, we need lose none of the music of the verse and may often discover rich harmonies of beauty resounding in the deeps' (Wicksteed 1928, 17–18).

Even when read on its own terms, *Works* does not quite do what it promises to. Truths' 'living fibres' can become hardened. Often in Ellis and Yeats's criticism of *Songs*, 'this = that', just one thing and not a hundred. 'London', for instance, is *tout court* 'the purely literary equiv-alent for the passage in *Jerusalem* [84.11–12, E243] – this really is all Ellis and Yeats say – (E-Y II.15); 'Infant Joy' is 'the same referred to' in *Vala* and *Jerusalem* (E-Y II.11). 'My Pretty Rose Tree', in a rare reference on to *Songs* itself, 'explains the worm' in 'The Sick Rose' (E-Y II.14). Crucially, the correspondence only ever runs one way: from *Songs* we are virtually always shuffled on to *Vala*, *Milton*, or *Jerusalem*; from *Vala*, *Milton*, and *Jerusalem*, we are never returned to *Songs*. For Ellis and Yeats, *Songs* remains tangential to Blake's larger myth. It is never allowed to be what we have seen Yeats call 'that point of view from which we choose to take the story' (E-Y I.287; see above).

BLAKE AND TRADITION: W. B. YEATS, 'WILLIAM BLAKE AND THE IMAGINATION' (1897), AND T. S. ELIOT, 'BLAKE' (1920)

It was in the broadly appreciative essay 'William Blake and the Imagination', first published in 1897 but subsequently collected in *Ideas of Good and Evil* (1903), that Yeats wrote of Blake as 'a symbolist who had to invent his symbols':

■ a man crying out for a mythology, and trying to make one because he could not find one to his hand. Had he [...] been a scholar of our time he would have [...] gone to Ireland [...] and chosen for his symbols the sacred mountains, along whose sides the peasant still sees enchanted fires, and the divinities which have not faded from the prayers of simple hearts; and have spoken without mixing incongruous things because he spoke of things that had been long steeped in emotion; and have been less obscure because a traditional mythology stood on the threshold of his meaning and on the margin of his sacred darkness. □
(Yeats 1903c, 172–3)

We may observe Yeats here setting light to his own straw man, as, influenced by his own increasing interest in Irish mythology, he turns his back on the idiosyncratically-named pantheon of beings that pop-ulates Blake's later writings, a pantheon he had himself, with Ellis, put centre-stage in *Works*. We could also say, in relation to *Songs*, that Yeats neglects the potential appeal to 'simple hearts' of its bare experi-ences (sorrow; joy), its humble, emblematic particulars (a clod of clay; a lamb), its communal spaces (London's chartered streets; England's echoing greens, places of play or festival). But in so far as *Songs* is also mystical, Yeats suggests that it cannot access living tradition, whether national or culturally appropriate. Mysticism might have a tradition, we might say, but it was no longer traditional – no longer a widely-accepted habit of thought.

Blake's relationship with tradition was also central to the poet and critic T. S. Eliot (1888–1965), in his essay 'Blake', published in shorter form as 'The Naked Man' in *Athenaeum* (13 February 1920) before being augmented and included in his essay-collection *The Sacred Wood* (1920). Eliot's Blake, like Yeats's, is cut loose from tradition. This is something that Eliot disparages in the longer, latter part of his essay – but which equally, at his essay's opening, seems to unsettle him and almost to force him to reconsider some of the seminal remarks he made earlier in *The Sacred Wood* in the celebrated essay 'Tradition and the Individual Talent' (1919).

In what has become the best-known passage of his essay on Blake, Eliot writes:

■ We have the same respect for Blake's philosophy [...] that we have for an ingenious piece of home-made furniture: we admire the man who has put it together out of the odds and ends about the house. □

(Eliot 1997a, 132–3)

He continues:

■ What his genius required, and what it sadly lacked, was a framework of accepted and traditional ideas which would have prevented him from indulging in a philosophy of his own, and concentrated his attention upon the problems of the poet. □

(134)

Eliot has a different idea of tradition from Yeats (see further, Larrissy 2006, 28–36). '[O]ur trolls and pixies' are objects of ridicule (Eliot 1997a, 133); what a writer needs is to be amid 'the Latin traditions', 'a framework of mythology and theology and philosophy'. Writing within this, Dante (an essay on whom succeeds the essay on Blake) is 'a classic'. Writing without it, Blake is 'only a poet of genius' (Eliot 1997a, 133–4). 'Tradition' has a special sense for Eliot; it is not simply about links to the past, as 'Tradition and the Individual Talent' shows. Instead, tradition has to do with the presentness of the past, with a 'historical sense' that would compel a man 'to write not merely with his own generation in his bones, but with a feeling that the whole of the literature of Europe from Homer and within it the whole of the literature of his own country has a simultaneous existence and composes a simultaneous order'. It is this 'historical sense' that informs the poet how to surrender himself to his art, how to extinguish his personality, and so write the greatest poetry (Eliot 1997b, 40–9).

To an extent Eliot is snobbish, condescending to Blake's 'meanness of culture' and want of 'education' (Eliot 1997a, 133, 130). While he insists that Blake was never, as his supporters would have had him, 'a naïf, a wild man, a wild pet for the supercultivated' (Eliot 1997a, 128), Eliot suggests equally, in the first part of his essay, that the self-taught Blake was 'naked', his verse exhibiting 'a peculiar honesty, which, in a world too frightened to be honest, is peculiarly terrifying' (131, 128). As an example of Blake's 'naked vision' Eliot cites the final stanza of 'London', and of Blake's 'naked observation', the first stanza of 'The Clod and the Pebble'. Blake's 'naked philosophy' is evident in *The Marriage of Heaven and Hell* (131–2).

Describing Blake's verse, Eliot repeats the adjective 'terrifying' twice; he emphasises the 'unpleasantness' of Blake's poetry; and of course there is that indecorous jolt of the poetry's nakedness (128). But curiously in the context of the criticism we have discussed so far, the disturbance Eliot registers is not a product of the 'formlessness' that, by implication, he thinks attends Blake's later writings (131). Instead, it is provoked by the kind of formal accomplishment he discerns in early writings such as *Songs*, an accomplishment of which Blake is capable even without the benefit of a traditional education. Eliot writes:

■ The Songs of Innocence and of Experience, and the poems from the Rossetti manuscript [*that is, the manuscript notebook*], are the poems of a man with a profound interest in human emotions, and a profound knowledge of them. The emotions are presented in an extremely simplified, abstract form. This form is one illustration of the eternal struggle of art against education, of the literary artist against the continuous deterioration of language. □

(130)

Eliot defines 'ordinary education' as 'the acquisition of impersonal ideas which obscure what we really are and feel, what we really want, and what really excites our interest' (130–1). The emotions that *Songs* presents are not, however, by consequence Blake's personal emotions. Not only, as we have seen, are they 'human'; they are also presented in 'an extremely simplified, abstract form', 'a medium', perhaps, 'in which impressions and experiences combine in peculiar and unexpected ways', to quote from 'Tradition and the Individual Talent' (Eliot 1997b, 46–7). There, Eliot writes that '[t]he emotion of art is impersonal'. But he also writes that the poet 'is not likely to know' how to surrender himself to his art without access to tradition (49). Blake is, then, an unsettling counter-example. Were it not for the Achilles heel of his home-made philosophy, he would be a potential flaw in Eliot's theories, a talent without tradition. Perhaps, then, Eliot exiles Blake from tradition deliberately, in order to punish him for being able, almost, to surrender himself to his art without it.

S. FOSTER DAMON, *WILLIAM BLAKE, HIS PHILOSOPHY AND SYMBOLS* (1924)

S. Foster Damon's *William Blake, His Philosophy and Symbols* (1924) was the first sustained scholarly account of Blake's writing as a system. So authoritatively did Damon's study embed Blake's writings amidst their intertexts that in its wake it would strain credulity to treat Blake as a writer (and for Damon, Blake was, above all, a writer) without either tradition or culture.

Samuel Foster Damon (1893–1971) was a North American academic, poet, and critic, 'a specialist in hard-to-find books by forgotten authors' who wrote widely on a range of literary and cultural topics (Cowley 1969, xv). His central achievement was perhaps to make Blake 'academically respectable' (Damon 1967–8, 2), although this by no means happened overnight: Harvard, his university, did not even allow him to submit *William Blake, His Philosophy and Symbols* 'in partial fulfilment […] of the requirements' of his Ph.D. (Cowley 1969, xxii). This was not exactly because Blake was one of Damon's 'forgotten authors': 'almost everyone had read *Songs of Innocence* and *Songs of Experience*', recalls his friend Malcolm Cowley; 'but Foster introduced me to the poems in the Rossetti and Pickering Manuscripts and to *The Marriage of Heaven and Hell*. He couldn't persuade me to follow him into the later Prophetic Books' (xv).

Damon picks out the same differential reception in the opening pages of *Philosophy and Symbols*:

■ The *Songs of Innocence* are read everywhere; yet we lack a correct text of *The Four Zoas*! The lyrics are in every anthology; yet professors of literature wonder if the epics are worth reading! □

(Damon 1924, ix)

It is possible Damon overstates the contemporary popularity of *Songs* just a little; certainly, when discussing 'The Tyger' later on he declares that it was 'circulated everywhere' in Blake's lifetime, which we know to be untrue (Damon 1924, 276). However, Damon's broader assertion that in the early twentieth century *Songs* was known and valued above all of Blake's other written works is borne out by the criticism we have discussed so far. So too is his broad suggestion that poems from *Songs* were more widely anthologised – and in fact this had been going on for a while. In Chapter 4 we saw that even before the publication of Gilchrist's *Life*, Allingham included some of its verses in *Nightingale Valley* (1860), although by the same token *Songs* was overlooked the following year by Francis Turner Palgrave, editor of 'the best-known and the best-selling anthology of English poetry ever', *The Golden Treasury* (1861) (Palgrave 1991, n.p.n.). Still, poems from *Songs* and *Poetical Sketches* were included, to name but a few publications, in Richard Chevenix Trench's *A Household Book of Poetry* (1868), Alfred H. Miles's *Poets and Poetry of the Century* (1891–7), Henry Charles Beeching's *A Paradise of English Poetry* (1893), William Ernest Henley's *English Lyrics, Chaucer to Poe, 1340–1809* (1897), and Arthur Quiller-Couch's *Oxford Book of English Verse, 1250–1900* (1900). Moreover, Palgrave too was to succumb, adding 'Infant Joy' to a revised edition of *The Golden Treasury* in 1883 and further lyrics from *Poetical Sketches* in 1890 (Palgrave 1991). The practices of anthologists give us one indication of how *Songs of Innocence and of Experience* was beginning to be absorbed into the heritage of English-speaking cultures.

Damon himself was inclined to favour Blake's later prophetic books, *The Four Zoas*, *Milton*, and *Jerusalem* ('the last of Blake's works are the greatest') (Damon 1924, ix). However, he does not stint, as Ellis and Yeats did in *The Works of William Blake*, to spend time analysing *Songs*, and manages to bind it more tightly and more persuasively into the larger mystical system of which he, like his precursors, thinks it is a part. For Damon the system that was bodied forth by Blake's writings was patterned after a five-stage 'Mystic Way':

■ (1) the awakening to a sense of divine reality; (2) the consequent purgation of the Self, when it realizes its own imperfections; (3) an enhanced return of the sense of the divine order, after the Self has achieved its detachment from the world; (4) the 'Dark Night of the Soul', or the crucifixion of the Self in the absence of the divine; (5) and the complete union with Truth, the attainment of that which the third state had perceived as a possibility. □

(Damon 1924, 8, 2)

Damon designates these states as 'Innocence' (associated with childhood in man and historically, with eternity), 'Experience' (which he later calls 'Disillusionment', associated with manhood and the Fall), 'Revolution' (the 'New Birth'; the life of Christ), 'The Dark Night' (despair; the eighteen centuries AD); and 'The Ultimate Union' (attainment; the 'New Age'). This fifth state, he adds, 'was a return to "Innocence" with the added wisdom of "Experience"' (2, 12, 43). Damon's extension of the vocabulary of innocence and experience to describe the final, most glorious stage of the 'Mystic Way' implies some complex temporalities. That the fifth stage entails the first stage seen anew suggests that time might not be linear but cyclical. It also suggests that *Songs of Innocence and of Experience*, read and re-read, might operate as a synecdoche of the 'Mystic Way' as a whole. Damon's aim, though, is straighter: stage succeeds stage in accordance with the development of Blake's life and writings over linear time. Thus *Innocence* belongs to the first stage of the 'Mystic Way' and *Experience* to the second; prophetic books, including *The Marriage of Heaven and Hell* and *America*, occupy the third, *Urizen* the fourth, and the last prophetic books and *Job* the fifth. There is some fudging of dates here to make the system fit: even though he thinks that *Marriage* and *America* were first printed in 1793 (in fact *Marriage* probably appeared in 1790, as previous critics such as Sampson, discussed below, had realised), Damon places them after *Experience* in his scheme (*Experience*, of course, being printed in 1794).

For all this talk of mysticism, Damon's *Philosophy and Symbols* is a much easier read than Ellis and Yeats's *Works*. This is partly because Damon's system-building is more omnivorous, and because many of the writers he aligns with Blake are more canonical – for *Songs*, these include not only Paracelsus, Boehme, and various alchemists, but also the Old and New Testaments, Dante, Milton, Traherne, Watts, Gray, Goldsmith, Shelley, Whitman, and (unusually) the Romantic-period Gothic writer Ann Radcliffe – even the nursery rhymes, *Mother Goose's Melodies* (40, 268–86, 41). For Damon, Blake's 'very definitive system of symbols' is not the only 'ke[y]' to his thought; it is joined by an extensive network of 'literary sources' (vii). Perhaps the main reason that Damon's criticism is relatively clear, though, is that it abides by many of the criteria for proper academic writing that we still abide by today. Poetic works such as Blake's 'To Tirzah' may be 'deliberately obscure', albeit that this obscurity had a communicative intent, that is, '[to] stimulate its readers to search the other poems [in *Songs of Experience*] for concealed meanings' (281). But the duty of the critic was to be explicit. Rather than gesturing towards the *Songs'* intertexts, Damon cites the evidence to support his assertions. Rather than riding a hobby-horse, he musters objectivity, situating his own arguments within a critical field. Indeed, Damon's is the first criticism we have come to whose work of vindication is almost done (Blake has been crowned as 'Poet' and 'Painter', if not yet 'Philosopher') (xi); his text bristles with the names of Blake critics historical and contemporary. A few years later Helen C. White would write, 'Time was when a book on William Blake had to open with a very explicit account of the remarkable poet-painter-mystic.' By 1927, though, the year of her writing and the centenary of Blake's death, 'the volume of comment and exegesis and reprint and appreciation continues to swell almost daily, so that today the question which the Blake student must answer is no longer "Who is Blake?" but "Why another book on Blake?"' (White 1927, 7).

Damon had not to make a case for this; his was one of the 'brilliant and learned books' White praised for what it had done to bring Blake's mysticism to light and to confirm that even his later writings were motivated by connected method rather than madness (White 1927, 7). The 'mysteries' of which Blake wrote, says Damon – and 'Mysticism was *always* the inner impulse of everything Blake wrote or painted, from the *Songs of Innocence* to his last works' – are not morbid, unbalanced ravings; they contain definite ideas expressed as Blake thought best' (Damon 1924, 8, 9–10). Furthermore, Blake always kept his feet on the ground:

■ The normal life, *heightened*, was his ideal. He never lost his grip on this world. [...] He left no systems of meditation or magical ceremonies to invoke deity; prayer was his sole method. And at the highest moments of the ecstasy, he puzzles in the back of his mind: 'How can I make other men see this?' □

(Damon 1924, 10)

After outlining Blake's mystical beliefs, Damon's next step is to put man and works into their historical context – or more precisely, to set them up in opposition to it. 'His was a type which is never in tune with the times; but one cannot imagine a century [*the eighteenth*] more definitely opposed point by point, to everything in which he believed' (13). This age of 'Reason', of 'wars, social disturbances, Materialism, offset by obscure false prophets, was no age for the arts' (15, 18). Hence, in an achingly-familiar narrative, Damon's Blake seeks consolation, which for Damon emphatically does not reside in art ('[h]is arts were tools, not ends in themselves') but in mysticism:

■ Rather than accept conditions as they were, he endeavoured to remodel them to his heart's desire, and this very attitude, predestined to failure, quickly cut him off from contemporary life. Here his mysticism aided him to create his own universe. □

(xi, 18)

Latent in Damon's description of the eighteenth century are historical-contextual links to Blake's writings which egregiously he neglects to amplify – one can almost feel the later criticism of Erdman as well as more obviously Frye taking root (see Chapter 6). There are generic connections latent too. When he comes to discuss *Songs*, no sooner has Damon said that 'all the influences of other writers [...] vanish' than he remarks on the affinity of *Songs of Innocence* to pastoral and to children's literature (Damon 1924). Mulling over the meaning of *Innocence*'s 'Chimney Sweeper', he concedes that '[t]his "broadsheet gone to Heaven" was inspired by the agitation that was then trying to pass laws against the use of children as chimney-sweeps' (269).

Damon's direct criticism of *Songs* is confined to two brief, early chapters, and an appended thicket of commentary on each of Blake's book's texts and 'decorations' in turn (this description showing his subordination of composite art to text) (271, 284). In the chapters it is noteworthy that Damon detaches the child speaker of *Innocence* from Blake himself: 'in writing about Innocence', Blake 'was describing a mystical state, rather than childhood; but he identifies the two so closely that his poems seem to be spoken by the very children themselves' (40). His local comments on the relationship between *Innocence* and *Experience* also nuance our understanding of the 'Mystic Way'. The former book, for example, anticipates the latter when in the 'Introduction' to *Innocence* the child (who for Damon symbolises the 'Poetic Genius') weeps upon hearing the piper's song for a second time (l. 8, E7) (40). Furthermore, and as the joint *Songs'* sub-title suggests, the second stage of the 'Way' (*Experience*) continues with the first (*Innocence*) in counterpoint: 'Blake was certainly not trying to reverse the lesson he had so beautifully taught; instead he retained them both', the 'happy past' continuing alongside the 'pessimistic present' (43).

It is Damon's later poem-by-poem commentary, though, that is from the point of view of *Songs* the real treasure-chest of his study, not least in its excavations of literary intertexts. His interpretations are also smart and authoritative. He refers to the prophetic books judiciously, spying below the text in 'The Human Abstract', for example, 'an old man, instantly to be recognized as Urizen, [...] struggling in the net of religion, his own weaving' (Damon 1924, 286; see *Urizen*, E82). He is not immune to levity when explaining the necessity of reading Blake's writings figuratively rather than literally: the questions of 'Earth's Answer', 'Does spring hide its joy | When buds and blossoms grow? | Does the sower? | Sow by night? | Or the plowman in darkness plow?' (E19, ll. 16–20), for instance, '[do] not mean that the acts of love should be performed in open daylight. "Night" throughout this book is used symbolically, as the absence of the true Light, or spiritual darkness' (274). He is on occasion attentive to the lyrics' form, as when he notes that with 'The Fly' Blake 'compresses his thought into miniature lines which by their prosody suggest the flitting of the insect' (Damon 1924, 274). But he is, above all else, instructive, his interpretations sure of themselves as 'answer[s]' (278). Damon's was not, of course, the last word. But in some respects it was the first: the font from which much subsequent scholarship would flow.

FIRST SCHOLARLY EDITIONS BY JOHN SAMPSON (1905) AND GEOFFREY KEYNES (1925)

Just as scholarly and influential as Damon's study, and arguably more enduring in its impact, was Geoffrey Keynes's authoritative textual edition of Blake's writings, first published in 1925. When identifying 'essential criticism', as we must for this guide, interpretations of Blake's *Songs* take precedence. But equally, as we have tried to show, we need to ask questions about how available Blake's books, or at least transcriptions of their texts, actually were, as well as surveying what was written about them. This section of the chapter introduces a new consideration: that of accuracy. For we need to understand editions of Blake's *Songs* as 'criticism' too. In the lines, letters, and punctuation marks they select, as well as in their editorial apparatus (such as introductions and notes), they evaluate Blake's state of mind or his prosodic skill. They also categorise *Songs* as more lucid or more obscure, lyric or prophetic, and either insert Blake's writings into historical time, or assert the importance, against this, of the contrary song-books' inter-relationship.

Literary historians have tended to track the progress of Blake's works through six major textual editions. The first (eliding Wilkinson's edition, discussed in Chapter 3) came with Volume 2 of Gilchrist's *Life*, edited by Gabriel Rossetti, which marked 'the first time' Blake's writings could 'readily be bought and read' (D 101). Five subsequent editions are usually identified in short-hand, whether by the names of their publishers, the place of their press, or the series of which they were a part: Pickering, Aldine, Quaritch, Oxford, and Nonesuch.

'Pickering' signifies *Songs of Innocence and Experience, with Other Poems*, an edition issued by the publisher Basil Montagu Pickering (1835–78) under the editorship of R. H. Shepherd in 1866. Pickering's father, William (1796–1854), had published the first edition of *Songs* in type in 1839, edited by John James Garth Wilkinson. Basil Montagu's 1866 volume answered to a gap in the market, as Shepherd explains: Wilkinson's edition 'had become very scarce', and Gilchrist's was 'beautiful and costly' (Shepherd 1866, viii), its 'mass of extraneous matter' placing it 'beyond the reach of many readers who might desire to possess the Poems in a separate form' (Shepherd 1874, vi). However, the chief fault of the *Life*, as Shepherd saw it, lay in Rossetti's editorial practice. Increasingly vociferously, as the Pickering Blake was slightly enlarged, retitled, and reissued in 1868 and 1874, latterly called *The Poems of William Blake*, Shepherd asserted the importance of scholarship and of textual fidelity. Gabriel Rossetti's interventions were 'unwarrantable' and 'destroy[ed] to a certain extent the historical value of the poems' (Shepherd 1874, xiv; see further D 110–12).

It was not, however, the Pickering but the Aldine Blake that saw out the nineteenth century as 'the definitive edition of Blake's lyric poems' ('lyric' because, like its precursor, it largely excluded the prophecies) (D 112). The Aldine Blake was, as we have seen, the work of William Rossetti; it signifies *The Poetical Works of William Blake, Lyrical and Miscellaneous* published in The Aldine Edition of the British Poets series in 1874. Grudgingly, Rossetti followed Shepherd in reprinting Blake's *Poetical Sketches* without his brother's 'emendations' (W. M. Rossetti 1874, cxxxi). Many of the *Life*'s presumed corrections to *Songs*, however, found their way into the Aldine edition. Reasserting Blake's own text of 'The Tyger' in 1905, for example, John Sampson noted how the line 'What dread hand? & what dread feet?' had been fashioned by Blake to parallel 'What the hammer? what the chain?', the line which begins the poem's next stanza (ll. 12, 13, E24–5). He laments:

■ The terrible, compressed force of these two short sentences, which burst forth with a momentary pause between them like shells from a mortar, is altogether lost in the languid punctuation of the Aldine edition – 'And, when thy heart began to beat, | What dread hand and what dread feet?' □

(Sampson 1905, 112)

The 'smoothd up & Niggled & Poco Piud' texts of even the Aldine edition, to borrow from Blake's own idiom in the *Public Address* (E576), show the hazards of treating *Songs* as what William Rossetti calls 'lyric outflow', whether of the 'babe' of *Innocence* or the 'prophet' of *Experience* (W. M. Rossetti 1874, cxii, cxv). This Blake does not possess sufficient technical skill and self-mastery to make authoritative decisions about form, language, or grammar. The Quaritch Blake, too, denies Blake such agency. Bernard Quaritch (1819–99) was the publisher of Ellis and Yeats's *The Works of William Blake, Poetical, Symbolic, and Critical* in 1893. The chief value of the *Works*, as we have seen, was in some of their interpretations rather than the accuracy of their quotation, and it is of little surprise that it did not challenge the hegemony of the slimmed-down Aldine. Yeats's smaller Muses' Library edition, of 1893, did not do this either (D 224) – although, as Sampson notes, its text of *Songs* was 'different and more accurate' than that in the Quaritch (Sampson 1905, 79). Ellis and Yeats's Blake has even less conscious agency than the Rossettis'. Albeit that 'a unity of significance' underlies Blake's myth, and albeit that 'the un-visionary or purely intellectual part of Blake's mind' was able 'to have caught the idea of the language which the visionary portion was talking, and talks it too', the upshot was that Blake's verses were 'dictated' (E-Y I.95). '[W]ithin twenty-four hours' of composition, he 'would not have known' what he had written (E-Y, quoted by Symons 1907, 68).[6] Such talk, whether of childlikeness or of automatism, was grist to the mill of Blake's detractors. '[Blake's] use of single words is often so strained and unnatural as to rouse a suspicion that really he did not know the precise meaning of some word employed,' writes Arthur Christopher Benson in *Essays* (1896). Picking on the word 'chartered', for instance, a word that occurs in the 'childish' poem 'London', Benson wonders:

■ Is it possible that Blake confused it with 'chart', and meant 'mapped out' or 'defined'? Conjecture is really idle in the case of a man who maintained that many of his poems were merely dictated to him, and that he exercised no volition of his own with regard to them. □

(Benson 1896, 151–2)

On into the twentieth century, then, Blake continued to stand in need of a good editor. One finally arrived in 1905 in the shape of John Sampson (1862–1931), scholar and librarian at the University of Liverpool. Sampson arguably did more than any other to deliver Blake's *Songs* into the hands of tradition – he is used, for example, by T. S. Eliot to rebut Berger's mystical claims about Blake's automatic writing (Eliot 1997a, 130fn). We focus here on his first edition, primarily of Blake's early writings, published by the Clarendon Press, which carries the full weight of its scholarliness in its title: *The Poetical Works of William Blake: A New and Verbatim Text from the Manuscript Engraved and Letterpress Originals, with Variorum Readings and Bibliographical Notes and Prefaces*. This was succeeded in 1913 by Sampson's expanded edition (the Oxford edition proper) of Blake's poems, which included the minor prophetic books as well as selections from *The Four Zoas, Milton,* and

Jerusalem (some of these last included in the 1905 edition) – although a portion of the notes which buttress the earlier edition are stripped away. The 'primary object' of the 1905 *Poetical Works of William Blake* was 'to recover and present Blake's own version of his poetry without the customary attempts of emendation' (Sampson 1905, v). Lists, tables, lengthy prefaces and footnotes to Blake's early poetical writings (Sampson takes only snippets from the prophecies) raise for the first time before the eyes of readers of *Songs* the kinds of bibliographical issues that we discussed in Chapter 1 of this guide. Going back to the copperplates and comparing multiple copies of *Songs*, Sampson notes how deliberate is Blake's spelling. Words like 'tyger' and 'lilly', for example, are not misspellings, but 'pleasant archaisms'; Blake 'system[atically]' spells out the ending of 'ed' (rather than the elided ''d') in the participle or preterite 'only when he intended the final syllable to be separately pronounced' (Sampson 1905, viii). Sampson also makes extensive reference to Blake's manuscripts, including his drafting of poems from *Experience* in the notebook and their inclusion in *An Island in the Moon* (see Chapter 1). This led readers such as Symons to conclude that 'Blake was as great a corrector as he was an originator' (Symons 1907, 68–9), although we should remember that no such drafts have been found for the bulk of Blake's poetry.

What Sampson had begun with *Songs* and some others of Blake's early writings, Geoffrey Keynes amplified and brought to near-completion in *The Writings of William Blake*, published in three volumes by the Nonesuch Press in 1925. Keynes (1887–1982) was a surgeon and literary scholar; in 1921 he produced *A Bibliography of William Blake*, and his edition of the *Writings* was succeeded by a series of editions 'culminating in that for the Oxford Standard Authors in 1966. These in turn were supplemented by editions of the drawings, studies of plates, a new census of the illuminated books [...], an edition of the letters [...], and an iconography of Blake and his wife' (*ODNB*). The 1925 Nonesuch edition includes the prophecies, and indeed all of Blake's writings that were then known. Eschewing Sampson's cumbersome editorial apparatus, Keynes cleared all but indications of Blake's own additions and deletions from the pages of his folio text, so best displaying, he thinks, Blake's 'real meaning' (Keynes 1925, i.xi). Archaic spellings, capital letters, and ampersands were there because Blake intended them to be. Only Blake's practice of punctuation remained perplexing, 'often with the effect of rendering passages unintelligible'. Keynes therefore exercised 'editorial discretion' (Keynes 1925, i.xvi).

Something as simple as the Nonesuch page of contents marks Blake's entrance into history. In its list of Blake's writings, printed in an approximation of their dates of initial printing or, if unpublished, com-position, *Songs of Innocence* is for the first time, to our knowledge, not followed immediately by *Songs of Experience*. Instead a gulf is marked, of fifteen texts in length. '[T]he contrary states of the human soul' the books may be, but now they are separated by the five years of histori-cal time that separated their first inscription on copper. The grounds had now been laid out for the post-war foundations of Blake criticism in the academy.

CHAPTER SIX

The Post-War Foundations: System, Myth, and History

Damon's *Philosophy and Symbols* was a major turning point in Blake criticism. At a time when English Literature was establishing itself fully as a subject in Anglo-American universities, the book offered Blake's poetry as a corpus that merited serious academic study. Damon's account of Blake's work as a coherent structure may have foregrounded his mysticism, but it also provided a sense of a complex philosophical system, not easily dismissed as insane ramblings. This systemic approach proved very influential on post-war criticism, most notably Northrop Frye's *Fearful Symmetry* (1947), a book that remains a key text on any reading list for *Songs*. The other major development was the emergence of a historical school of criticism, concerned especially with placing Blake in the context of the reaction to the French Revolution. For this tradition, most obviously represented early on by Jacob Bronowski, Mark Schorer, and later David V. Erdman, historicising Blake was part of a political programme that was as enthused by the continuing visionary potentiality found in the poetry as by its relation to Blake's lifetime. In terms of the *Songs*, this critical tradition was obviously drawn to the social criticism apparent in a poem like 'London', but also to the utopian possibilities of 'Innocence'. Although there was a great deal of communication between the two traditions, the idea of Blake as a political poet was distinct from Frye's emphasis on the human imagination and, especially, Harold Bloom's account of Blake as part of a visionary company for whom apocalypse within the individual consciousness was the primary site of romantic revelation.

SONGS AND THE POST-WAR POLITICS OF HOPE

The context of global crisis in the 1930s and 1940s added urgency to the reception of Blake in those decades. Jacob Bronowski's work was among the earliest of several leftist responses at the time. A Jewish immigrant, educated at Cambridge, Bronowski (1908–74) was also a distinguished mathematician whose commitment to humanist values was sharpened by a sense of Europe tending towards barbarism. His first book, *The Poet's Defence* (1939), examined and attempted to reconcile the truth-claims of science and poetry, bringing Blake forward as a key figure in a history of enlightenment as something more than rationalism. His major book *William Blake, 1757–1827: A Man Without a Mask* (1943) – which takes its sub-title from Samuel Palmer's characterisation of Blake as quoted by Gilchrist in the *Life* (see Chapter 4) – was deeply influenced by the sense of a need to preserve liberal values amid the general conflagration, but also retained a strong Marxist-inspired commitment to building a new world out of the ruins of the past. Blake's value for Bronowski lay in his fearless engagement with the world around him, not with the arcane system-building that had attracted Damon. His mysticism was uncommon because 'alone among such other-worldly thinkers, he founded it on a harsh understanding of the actual' (Bronowski 1972, 33). In this regard, especially, Bronowski saw Blake as responsive to fundamental shifts in economic and social structures, specifically, the Industrial and French revolutions. *Songs* and the later prophetic writings are responses to the change from 'village to factory industry' and 'from a society of money to one of capital', and it 'was overwhelmingly in Blake's lifetime that industry moved to the factory; that farming enlarged its scale; and that iron and coal gave England her new skeleton' (45, 173).

Within this loosely Marxist sense of *Songs* as responsive to deep-seated changes in the means of production, Bronowski gives special emphasis to its representation of childhood. Cementing the idea of Blake as a paradigmatically Romantic thinker, linking the *Songs* to work by Wordsworth, Coleridge, and Shelley, Bronowski sees the poems as part of an eighteenth-century 'cult of the child' predicated upon 'growing dislike of social man'. Downplaying the distinctively urban nature of their pastoralism, this account represents Blake as writing 'against towns and against industry, in which children played their pitiful part'. For 'humanitarian dissenters' like Blake and Coleridge, 'the child became a twofold Christian symbol: innocence, the symbol of pity; and experience, Christ the child teacher become a teacher of children'. The humanitarian impulse in poems such as 'The Chimney Sweeper' both in *Innocence* and in *Experience* was to be read in the light of contemporary efforts such as the establishment of the Foundling Hospital in 1739 and attempts to free apprentice chimney sweepers from their 'dangerous and cancerous work' (147–8).

In practice, Bronowski's analysis of the *Songs* struggles fully to incorporate them into his narrative of the dehumanising effects of industrialisation, usually relying upon passages in the prophetic epics to dramatise this part of his thesis. More fundamentally, Bronowski sees the poems as anticipating the critiques of Hegel and Marx in their responsiveness to deep social changes (180). Muted its Marxist influences may be, but *Man without a Mask* represents one of the earliest critical texts to attempt an understanding of Blake's contrary states of the human soul as a form of dialectical thinking. His account of the states of Innocence and Experience, for instance, shadows Marx's contrast between society organised under communist and capitalist principles:

■ Blake believed that society has no ends. Like his machines, it is a means become master. He thought the more deeply of the ends of man. □

(179)

Innocence and Experience represent opposed forms of social relationships, exemplified for Bronowski in the contrast between the humanistic altruism of 'The Divine Image' in *Innocence* and the terrible alienation of these virtues 'grown inhuman in self-interest' in 'The Human Abstract' and 'A Divine Image' of *Experience* (155).

For Bronowski, the states of Innocence and Experience contrast human potential with its restriction under the reality of oppressive social forces. Invested in values of progress and improvement, Bronowski's analysis tends to privilege the emancipatory vision of *Innocence* as against the starker sense in *Experience* of the restrictions of the world Blake occupied. Despite this emphasis, the book does pay attention to the idea that *Songs* also manifests the poet's response to the history of the French Revolution unfolding in the England of the 1790s. Bronowski imagines *Songs of Innocence* as completed in a 'happy child mood which the French Revolution seemed [about] to fulfil'. The *Songs* are situated in the world of Joseph Johnson's radical bookshop, amid the influence of writers like William Godwin, Thomas Paine, and Mary Wollstonecraft, although not with the contextualising detail that was to mark David Erdman's crucial study a decade later. Only 'English opposition to the French Revolution' explains the bitterness of *Experience* and its attack on 'the mind of the hypocrite'. While Innocence is symbolised by the child, 'the symbol of experience, mazy and manifold as the hypocrite, and as fascinating, is the father' (156). The *Experience* poems are 'at bottom, songs of indignation' etched in 'acid' with 'fluid grace' like the copper plates themselves (164).

Bronowski does recognise the fluidity of the order of the collection, which has become such an important aspect of their fascination for more recent criticism (see, especially, Chapter 8). Innocence is the potential for social renovation that can still find articulation against 'that false experience whose form is fixed in societies' (159). He sees Blake's decision to move 'The Little Girl Lost' and 'The Little Girl Found' into *Experience* as a sign of 'a new depth', in which Innocence can become a robust commitment to change. It is insufficient:

■ for the innocent boy to go from false experience to true, by chance. Experience itself must learn, fasting in the desert, to follow a greater innocence, by choice. What began as a fable in the child cult has become, in its new setting, a searching test of faith. □

(158)

In *Experience*, Bronowski sees figures such as the Chimney Sweep, the Little Vagabond, and the child in 'Infant Sorrow' as victims, whose Innocence fails to transform their society. He interprets 'The Lamb' and 'The Tyger' in the light of this impasse: 'the child, the lamb of God' must 'learn to lead her parents home to the Tygers of Wrath'. 'Christ is become the Tyger, symbol of energy burning in a darkening world' (158).

Bronowski's most penetrating insights are not all to do with the broad sweep of historical processes. His comparisons of *Songs* with Isaac Watts's *Divine Songs* (1715) and the Methodist hymnody of John and Charles Wesley explore a lineage that has remained an important strand of critical responses to Blake's poems. Bronowski links the opening two stanzas of 'The Divine Image' to John Wesley's 'Thou hidden love of God, whose height' (c. 1736, a translation from a German original). Wesley's hymn begins:

■ Thou hidden Love of God, whose height,
Whose depth unfathomed no one knows,
I see from far Thy beauteous light,
And inly sigh for Thy repose;
My heart is pained, nor can it be
At rest, till it finds rest in Thee. □

The third stanza of Wesley's hymn is key for Bronowski's comparison with Blake:

■ 'Tis mercy all that Thou has brought
My mind to seek its peace in Thee;
Yet while I seek, but find Thee not,

No peace my wandering soul shall see.
O when shall all my wanderings end,
And all my steps to Theeward tend? □

According to Bronowski, it appears scarcely changed in Blake's 'The Divine Image':

■ To Mercy, Pity, Peace, and Love
All pray in their distress;
And to these virtues of delight
Return their thankfulness. □

Blake's radicalism comes in the satirical development of two lines of thought from Wesley's hymn. One is the recognition of virtue grown inhuman in 'the Human Abstract' of *Experience*: 'Pity could be no more, I If we did not make somebody poor' (155). The other is to translate the abstract virtues into their human forms in 'A Divine Image':

■ Cruelty has a Human heart,
And Jealousy a Human Face;
Terror the Human Form Divine,
And Secrecy the Human Dress □

For Bronowski, this movement from the Christian virtues of Wesley's hymn to the sharp focus on the desacralised forms of the human body is paradigmatic of the shift from the *Innocence* to the *Experience* poems of pairs like 'The Ecchoing Green' and 'The Garden of Love'.

Although revealing, this source analysis is not fully integrated into the broader account of Blake's relation to industrial and political revolution, and it would take revisionist histories like E. P. Thompson's *The Making of the English Working Class* (1963) to link Methodist and capitalist disciplinary mechanisms into a broader picture of Blake's resistance to a new form of modern subjectivity (see Chapter 7). Humanistic values are paramount in Bronowski's account, which closes with an impassioned defence of the idiosyncratic individualism associated with the artist and particularly the sort of dissenting mind that he takes Blake to represent:

■ This is why the designers of Utopias, of whatever kind, have feared their cast of mind more than their writings. If you want to run a state for ever without trouble, says Plato, says Hitler, get rid of those whose make-up is odd, questioning, dissenting. Get rid of truth, get rid of literature, because their common interest is dissent. □

(188).

The emphasis on the imagination was, for Bronowski, the significant element which stimulated Blake's resistance to such totalitarianism: 'The imagination sets the worth for which societies reach and fail: pity and justice, order and happiness, peace with passion. It is the worth which man knows, for it is *The Divine Image*' (184).

Mark Schorer's *William Blake: The Politics of Vision* (1947) reiterated and expanded Bronowski's sense of Blake's relation to 'the major currents of opinion of his time' (Schorer 1946, xi). For Schorer (1908–77), 'the content of Blake's poetry is primarily social and [...] his criticism of society is radical' (151). Critics like Damon were guilty of isolating Blake from his contemporaries in order to distil his 'pure doctrine' (xii). *Songs of Innocence* had 'nothing to do with sanctity or even piety'. Schorer also examines *Songs* in the light of William and Catherine Blake's dalliance with the Swedenborgian New Jerusalem Church, as had Bronowski, but takes pains to point out their differences: 'Swedenborg's "Human" related man to God, whereas Blake's "human" relates God to man, and especially to artists. The "Human" is a concept by which Swedenborg separates man's good from his bad; the "human form divine" is the symbol by means of which Blake prohibits any such separation' (116).

Anticipating David Erdman's work in this regard, *The Politics of Vision* gave new detail to Blake's position within the ferment of liberal and radical thought during the 1790s, in particular the circle that gathered around the publisher Joseph Johnson. Conjecturing that the encounter with this group dated from c. 1788, Schorer sees the publisher's circle as the major springboard for the creative leap into *Songs*, but distinguishes Blake from the rationalism of Godwin and Paine (Schorer 1946, 456), an issue to which Robert Essick (1991) and Saree Makdisi (2003) have given new emphasis more recently. Significantly, Schorer saw this divergence as the source of Blake's idiosyncratic art: 'To trace the dialectic of innocence and experience, he tried to express (and to correct) the ideas of political thinkers like Paine and Godwin in the vocabulary of religious thinkers like Boehme and Swedenborg' (Schorer 1946, 3). Schorer sets Blake's *Songs* against the realities of social and political change ushered in by the Industrial and French revolutions. He agrees with Bronowski that Blake's lifetime corresponded to the change Marx identified between 'the age of manufacture' and 'the factory age'. Blake's opposition to these social developments was registered in his attacks on 'the substitution of mechanical for living values' (195, 202). This opposition maps onto Schorer's portrayal of Innocence and Experience. He finds much of the political meaning of Innocence in Rousseau, despite recognising Blake's antipathy to any notion of

'Natural Piety' (132–3). *Songs of Innocence* serves as a Rousseauvian rebuke to the corrupting power of commerce and luxury.

In what Schorer sees as the satire of *Songs of Experience*, the children of *Innocence* 'have become captives who cry for liberty, and, denied it, suffer a deterioration of natural virtue'. In 'Infant Sorrow', 'The Schoolboy', and 'The Little Vagabond', Schorer sees Blake making an attack similar to Godwin's on authoritarian education as the root of adult prejudice. These poems protest 'against authority because it ignores individuality by restraining natural impulse' (237). Like Bronowski, Schorer looks to the renewal of a higher form of Innocence dramatised in the opposition of 'The Lamb' and 'The Tyger'. The curbing of the lamb's innocent impulses and energy produce the tiger by a dialectical process:

■ Energy can be curbed but it cannot be destroyed, and when it reaches the limits of its endurance it bursts forth in revolutionary wrath [...]. The tiger is necessary to the renewal of the lamb. □

(250–1)

If Schorer's reading of the individual songs is underpinned by his sense of them as part of a set of dialectical relations structuring the collection as a whole, his historicism is far from insensitive to more local questions of form. *Experience* represents an advance in Blake's thinking and also marks a crucial stylistic development. Acknowledging with many others the importance of Watts to Blake's style, Schorer sees in *Experience* the emergence of 'one of Blake's most characteristic qualities, the ability to make intense verse out of abstractions'. Although he delights in the symbolic density of poems like 'London', Schorer worries that 'the intellectual content is coming into the ascendancy, and the treacherous allegorical element is about to become a necessity'. If 'London' represents Blake's triumph in pressing 'the lyric precisely as far as it could go', the judgement also marks the sense in Schorer's work that the prophetic books represented the disappointing ascendancy of intellectualisation and abstraction over feeling. For Schorer, what comes after *Songs* is a decline: 'The difference between the compressed and lovely lucidity of an early poem like "Ah! Sun-flower" and the prolix and endless involutions of the later work reveals the extent of this derangement' (49).

HUMAN IMAGINATION

If for writers like Bronowski and Schorer the ability of the *Songs* to tap into fundamental human desires and anxieties was crucial to its distinctive political vision, in Northrop Frye's seminal *Fearful Symmetry*

(1947) the same qualities were deemed to make them a paradigmatic of the western literary tradition. As well as being an academic, Frye (1912–91) was an ordained minister of the United Church of Canada, who later claimed that he had become hooked on Blake because 'I had been brought up in much the same evangelical subculture' (Frye 1976, 103). Deeply committed to a systemic study of Blake, Frye's book represented the poems not as the expression of a singular hermetic imagination, but as manifestations of a patterning fundamental to literature and myth as general human categories. Where Eliot (see Chapter 5) described Blake as a poet compromised by idiosyncratic mythopoesis and a failure to relate to any broader tradition, Frye took Blake's poetry to reveal what he saw as the very foundations of literature.

Rejecting notions of Blake's poetry as mystical, Frye repudiated any 'attempt to explain them in terms of something that is not poetry' (Frye 1947, 6). Although influenced by Damon's book, Frye claimed to be resisting any description of Blake's ideas as a fully elaborated 'system' as such:

■ One should never think of Blake as operating or manipulating a 'system' of thought, nor should we be misled by his architectural metaphors to think of his symbolic language as something solidified and crustacean. □

(ii)

Nevertheless, he did present a 'canon' of the engraved works as part of a 'unified scheme' that was also 'in accord with a permanent structure of ideas' (14). Frye attempted to map out Blake's poetry as a personal myth that exemplified what he thought of as the human imagination in itself. Consequently, Frye also necessarily tends to read the individual poems as insights into the greater poetic system he later elaborated in *The Anatomy of Criticism* (1957). This method found little space in practice for close textual analysis, nor for Blake as printmaker, but, in treating the poetry as representing a vital contribution to human culture, aimed to make it difficult for anyone to dismiss Blake with the charge of madness ever again.

Part of the affinity Frye felt for Blake was a shared background in Christian nonconformity, a background that also helps explain the sense of the human imagination as saturated with biblical resonances, but the methodology of *Fearful Symmetry* also shows the influence of contemporary developments in structural anthropology. Study of comparative religion and 'a morphology of myths, rituals and theologies' would unearth 'a single visionary conception which the mind of man is trying to express, a vision of a created and fallen world which has been redeemed by a divine sacrifice and is proceeding to regeneration' (Frye 1947, 424). Blake's greatest value is the degree to which 'he insists so urgently on this question of an imaginative iconography, and forces us to learn so much of its grammar in reading him' (421). Although Frye makes it clear that Blake thought a narrow faith in the authority of the Bible an egregious error, it remains the case that the version of literary tradition and competence to which he primarily appeals in *Fearful Symmetry* – familiarity with Dante, Shakespeare, Spenser, Milton, and Gray, and, above everything else, the Bible – might be taken to be an elite and geographically limited 'literary' system of knowledge produced in place of Damon's mystical system.

In terms of *Songs*, Frye focuses upon Blake's linkage of the categories of Innocence and Experience with the Biblical narrative of the Fall, not as a biblical event or even trope as such, but as an early statement of a fundamental insight of the human imagination. Characteristically, Frye refracts these readings of Innocence and Experience through Blake's attack on Lockean psychology. Innocence consists of the subject's imaginative unity with the world being perceived, whilst Experience represents a Lockean mode of engagement with the world, characterised by the alienation of a perceiving subject and a perceived object. This psychologised version of the Fall informs Frye's reading of paired opposites of poems:

■ The universal perception of the particular is the 'divine image' of the *Songs of Innocence*; the egocentric perception of the general is the 'human abstract' of the *Songs of Experience*. □

Innocence weaves an idealistic strand into Blake's thought, which Frye particularly associated with the pastoral genre, an insight that was to inform later critics like Bloom and Wagenknecht (see below and Chapter 7). This state provides a co-operative, humanised vision of nature:

■ The world of imagination in its pitying, tender, sympathetic and feminine aspect is in *The Book of Thel* as well as the *Songs of Innocence*; but [...] real children are not symbols of innocence: the *Songs of Innocence* would be intolerably sentimental if they were. One finds a great deal more than innocence in any child: there is the childish as well as the childlike; the jealousy and vanity that all human beings naturally have. □

(235)

Identifying the affinity of these songs with the pastoral genre, Frye sees Blake knowingly exploiting a potential for satire in the disparities between the fallen world and its vision of wholeness, but also recognising its potential for recuperation into the present. Such recuperation recurs when 'in every attempt of an adult to console a crying child' there is an imaginative recognition that the world is not good enough (237, 236).

Crucial to Frye's method is his incorporation of these individual poems and the states of Innocence and Experience into the larger structure of Blake's myth. Frye's method implies the impossibility of reading the *Songs* before knowing the later prophecies and the myth behind them. For instance, Frye reads the state of Innocence as an articulation of the Beulah of later epics, a restful mid-point between the furious energies of Eternity and the fallen world of Ulro. Beulah's cocooning world is fragile and potentially delusive. The pastoral aspects of the *Innocence* poems link them, for Frye, as for Ellis and Yeats (see Chapter 5), to the figure of Tharmas in the longer epics:

■ the pastoral side of eternal existence, the Zoa of Jesus which makes him the Good Shepherd and the Lamb of God – not the Lamb as a sacrificial victim, which is Luvah, but as the symbol of the ideal Beulah existence portrayed in the twenty-third psalm. □

(284)

The poems in *Songs of Experience*, on the other hand, are 'deeply acid-bitten' satires, opposing the comforts of Innocence with the disillusioned perspective of Experience in the fallen world (74). In the process, they dramatise the distortion of Innocent values. 'London' demonstrates Blake's perception of wasted potential in the harlot. The key word 'chartered' is read via a wealth of ironies (74, 181), later unpacked in historical terms by David Erdman and E. P. Thompson, among others (see the next section and Chapter 7), but for Frye the particularities of individual poems are to be more appropriately understood in terms of Blake's myth and the archetypes behind it. Frye associates the contrary states of Innocence and Experience with the Orc cycle, the major mythic dynamic he sees at work in the later prophecies. Frye identified in Blake's core myth the ascendance of revolutionary human energy (identified with the figure of Orc) over the fallen world and its inevitable corruption into new forms of enslavement. The figure of Los and the valorisation of an interiorised imagination were Blake's route of escape from the nightmare of historical recurrence. This has proved a lasting legacy to Blake studies, although its tendency to see political change as an inevitable dead end has often been criticised (see, for instance, Hobson 1998). When it comes to the *Songs*, its centrality for Frye means necessarily reading them as anticipating the fully elaborated version of the Orc cycle in the later prophecies.

Despite these lingering questions, Frye's approach made the decisive contribution to the rising fortunes of Blake's poetry in the twentieth century. By linking *Songs* to Blake's broader project, he placed the collection at the centre of his account of the literary imagination as a whole. There is a consistently iconoclastic strain throughout *Fearful Symmetry*, especially in relation to 'priestcraft', which may now be difficult to recognise in what has become a classic of literary criticism. The prestige it won for its author makes it easy to overlook the scandal of choosing to make an outsider like Blake the key to the fundamental processes of the human imagination. As Frye himself acknowledged on the first page of his book, Blake had always been treated as 'an interruption in cultural history, a separable phenomenon'. Now he was being offered as the key to the human imagination as a whole. Staking everything on such a marginal figure paid off, as *Fearful Symmetry* proved hugely influential, not just on Blake criticism, but on literary studies and poetry more generally. Harold Bloom recalled it as 'the best book I'd ever read about anything' (quoted in Frye 2004, xxxvii).

Bloom's engagement with Blake pervades nearly everything he ever wrote, perhaps unsurprisingly since he claimed to have been reading the poet before he heard English spoken (Frye 2004, xxxvii). Born into a Yiddish-speaking family in 1930, Bloom (b. 1930) was a member of faculty at Yale from the mid-1950s. He played a crucial role in the development of Romanticism as a critical discipline, placing Blake at the centre of this understanding. The influence of *Fearful Symmetry*, acknowledged in the preface, pervades Bloom's *Blake's Apocalypse* (1963), which expands upon Frye's insights and methodology in distinctive ways. Bloom shared Frye's preference for thinking of Blake's work as a form of universal poetry. Bloom radically develops Frye's account of Blake's antipathy towards natural religion and deism, including what he called 'Constructive Deism', the wider assimilation of natural religion into mainstream Christianity. The apocalypse of Bloom's title is Blake's rejection of nature and naturalism in favour of a prophetic vision that roots authentic poetic imagination in scriptural tradition. In his discussion of *Songs of Innocence*, Bloom's primary focus is on pastoral, but sharply distinguished from the classical tradition that begins with Theocritus and Virgil (Bloom 1963, 36). More important is the biblical pastoral of the Song of Songs and St John's Christ the good shepherd as well as the 'English Puritan' absorption of the classical tradition into a vision of prelapsarian innocence, typified, as it had been for Frye, by the works of Edmund Spenser, John Bunyan, and particularly John Milton (37–8). What is good about the pastoral for Bloom must be understood as 'a self-consuming light that momentarily transforms natural reality into an illusion of innocence'. The child of *Innocence* is thus 'a changeling, reared by a foster nurse who cannot recognise his divinity, and whose ministrations entrap him in a universe of death' (37). Not only does such anti-naturalism retrospectively impose Blake's later notion of 'the Female Will' onto the *Songs*, it also illuminates a misogynistic tendency in Bloom's basic terms of reference that feminist critiques of Romanticism have since done much to uncover (see Chapters 7 and 9). Whether these critiques are more appropriately aimed at the Bloomian criticism, or at the poems themselves, remains an ongoing matter of debate.

Innocence as a category associated with a feminised nature is certainly suspect for Bloom. As a result, he sees Blake developing a subtly ironic approach to pastoral with a paternal inheritance derived from Milton (38). For Bloom the Christian pastoral evident in 'Introduction', 'A Dream', 'The Lamb', and 'The Shepherd' reflects a harmony between the child and nature, the former not having 'sundered itself to self-realization'. A more ironised perspective begins to emerge in poems like 'The Blossom', according to Bloom, where the lack of response to the robin's situation undermines the harmony of man and nature evident in other songs (Bloom 1963, 40). What Bloom regards as 'realization' is a higher state of consciousness that 'depends upon a severing between the natural and the human' (46).

Inevitably, given this perspective, *Experience* is the great achievement. Linking these poems to Blake's later scheme of the Reprobate (antinomian and prophetic), the Redeemed (the imaginative who require redemption), and the Elect (the orthodox, dogmatic, and judgemental) in *Milton*, Bloom proposes three different narrative voices in the collection:

> ■ The Bard's songs are, besides the *Introduction*, notably *The Tyger, A Poison Tree*, and *A Little Girl Lost*. Blake's own songs, in which he allows himself full Reprobate awareness, are *Holy Thursday, Ah! Sun-Flower, London, The Human Abstract*, and the defiant *To Tirzah*. The remaining poems in *Songs of Experience* belong to various other Redeemed speakers. □
>
> (132)

The Bard of the 'Introduction' has 'considerable capacity for vision, and has much in common with Blake, but he is *not* Blake, and his songs are limited by his perspective' (130). The Bard sees 'Present, Past & Future', but his inability to 'see them all as a single mental form' is a 'tragic mental error'. The past tense in relation to 'the Holy Word' indicates that 'he does not hear that Word now'. The Bard 'thinks of man as a "lapsed Soul," and Blake of course does not, as the *Marriage* has shown us' (130). The Bard's call to Earth to arise 'is what ought to be, but Earth can no more arise "from out" the grass than man's "lapsed soul" can rise from the "slumberous mass" of his body'. 'Earth's Answer' reflects the inadequacy of the appeal to nature; for Bloom 'Earth gives the burden back to whom it belongs: the Bard, and all men, must act to break the freezing weight of Jealousy's chain' (133). The harmony of man and nature in Innocence is disturbed in Experience, exemplified in 'Ah! Sun-flower' in the plant's agonising 'heliotropic bondage' and the unnecessarily 'vegetative existence' brought about by the Youth and Virgin's attempts to repress their energies and aspire to heaven like the flower (140).

Bloom devotes most discussion to 'The Tyger', which sees 'the Bard of Experience' returning 'in all the baffled wonder of his strong but self-fettered imagination' (137). The confrontation with a mythic beast and the 'series of increasingly rhetorical questions' is understood in terms of a theodicy, that is, the question of the place of good and evil in the world, derived from the Book of Job. The Tyger is Blake's version of the Behemoth and the Leviathan in Job, 'emblems of the sanctified tyranny of nature over man'. The Bard – identified with the poem's speaker, but not with Blake – is a figure confused by the coexistence of 'love (the Lamb) and fright (the Tyger)' in the visible world, who comes to a deeper understanding over the course of his questioning, revealing the origins of these categories in the human breast (138–9). *Blake's Apocalypse* draws the *Songs* into a larger myth, elaborated by Blake in the later epics, often at the cost of any sense of individual complexity in the lyrics (compare our discussion of Ellis and Yeats in Chapter 5). Thus 'The Sick Rose' discovers the psychology of 'a Leutha-figure subservient to the Enitharmon of nature, and the frustrations of male sexuality strike back in the worm's Orc-like destructiveness' (135). Like Frye, Bloom also extends patterns of meaning into a wider Biblical and mythological complex. 'To Tirzah' becomes a 'condensed summary of the entire cycle of *Songs of Innocence and of Experience*'. While Jerusalem was the capital of Judah and the two redeemed tribes of Israel, Tirzah was the capital of the kingdom of Israel and the ten lost tribes. Bloom believes the former equates to Milton's Christian Liberty, 'the spiritual freedom of man', but the latter 'stands for man's bondage to nature'. The lyric repudiates the 'generative cycle' of nature just as Jesus announced his freedom from mortality by repudiating his mother. Bloom's version of Blake consistently chooses an apocalyptic and imaginative perspective gendered as masculine over the natural religion gendered as feminine. Moreover, political perspectives in Blake are acknowledged by Bloom but always subsumed 'as a single element in a more complex vision' understood in terms of distinctive rendering of the poetic as a function of the apocalyptic with the imaginative.

Both Bloom and Frye tended to emphasise a Blake whose apocalypticism is distinctively anti-dualistic. In so doing, they were repudiating the Blake which Damon and others understood as part of a hermetic Neoplatonic tradition that saw a spiritual world beyond this one. This version of Blake remained appealing and received renewed attention in G. M. Harper's *The Neoplatonism of William Blake* (1961), Desiree Hirst's *Hidden Riches* (1964), and Kathleen Raine's capacious *Blake and Tradition* (1969). Using a procedure similar to Frye's in so far as they construed Blake's poems to be manifestations of a larger system, prior to them, both Harper and Raine believed that Blake was familiar with at least the writings of Thomas Taylor (1758–1835), a London contemporary and translator of Plato's works into English. Harper is the more cautious, focusing on Taylor and other Neoplatonists 'to demonstrate the fundamental ties' with 'Blake's basic ideas' (Harper 1961, vi). By contrast, Raine, an important British poet in her own right, for whom Blake was a major inspiration, confidently identifies sources for Blake's ideas within a mystical tradition comprising Swedenborg, Jacob Boehme, Paracelsus, Plato, Plotinus, Gnosticism, and the Hermetica. Raine's project was in many respects deliberately polemical, and spurning of recent academic developments. She represented herself as returning to essential premises of Blake's work that Ellis and Yeats (see Chapter 5) had at least grasped as part of a reaction against modern materialism. Few of the critics looked at in this chapter would have dissented from this notion broadly stated, but Raine's version of Blake was a votary of a secret tradition 'whose sources were not divulged, as knowledge of the ancient mysteries was kept secret among initiates' (Raine 1969). Both Harper and Raine tend to approach *Songs* in terms of a key that can unlock their treasures once it has been provided. Where Bloom, Frye, and most historical critics have read Blake as profoundly anti-dualistic, the Neoplatonic school of Blake criticism has always seen the poems as validating spirit above matter. 'Ah! Sun-flower' thus becomes a homage to the yearning of the spirit for transcendence, rather than an attack on this impulse. Harper finds the source for this poem in Taylor's translation of the *Hymns of Orpheus*, where the sun is the chief Neoplatonic symbol demonstrating the participation of earthly things in the divine order, and their desire to return to it (Harper 1961). Raine sees it as 'a poem on the theme of love as prayer' and 'as a mediating spirit, which leads, through the attraction of earthly beauty, to the heavenly original', whose origins lie in Plato's *Phaedrus* (Raine 1969, I.220). For Raine, the starting point of Blake's mystical symbolism lies in his early fascination with Swedenborg, who she sees as an offshoot from the main branch of Neoplatonic tradition (I.4). The symbolic logic of Swedenborgianism influences not only the poems but also the designs, including even the colours chosen by Blake (I.6). Harper and Raine identify numerous sources in the esoteric tradition for individual poems, even though Blake's own mentions of occult writers are sporadic and limited largely to Swedenborg, Boehme, Paracelsus, and Plato. In this context, the largely anecdotal evidence for Blake's relationship with Taylor becomes key to their project. Otherwise Blake's relation to his own times or to more mundane aspects of his literary predecessors is largely ignored, although for Raine this search for a truth above the everyday world of getting and spending is precisely what makes Blake such an urgent poet for her times.

THE REASONING HISTORIAN

Most accounts of Blake from the first half of the century still viewed him, in Frye's words, 'as out of touch with his own age, and without influence on the following one' (Frye 1947, 3). Frye's emphasis on universal myth scarcely adjusted the situation, at least not beyond a very generalised sense of reacting against eighteenth-century philosophy and the French Revolution. The relative paucity of reliable biographical material relating to Blake posed a barrier to understanding the conditions in which he wrote his poems, although books such as Margaret Ruth Lowery's *The Windows of the Morning* (1940) had examined Blake's family and upbringing. During the 1950s, the American scholar David V. Erdman (1911–2001) began to build upon the work of Bronowski and Schorer to undertake close research into the historical context in which Blake wrote. He brought a new historical rigour to the study of Blake, refuting the pervasive myth built up by biographers that Blake's childhood was spent in a family saturated with Swedenborgian reading and that he had composed 'A Divine Image' in the New Jerusalem Church in Hatton Garden (Erdman 1953).

The culmination of this detailed research was *Blake: Prophet Against Empire* (1954), still routinely the first port-of-call for those who wish to relate *Songs* to its historical context. In the Preface to the first edition, Erdman explains how he had delved into contemporary newspapers, prints, caricatures, paintings, debates, and pamphlets to 'get close to the eye-level at which Blake witnessed the drama of his own times'

(Erdman 1977, ix). Despite Blake's often-obscure symbolism, Erdman asserts that he has traced 'through nearly all of his work a more or less clearly definable thread of historical reference' (x). Interpreting Blake's poems within a wider discursive context, Erdman differs from Frye in his focus on specific historical, social, and political material to provide larger cultural structures upon which to build his readings of the texts, as opposed to the latter's foundation in universal myth. Within these large differences, there were affinities between these two major projects of the first wave of post-war Blake criticism, not least their valorisation of Blake the iconoclast. In fact, Frye read drafts of Erdman's book and encouraged him in his endeavour (xv). No less than Frye, Erdman was driven by a sense of relationship between the events of Blake's times and his own. Where they differed was that Erdman continued to see a commitment to revolutionary political change as fundamental to Blake's artistic enterprise. The Orc cycle as it appears in various specific places is to be understood, in muted criticism of Frye, not as 'a fatalistic generalization but as a description of the period' (308).

In his readings of individual poems, Erdman's sense of the 'divinity of the creative individual' also overlaps with Frye's sense of the priority of the human imagination, although Erdman is much more concerned with the relation of the poems to a spirit of liberation stirring in their time (and in his own) (143). The social concerns of late eighteenth-century philanthropic movements become foundational to Blake's enterprise in *Songs*. 'The Chimney Sweeper', for instance, is the product of agitation for a 1788 Parliamentary bill intended to give some protection to the 'climbing boys' and restrict the use of young children. Erdman perceives the angel's 'bright key' opening the coffins as a reference to the bill. 'The Little Black Boy' likewise becomes a contribution to the early efforts of the Society for Effecting the Abolition of the Slave Trade (132). Contrary to earlier accounts of *Innocence* as a pastoral idyll (see the previous section), Erdman believed the poems were deeply engaged with the pain and suffering of the world around them, and conceived from the very beginning with their contrary in mind. Erdman agrees with Frye that the poems in *Innocence* provide a kind of satire on the state of Experience, exposing 'its hypocrisies by contrast' (117). The origin of several songs in *An Island in the Moon* indicates for Erdman an acute sense of social critique at play in the poems (115–17). He sees irony, for instance, in Blake's decision to make Obtuse Angle the singer of 'Holy Thursday' (later of *Innocence*) there. He obtusely and uncritically 'accepts the annual regimented singing of London charity-school children as evidence that the flogged and uniformed boys and girls are angelically happy' (121). Reports from *The Times* in 1788–9 of the London charity school Holy Thursday services held in St Paul's Cathedral provide many of the details Erdman uses in his analysis. He notes the harsh realities underpinning the spectacle: the children had sometimes been 'benevolently' separated from their 'wicked parents'; parents and other 'improper company' were sometimes ejected from the event; and children were 'trained to useful servitude'. The *Times* reporter's bland certainty that the services 'must raise the mind to sympathy and to brotherly love' is the corollary of Obtuse Angle's concern with the superficial arrangements for the event. By contrast, this 'obtuse, roseate view is refuted point by point' in the 'Holy Thursday' of *Experience*. Erdman associates this voice with Blake's own outrage at this snapshot of 'a land of poverty'. Only 'the sentimental can call "that trembling cry a song" or be complacent about the "thousands of little girls & boys" in uniform who are "so many children poor"' (122).

For Erdman *Songs* is to be read alongside Blake's other writings of the same time as signs of the developed social outlook that underpins *Experience*. The annotations Blake made to his copy of Johann Kaspar Lavater's *Aphorisms on Man* (1788) he regards as 'the nearest thing we have to a commentary on the songs themselves'.[1] *Innocence* reflects Blake's refusal to criticise superstition, 'which is ignorant honesty' and 'beloved of god & man', and he approves of Lavater's preference for 'heroes with infantine simplicity' as 'heavenly' (E591). 'True Christian philosophy' annotating the aphorism that the purest religion is 'the most refined Epicurism' indicates the liberal Christianity shared by both (E583–4), although Erdman sees Blake going further by praising exuberance and celebrating love and laughter (127). Erdman also suggests that the Lavater annotations contain 'important themes that belong to the *Songs of Experience*' further bolstering the argument that Blake 'had both contraries in mind all along' (129). Key to Erdman's understanding of the poems in *Experience* is that they have within them not only a critique of social and political conditions, but also something like a Marxist critique of false consciousness. These poems do not simply expose suffering, but also the way that sufferers are forced to collude with their own situation by understanding it as the way the world has to be. In this regard, Erdman's book is an early account of Blake's poems as staging their own form of ideology critique, revealing the way 'mind forg'd manacles' have prevented the oppressed from understanding their own oppression (see Chapter 7).

The French Revolution is understood by Erdman as the catalyst for Blake's move into a prophetic form of art that looks to liberation from false consciousness. While the works etched or dated in 1789 'all bear the pre-revolutionary emphasis on the plight or energy of the individual', Blake's subsequent poems – especially *The French Revolution* (1791) – are 'alive with the sense of a new and revolutionary break with the past and a great hopeful movement of the people' (130). Although Erdman does not find reliable evidence that Blake was significantly involved in the Johnson circle, he discerns wry parodies of Anna Laetitia Barbauld's educational book *Hymns in Prose* (1781) in poems like 'Nurse's Song', 'The Ecchoing Green', and 'Laughing Song' (123–5). More importantly, Blake's writings are shown to be thoroughly imbued with what Erdman calls 'the *ideas* of the Paine set'. What remains less clear among the welter of minute particulars, as the account of the parody of Barbauld suggests, is exactly who constitutes this 'set' for Erdman and how Blake agrees or disagrees with particular principles held by its participants. In contrast to what he describes as the 'Whiggish radicalism' of Wordsworth and Coleridge, Erdman finds a 'warmth of republican enthusiasm' in Blake that he identifies with the popular reform societies, although there is even less evidence for any actual involvement in political agitation than for either of the other two poets (161–2). Erdman's point is that the tone and temper of Blake's outlook, rather than any practical affiliation, are what make his radicalism distinctive among 'literary' sympathisers with the French Revolution, a line of argument developed more explicitly in Jon Mee's *Dangerous Enthusiasm: William Blake and the Culture of Radicalism in the 1790s* (1992) and, more recently, in Saree Makdisi's account of Blake's resistance to reformist ideas of improvement in *William Blake and the Impossible History of the 1790s* (2003).

If Erdman reads *Innocence* as an effusion of revolutionary optimism, he makes the government's moves to repress the radical movement after 1792 the context for his readings of *Songs of Experience*. The nonpublication of *The French Revolution* (1790), which only exists in what seems to be proof copy, is used to show that Blake was directly affected by this climate, and pushed towards anxiety about his own fate, although 'in his bardic self he remained bold' (153). The key poems for Erdman inevitably become those that articulate a bardic indignation Blake felt unable to articulate in his own voice:

■ the fused brilliance of *London* and *The Tyger*, the sharp, poignant symbolism of *The Garden of Love*, *Infant Sorrow*, and many another 'indignant page' were forged in the heat of the Year One of Equality (September 1792 to 1793) and tempered in the 'grey-brow'd snows' of Antijacobin alarms and proclamations. □

(272)

In the 'chartered' streets and Thames of 'London' Erdman finds evidence of Paine's attack on charters as restrictions of rights, made in Part Two of *Rights of Man* (see Chapters 1, 7, and 8 on Blake's use of this word in the Notebook). Likewise he asserts that the 'mind-forg'd manacles' refer to anxieties promoted by government spies and informers, the gathering of troops on the outskirts of London, and Pitt's proclamations against sedition. He suggests that the phrase 'german-forg'd links' in the notebook draft of the poem points towards George III's Hanoverian origins, the British military alliance with Prussia, and fears that Hanoverian and Hessian mercenaries would be used by the government (276–7).

For Erdman, *Songs* shows Blake 'firm in the belief that the blighting Code of War & Lust is historically negatable'. Readers 'in the future age', as Blake puts it in 'A Little Girl Lost', will be shocked to learn 'that in a former time, Love! Sweet Love! Was thought a crime' (272). 'The Human Abstract' explains the propagation of this ideology, with the evil tree planted in the brain 'by priest and king, who use the virtuousness of pity as an excuse for poverty and who define peace as an armistice of fear – and thus "promote war"' (273). 'The Chimney Sweeper' of *Experience* points at 'God & his priest & King' as the sources of this oppression and Erdman views his resultant punishment as part of the reactionary backlash: 'King, priest, god, and parents do not reckon the revolutionary potential in the multitude they are stripping naked' (275). Despite this onset of winter and its mental bondage, the Bard – who Erdman identifies as the narrator of the second volume of poems – 'is determined that the spring *shall* come' (270–1).

Along with his 'reconstruction' of the historical contexts that he sees as shaping the twinned vision of *Songs* as a collection, Erdman recovers a wealth of contemporary allusions and implications for individual poems. These allusions are particularly important for his reading of 'The Tyger', Blake's 'great revolutionary lyric', which is 'apocalyptic in its implications':

■ On the level of practice it is clear that 'The stars threw down their spears' means: the armies of counterrevolution were defeated. On the level of theory it is clear that Reason, when it refuses to assist but attempts to hinder Energy, is overthrown. Denied the peaceful accommodation of the Steeds of Light, the just man seizes the Tigers of Wrath. □

(189, 194–5)

These lines represent an apocalyptic 'day of repentance' when regal, aristocratic, and priestly impositions are driven out by 'dread power as well as daring and art'. Erdman suggests that Blake saw this wrathful aspect as a necessary stage in achieving liberty, albeit one tempered by its role as a contrary. Although he denies that his reading of 'The Tyger' is 'political allegory' (196), it certainly influenced numerous critics in their hunt for tigerish multitudes in contemporary texts (see Crehan 1984 and Pedley 1991). More importantly, Erdman's account of the late prophecies certainly tends towards reading them as a kind of commentary on contemporary events, and this tendency also shapes his interpretation of the *Songs*. Often there is a tension between the wealth of historical context and specific references he adduces for each poem and the larger readings he produces for them. The latter often adopt similar positions to Frye in general terms without entirely integrating them with the detailed contextual work that makes up most of his study. Nor does the acute sense of historical resonances in the language always follow through to the question of form and what it might imply about the politics of the poems, a path followed much more successfully by later critics such as Heather Glen (see Chapter 7), whose work both uncovers new sources for the 'Holy Thursday' poems and closely investigates the transformative work Blake's lyric form undertakes. Nevertheless, *Prophet Against Empire* was a major work, which, like *Fearful Symmetry*, has had a lasting impact upon Blake criticism, deepening the sense of relationship between the songs and their times. For Frye, the *Songs* managed to see into the deepest wells of human creativity. Erdman in many ways confirmed this understanding of Blake, but as the product of a multiplicity of interactions with his own time. The next generation of critics took these insights to new levels of complexity, but few of them were not in one way or another indebted to *Fearful Symmetry* and *Prophet against Empire*.

CHAPTER SEVEN

Freedom and Repression in the 1960s and 1970s: Form, Ideology, and Gender

With the publication of major books by Frye and Erdman, the 1940s and 1950s had witnessed two of the enduring keystones of Blake criticism being put into place. Little written on Blake in the decades that followed did not orient itself in relation to these two monumental achievements in one way or another, but neither Erdman nor Frye had gone far into the minute particularities of *Songs*. Frye's systemic approach tended towards elaboration of the mythology of the later prophecies, which provided the retrospective lens through which he saw the earlier collection. Erdman's historical approach seemed most comfortable when matching Blake's epic scale against the events of his time. With literary criticism beginning to develop seriously as a post-war academic subject, formal or close analysis of individual poems increasingly came to define its remit. This encouraged the analysis of the lyrics in *Songs*, and produced some wonderfully nuanced critical work by a host of scholars, attentive not just to the textual interplay that sustained individual poems, but also to the way these echoed between poems and across the collection. The first section here discusses the development of formal analyses of the poems, particularly in the work of the American scholar Robert F. Gleckner, noting its affiliation to Frye's idea of the 'human imagination' as the ultimate meaning of Blake's texts.

In fact, whatever its claims about attention to minute particulars, much of the criticism of the 1960s and 1970s was influenced by general assumptions about Romanticism as a framework within which Blake was read. This trend reached an apotheosis in M. H. Abrams's *Natural Supernaturalism: Tradition and Revolution in Romantic Literature* (1973). Blake's place as a canonical figure in Romanticism was confirmed by the 1960s and 1970s. He provided for Abrams a key example of the 'doctrine ... of the active existence by which man, exhibiting the cardinal virtue of "energy" must earn his way from simple innocence back and up to a higher paradise of "organized innocence"' (Abrams 1973, 261). Ironically, despite its use of these terms, the commitment to Frye's account of the later prophecies in *Natural Supernaturalism* meant it found little room for any actual discussion of the *Songs* beyond this notional dialectic of Innocence and Experience.

For both Erdman and Frye, Blake mattered because he was understood as a prophet who had things to say of a moral and political nature to their own post-war society. Together with the increasing complexity and sophistication of formal analyses, this assumption continued to flourish in criticism of *Songs*, not least in the context of the progressive movements of the 1960s, for which Blake became a major icon. 'The tigers of wrath are wiser than the horses of instruction,' one of the 'Proverbs of Hell' in *The Marriage of Heaven and Hell* (E37), became a mantra for the counter-culture suspicious of the covert perpetuation of traditional values through educational institutions. This context influenced the interest in ideology explored in the second section of this chapter, not just as something that *Songs* was about, but also as something shaping the way it worked in Blake's poems to rouse the reader's faculties, freeing them from 'mind-forg'd manacles'. These approaches gave new urgency to Blake's critique of his contemporary society, giving more emphasis than Erdman to his account of the way social arrangements corrupted the structures of the mind. For other critics, especially those influenced by Sigmund Freud and Carl Jung, this aspect of Blake's poems was less a matter of history and politics than of human psychology. The roles of repression and liberation in shaping consciousness, especially in relation to sexuality, were taken to be crucial to poems like 'A Poison Tree' and 'The Garden of Love'.

Influential books for the counter-culture of the 1960s, like Norman O. Brown's *Life against Death* (1959) and *Love's Body* (1966), made much of Blake as a harbinger of psychological and sexual liberation, but perhaps the most influential psychoanalytical account of the poetry in this period was provided by Harold Bloom's theory of revisionism. As set out in *The Anxiety of Influence* (1973), Bloom's general theory was grounded in his love of Blake, although it provided no reading of any of the *Songs* until the discussion of 'London' and 'The Tyger' in his *Poetry and Repression* (1976). For Bloom, Blake was fundamentally a revisionist poet, defined by the experience of belatedness understood as a form of Oedipal conflict. Bloom's theories primarily accounted for relations between poets in terms of a struggle between powerful geniuses for imaginative space. Others influenced by psychoanalysis identified versions of Freudian or Jungian analysis within the poems, especially in relation to the formation of sexual identities and the repression of more libidinous possibilities. Diana Hume George's account in *Blake and Freud* (1980) ended with the question of 'feminine psychology'. For George, Blake's theories on the subject did not just anticipate Freud's ideas but also saw beyond them because he did not see human possibilities as completely defined by biology.

Blake and Freud reflected a more general reorientation of criticism at the end of the 1970s towards the consideration of the question of gender in Blake's poetry. Despite his reputation as someone who broke through traditional ideology, Blake has continued to prove a troubling case for feminist criticism, often revealing an artist who was as much the product of patriarchy as its critic. Certainly the feminist critics discussed in the chapter's final section were sceptical of the critical tradition that celebrated Blake as the prophet of revolt against a nature gendered as feminine (as with Bloom and the critics most influenced by him). Whether the problem was Blake's or the assumptions of critics committed to an idea of the human imagination as a form of visionary transcendence is a question still being argued over.

FORM, STRUCTURE, GENRE

From at least the 1950s onwards, professional literary criticism began to pay much more focused attention to the precision of Blake's language in *Songs*, not least to the way his verbal registers changed within poems and between the two parts of *Songs*. Attention shifted from the larger focus of studies like Erdman and Frye's, and those of Swinburne, Ellis and Yeats, and Damon before them, into a series of book-length accounts devoted to *Songs* and other early lyrics. These include Hazard Adams's *William Blake: A Reading of the Shorter Poems* (1963), E. D. Hirsch's *Innocence and Experience: An Introduction to Blake* (1964), and John Holloway's *Blake: The Lyric Poetry* (1968) – although there had, of course, been studies focused on the collection, published before this, such as Joseph Wicksteed's *Blake's Innocence and Experience* discussed in our Chapter 5. This approach militated against reading *Songs* as a statement of a Blakean philosophy from which aphoristic truths could be harvested. A major figure in this development was the American critic Robert F. Gleckner whose *The Piper and the Bard* (1959) was, at this stage, one of only a very few books entirely devoted to *Songs*. Gleckner began his study by affirming F. W. Bateson's claim that the 'total intelligibility' of *Songs* was a 'modern discovery' (quoted in Gleckner 1959, vii). Although Frye is the critic most referenced in a book that reads the poems in terms of a journey through a series of states towards a 'higher innocence', Gleckner's analysis provided a detailed account of the interplay of different points of view within individual songs, between particular poems, and across the two parts of *Songs* as a whole. *The Piper and the Bard* originated in part from the essay 'Point of View and Context in Blake's Songs' (1957), often reprinted in anthologies of Blake criticism.[1] 'Points of View and Context' castigates the tendency to read the lyrics for moral content regardless of their relations with each other or the linguistic nuances within each poem. 'Context' for Gleckner refers primarily to the place of individual poems within the collection, not just in *Innocence* or *Experience*, but also in a series of smaller units, and then 'to each individual song within the series, to the symbols within each song, to the words that give the symbols their existence'. Gleckner particularly relates this question of symbolic patterning to 'a correct determination of speaker and perspective'. The most obvious of these perspectives are those of the Bard and of the Piper (that gave his book its title). Although they differ in 'the direction of their vision', as Gleckner puts it, 'both singers are imaginative, are what Blake called the poetic or prophetic character'. The aim of the *Songs* is to raise the reader to a perspective able to see across these different points of view. To see, for instance, that the Little Vagabond is a 'child of experience' who has to contend with the closed perspectives of his mother, the parson, and the 'father-priest-king'. Alertness to the different points of view comes from recognising the linguistic patterns Blake associates with the different characters (Gleckner 1957).

Gleckner's later work took its bearings from the passage addressed 'To the Public' in *Jerusalem*:

■ Every word and every letter is studied and put into its fit place: the terrific numbers are reserved for the terrific parts – the mild & gentle, for the mild & gentle parts, and the prosaic, for inferior parts: all are necessary to each other. □

(E146)

His essay 'Blake's Verbal Technique' (1969) notes that the quotation had often been used to justify study of the Blakean system as a unified whole, but less often to encourage critics to think about 'the peculiar appropriateness of Blake's verse, language, use of poetic forms, prosody – in short his poetry'. He attempts to rectify this omission by paying particular attention to Blake's 'poetry of adjectives' (Gleckner

1969, 321). Gleckner's point is that the patterns of symbolic meaning attached to particular figures like the child and the mother, which recur across *Songs*, are generated out of the interplay of distinctive sets of adjectives associated with the different states of being, for instance, 'happy', merry', 'tender', and 'mild'. These key adjectives 'carry the weight of nouns and verbs' (323). The connection with Gleckner's earlier work comes in the recognition that the key points of view explored in *Songs* are inherent in these adjective patterns. Indeed, he wants to claim, particular figures in the poems, like the child, are not to be understood as characters as such but as 'symbolic frames' on which the state of innocence is hung (323; compare the 'Symbolic System' developed by Ellis and Yeats discussed in Chapter 5). An entirely different semantic field defined experience, in contrast, as one might expect, where relations between nouns and adjectives seem much less settled.

Critics like Hazard Adams (1986) took Gleckner's insight into the relationship between language and mental states in the poems much further. Adams argued that Blake's manipulation of semantic fields did not simply generate meanings, but more fundamentally explored the way language structured the universe of perception. This sense of the productive nature of language was very different from the idea of the poems as manifestations of deep structures found in Frye's poetic theory. For Adams, whose earlier work had been very much indebted to Gleckner, Blake was an early 'symbolist', who believed that questions of freedom and repression were deeply bound up with the linguistic structures human beings created for themselves (or had imposed upon them) as ways of seeing the universe, a premise developed in the ideology criticism investigated in the next section of this chapter.

Gleckner's approach followed a rather different strain of thinking. The various semantic fields he explored in *Innocence* and *Experience* were meant to indicate a fundamental aspect of the Blakean Fall, 'not only equal to the fall of the Word into words but also of the disintegration of non-discursive unity into normal syntactic patterns' (1974, 561). Gleckner's work was related to Frye's in that he continued to understand Blake in terms of a perpetual search for a language that could transcend 'fallen sense perception', even while he argued poetry could never escape the determining limits of 'a time-bound, space-bound syntax that passively mirrors the shattered mind' (557). These reflections on his own earlier work appeared in an essay called 'Most Holy Forms of Thought' (1974), which pays little attention to *Songs* as such, but sees the problem facing Blake and all the Romantic poets as creating 'emblems of disjunctiveness', while at the same time 'providing us the paradigmatic conjunction or identification of All by which

the disjunctiveness can become meaningful' (561). For many later critics of *Songs*, especially those writing in the 1980s and after, influenced
by J. J. McGann's notion of a 'Romantic ideology' (see Chapter 8), this
'All' seemed to perpetuate a transcendent notion of truth that simply
reproduced the ideology it was supposed to be critiquing.

Robert Essick's *William Blake and the Language of Adam* (1989) acknowledged Gleckner's questions about Blake's conception of language as the
starting point of his enquiry (Essick 1989, 2–3). Essick's account of
Blake's early poetry, including *Songs*, looks at the idea of 'the motivated
sign' (3) as the beginning and end of language. The ideal form of language described in *Innocence* is one where the sign indicates something
of its meaning, both expressively and mimetically. So in various situations in the poems, children respond to their environment with verbal
and bodily signs that are expressively linked to their emotions and in
some way also to the experiences that produce them. 'The Ecchoing
Green' is representative of a situation where 'all acts – including utterance – bear a homologous relationship to all others' (107). The symmetry of the poem is the product of the responsiveness of the children
who participate in the playful circle. At least, Essick points out, this
understanding of the homology between world and sign 'is the innocent or primitive condition imagined by the speaker' (107). This consciousness has yet to be conditioned by the more abstract and logical
ideas of subordination and causation found in *Experience*, for instance,
in the 'differential logic' of the marking that takes place in 'London'
(134–5). Unlike Gleckner, Essick does not see any implied longing
for permanent forms of language at work in Blake. As someone who
has made major contributions to our understanding of Blake as printmaker, discussed in the next chapter, Essick never seems comfortable with the privileging of transcendence found in Gleckner's work.
Indeed, he summarises his own position as replacing 'transcendence
with incarnation, sublimation with immanence and questions about
how far even an ideal language can become a transparent medium of
something other than itself with questions about how far that other is
a reified projection of the medium' (5).

One of the few critics of *Songs* in the early 1960s who resisted the
powerful rhetoric of Romantic transcendence was Alicia Ostriker in her
Vision and Verse in William Blake (1965). Gleckner (1969, 332) recognises
Ostriker as a rare critic who had paid close attention to the verbal fabric
of the *Songs*, although he rightly describes their work as 'quite different'.
Ostriker's study begins by forcefully contrasting her attention to detail
with Frye's concern with archetypal meanings, 'to be everything in general and nothing in particular, might not have been so pleasing to the

poet' (Ostriker 1965, 4). *Vision and Verse* looks instead to the context of the literary (and popular) traditions of English poetics that had preceded *Songs*. For Ostriker versification and patterns of sound are central to poems. Significance, for her, is generated in *Songs* through metrical variations within and between the poems, but also in their variation from traditions of eighteenth-century versification more generally, divided into what she described as the 'liberal' and 'conservative' inheritances. Blake's experiments with metrical forms are, for Ostriker, fundamental to his investment in 'liberty', breaking away from what his contemporaries would have recognised as 'conservative' poetic practice, and broadly affiliating him with 'liberal' innovation (5–6).

Part II of her study is devoted entirely to the *Songs*, which she sees as marking a fundamental break with the conventionality of the lyrics published in *Poetical Sketches*. Taking off from T. S. Eliot's claim that Blake's 'peculiar honesty' derived from 'great technical accomplishment' (see Chapter 5), Ostriker identifies two key components to Blake's 'temerity' (Ostriker 1965, 77). First, he wrote 'serious poetry with the basic rhythmical and linguistic tools of a prattling child'. Second, 'he dared to think thoughts and hear melodies whose precise expression required breaking some universally accepted metrical conventions'. Ostriker notes the debt to Isaac Watts recognised by many critics before and after her. Blake adopted the metrical simplicity of Watts's children's verse, but developed from it a daring innovativeness, in Ostriker's opinion. Take her comparison of Watts's 'Cradle Hymn' and Blake's 'Cradle Song' (49–50). Ostriker notes that Watts uses a four-accent trochaic line to give a sense of childish simplicity to his poem:

■ Sleep, my babe; thy food and raiment,
House and home thy friends provide;
All without thy care or payment,
All thy wants are well supplied. □

The problem is that the simplicity in Watts 'marches boldly along'. Blake's poem, by contrast, 'is as full of repetition as a chant, and his crooning, hypnotic rhythms are the rocking of a cradle':

■ Sweet dreams form a shade,
O'er my lovely infants head.
Sweet dreams of pleasant streams,
By happy silent moony beams. □

The effect achieved by Blake conveys a sense of the 'sleepy sensuousness of maternal love', exploiting an internal rhyme that many contemporaries would have identified with light verse (50). Placing 'happy' and 'moony' in the same line would have been indecorous to Watts, whose range encompassed neither the easy switch from trochaic to iambic lines (Blake manages it twice), nor the long monosyllables of 'Sweet dreams'. In this readiness to dispense with decorum, Ostriker claims, there is more in common with popular nursery rhymes like 'Who Killed Cock Robin', which is the source of at least two birds (the sparrow and the robin) and a rhyme (sparrow/arrow) in Blake's 'The Blossom'.

The most striking of the sound effects Ostriker identified in *Songs* was 'their extraordinary use of repetition and parallel phrasing'. Ostriker drew on quantitative analysis to show that Blake's usage of these features was much heavier than that of most other poets from the period (56).[2] 'Bird', 'child', 'infant', 'lamb', 'little', 'laugh', 'mother', 'father', 'sweet', 'weep', 'sleep', and 'joy', all occur over twenty times, the intensity heightened by the way they cluster in particular poems (as with 'pipe' and its derivatives in the 'Introduction' to *Innocence*). In *Experience* the group of lexical repetitions is smaller, with only 'love', 'weep', and 'night' appearing more than ten times. The reason is that *Experience* explores a 'broader world, where the symbols can be more diverse, fewer terms repeat from song to song', but within particular poems there is still a lot of repetition. Ostriker identified several general functions performed by these effects:

■ They furnish a primitive esthetic pleasure comparable to that produced by a regular beat, and they accentuate, when placed in crucial positions on accents and especially at the end of the line, the poem's rhythmic structure. These effects are obvious, and have obvious value in Blake's style of lyric. In addition, and less obviously apparent, they serve to intensify emotion, and often help create it. □

(81)

Nowhere do they work more intensively than in 'The Tyger', where 'the degree of echo' is packed much more tightly than in most other poems in the collection; 'its last stanza is a musical miracle of rare device to express, through sound, the synthesizing energy of Creation, and the fearfulness of the thing created':

■ Tyger Tyger burning bright,
In the forests of the night:
What immortal hand or eye,
Dare frame they fearful symmetry! □

(Ostriker 1965, 86, ll. 21–4, E25)

Ostriker's analysis of the dense patterns of assonance, alliteration, and repetition concludes that they do not convey any sense of 'sensation' or 'physical effect', as might be found, for instance, in the odes of John Keats (89). Their concern is with a 'symbolic essence' that conveys 'glory and terror, and not a corporeal splendor'.

Despite the implication that Blake's aesthetics here tend towards symbolism, Ostriker's close reading of Blake's versification places him within the conventional practices of eighteenth-century poetry. David Wagenknecht's *Blake's Night: William Blake and the Idea of Pastoral* (1973) made a similar move at the level of genre, although he was keen to delimit the literary context to something closer to Bloom's visionary company of canonical male poets. Bloom had placed pastoral at the centre of his account in *Blake's Apocalypse*. Wagenknecht acknowledged Bloom's insight, but defined his own emphasis as 'literary' rather than the 'prophetic'. Pastoral is primarily a technical or generic issue concerned with the discovery of a poetic voice for 'expressing reconciliation' (Wagenknecht 1973, 5). Nevertheless, as we have hinted, Wagenknecht's downplaying of parallels with Watts and Barbauld in favour of those with Milton and Spenser aligns his criticism with a critical consensus, aligned with the work of Frye and Bloom, eager to place Blake within a 'strong' male line of poets.[3]

Wagenknecht also develops Gleckner's work on point of view by relating various voices and perspectives to his idea of different aspects of the pastoral tradition. He reads 'Spring' from *Innocence* as a poem in which the universe seems to sing unequivocally of the joys of Creation:

■ The jangling rhymes are meant to jangle, and to seem childish, because they represent the very first, inexperienced responses to the magic flute of the first line, responses which ring the natural world out of the silence of line 2 into the light (and dark) of quotidian day. □

(24–5)

The key transition in terms of points of view comes between the second and third stanzas of 'Spring' where the introduction of the 'Little Boy' and 'Little Girl' brings a split between the subject and the creation through a series of erotic innuendoes (like the crowing cock), which Wagenknecht (27) reads in terms of ideas of 'betrayal and sacrifice'. These darkening potentialities, of which the poem's joyful speaker seems unaware, are reinforced by the designs that accompany the text of the poem, marking Wagenknecht as part of a growing move among critics in this period towards offering sustained readings of the poems in terms of their 'composite art' (29). Pastoral for Wagenknecht is the genre that allows mediation between these innocent and darkening tendencies, an achievement understood at the level of form, rather than in terms of any system of meaning. From this perspective Blake's poetry is not so much about transcendence, but about the creation of a language in which 'the transcending fiction is reliant for its imagery upon the order being transcended' (100–1).

IDEOLOGY AND UTOPIA

For many critics, perhaps especially within the British critical tradition, the different points of view explored in *Songs* were understood as primarily questions about ideology. The Marxist historian E. P. Thompson had made Blake a kind of choric presence in his masterpiece *The Making of the English Working Class* (1963). A decade later, he published a major essay on the relationship of Blake's 'London' to the word 'charter'd' reiterated in its opening:

> ■ I wander thro' each charter'd street,
> Near where the charter'd Thames does flow.
> And mark in every face I meet
> Marks of weakness, marks of woe. □

> (ll. 1–4, E26)

Thompson showed that the term was a pivotal one in the dispute between Edmund Burke and Thomas Paine over the French Revolution at the beginning of the 1790s. Charters had long been understood as part of the constitutional tradition of British liberty, a means used by the Crown to grant freedoms to the people. Paine argued that such charters were not the Crown's to give and in fact were ways of limiting freedom:

> ■ It is a perversion of terms to say, that a charter gives rights. It operates by a contrary effect, that of taking rights away. Rights are inherently in all the inhabitants; but charters, by annulling those rights in the majority, leave the rights by exclusions in the hands of the few. □

> (Paine 1985, 220)

Despite the many differences between Paine and Blake, Thompson seized on their shared sense of the way language controlled perceptions, what are called 'mind-forg'd manacles' in 'London' (changed from 'german-forg'd' in the Notebook, a phrase more obviously critical of the Hanoverian monarchy, as Erdman had noted, see Chapters 1 and 6).

Thompson's work was a major influence on books like Heather Glen's *Vision and Disenchantment* (1983) and Stewart Crehan's *Blake in Context*

(1984) in thinking not only about the historical context, but also about relations between language and ideology in the poems. Glen's study adapted the interest in the relationship between Blake's songs and the poetry, for instance, of Isaac Watts, by now long-established as an important context for understanding *Songs*, to suggest that various poems manifested and undermined such points of view within themselves, even in some of the poems of *Experience* that had often been read directly as voices of protest. In this regard, Glen might be said to read the manipulation of points of view in *Songs* as part of a complex ideology critique rather than the organised progression through different states of being perceived by Gleckner. The speaker of 'London' is not taken simply to be Blake, prophesying against empire, as it were, but 'a lonely wanderer, who passes through the streets of a particular city, and sees it from a lamenting distance'. The point of view of the wanderer recognises, but does not fully comprehend, a new development in the rapidly expanding metropolis, 'a place of bewildering diversity, changing and growing rapidly, in which a new kind of anonymity and alienation was becoming a remarked-upon fact of life' (Glen 1983, 208). Acknowledging previous discussions of the word 'charter'd' in the poem, Glen concentrates instead on the function of the word 'mark', another repeated word, and linked to 'charter'd' by assonance (Glen 1983, 211). Here verbal patterns of the sort traced by Gleckner and Ostriker are used to place Blake in the context of various kinds of language circulating in his time, identified with particular social groups, specifically 'those artisan classes whose newly articulate radical politics were still intertwined with, and sometimes framed in the language of prophetic materialism' (211). This understanding of aspects of the language as a sociolect, a language circulating in particular ways in specific speech communities, was very different from the apocalyptic readings of Frye and Bloom. It would be an important aspect of the historical readings of Blake that emerged in the 1990s (see Mee 1992).

The subtlety of Glen's reading of 'London' went beyond simply identifying it with a distinctive sociolect. She placed it within an emergent drama of points of view. The shift is from the perspective of 'an alienated observer' in the first two stanzas to one where 'observation turns to revelation'. And there is a final turn to Glen's understanding of 'mark', one that was increasingly made in the criticism from this time on, that is, the relationship of the word to the marking of the copper plate in the engraving process that produced the illuminated books (see Chapter 1). Ultimately, in Glen's reading, 'London' is a closed structure that she says, quoting Thompson's essay, 'shuts like a box' (Glen 1983, 218). The possibility of prophetic transformation lies only implicitly in the 'negative articulation' brought to bear by the haunt-ing presence of *Innocence* in the 'new-born Infants' of the penultimate line. Against the closed box of 'London', Glen places 'the freely emerg-ing forward-pointing interplay' of poems in *Innocence* like 'Infant Joy', 'Nurse's Song' and 'The Ecchoing Green'. These she reads as a 'portrait of a society organized in ways characteristic of Innocence' (218–19). Glen understands this aspect of Innocence, primarily defined by an ethics of play and playfulness, as at least potentially more radical than what she calls 'protest', because it is committed to rousing its readers to the creation of values that are not already given, but future-oriented and 'collectively created' out of the world of experience, including the experience of reading *Songs* (164).

Glen's understanding of the role of open-ended play in the *Innocence* poems is partly elaborated by contrast to the children's verse of Isaac Watts. Glen sees Blake as not just taking a different path from Watts. Instead, she has Blake playing his poems off against the expectations of the tradition Watts had initiated:

■ And in frustrating those expectations, Blake is thrusting his readers' ten-dency towards simplistic moral categorizing before them as a problem. □

(18)

In this regard, Glen's account built upon work done in Zachary Leader's *Reading Blake Songs* (1981), which provided a sustained account of the relationship between the educational literature of the period and Blake's collection.

Glen's sense that *Songs* contained a complex interplay between the utopian promise of *Innocence* and the ideological critique of *Experience* was explored in a more explicitly theoretical way in John Brenkman's book *Culture and Domination* (1987). In a chapter called 'The Concrete Utopia of Poetry', Brenkman discussed Blake's poems in the context of the failure of mainstream Marxism to acknowledge the extent to which 'the practices of artistic production and aesthetic reception are embedded in moral-political relations and are a site of conflict over the moral-political valuations that inform our participation in social relations more generally' (102). Influenced by Frankfurt School think-ers like Ernst Bloch, Herbert Marcuse, Walter Benjamin, and T. W. Adorno, *Culture and Domination* deployed a more rigorous sense of the relations between ideology and utopia:

■ For Blake, poetry is an active imposing of imagination or fantasy against dominant values and institutions. Casting himself in the double role of visionary and voice of condemnation, he attributed both a utopian and a negative power to poetic writing. □

(104)

The dynamic between utopian possibility and ideological critique sustains a brilliant analysis of 'A Poison Tree' predicated on the poem's double perspective, on 'action *then* and his judgment *now*', set up in the first stanza:

■ I was angry with my friend;
I told my wrath, my wrath did end.
I was angry with my foe:
I told it not, my wrath did grow. □

Out of this double perspective a moral seems to emerge something along the lines of 'telling one's wrath is healthy and not telling it is harmful and even self-destructive' (112). What complicates this double perspective even further is the emergence of a contradictory train of thought that seems to relish the destruction of the foe, culminating in the final couplet:

■ In the morning glad I see;
My foe outstretchd beneath the tree. □

Both these meanings can be generated from within the poem, Brenkman argues; their 'undecidability', as he puts it, 'represents two contradictory experiential situations, remorse and remorselessness, condemnation and coldness' (113). The key is the central passage that provides the circuitous route that translates 'wrath into fear, duplicity, and finally deception':

■ And I waterd it in fears,
Night & morning with my tears:
And I sunned it with smiles,
And with soft deceitful wiles.

And it grew both day and night.
Till it bore an apple bright. □

(E28)

The produce of this tortuous logic is 'an apple bright', but it is not obvious how it is the fruit of what has come before it. For, as a fruit, it seems the product of the speaker's unexpressed wrath, but also the cause of the antagonism that generates the poem. This central image, then, confuses different levels of the narrative order, in 'a figurative swerve' that Brenkman identifies with the figure of speech known as 'metalepsis' (115). Brenkman perceives the 'bright apple' as illuminating the contradictory experience of social relations in bourgeois society, where individuals become 'interchangeable by the market-mediated relations in which they meet [...] deprived of the very individuality in the name of which they act'. The 'apple bright' becomes the utopian articulation of poetic speech that reveals the contradictions of the lived social relations. Measuring his distance from Herbert Marcuse's ideas, Brenkman's point is not that the aesthetic utterance of the poem itself stands in contradiction of the fallen world of capitalist social relations. Rather its 'concrete act of speaking' reveals these contradictions. The figure of metalepsis provides Blake's readers with a glimpse of 'a morality that cannot yet be lived in society or represented in poetry'. Precisely by taking up the discourses of actually existing social relations as the organising principles of its structure and language, it also provokes 'an *alternative* interaction' that goes beyond those values.

Brenkman's chapter ends with a return to 'London' where he marks his own difference both from the historicism of Thompson's intrepretation and from Bloom's desire to read the poem in terms of eternal dualities. Perhaps the divergence from Thompson may be the more surprising of the two, given their ideological affinities. Brenkman's point is that Thompson's reading of the poem as a 'closed box' attributes the perspective of the speaker to Blake (129). Accepting Thompson's important explication of the connotations of the word 'charter' in the 1790s, Brenkman refuses Thompson's assertion that the expectations of his contemporaries provided a semantic unity to the poem. For Brenkman (as with Glen), the idea of semantic unity closes Blake's poem off from the utopian possibility of a future beyond the social conditions that Thompson sees the poem as critiquing. The poem becomes a statement rather than the kind of opening up to the future that Glen had identified as the distinctive quality of Blake's collection.[4] The importance of *Songs* lies in the fact that it anticipates a revolution in social relations that did not occur; 'his poetry still speaks to us because we have not been freed to hear it' (138).

DESIRE AND REPRESSION

In his closing discussion of 'London', Brenkman engages not only with Thompson, but also with Harold Bloom, whose denial of the political possibilities of the poem had been reiterated in his *Poetry and Repression* (1976). Far from understanding the poem as the voice of prophetic protest, Bloom understood it as structured by a painful awareness of its own belatedness. 'London' is defined by the 'anxiety of influence', that is, the tension between the belated poet and his 'strong' precursors, specifically, in the case of 'London', Ezekiel 9.4:

■ Go through the midst of the city, through the midst of Jerusalem, and set a mark upon the foreheads of the men that sigh and cry for all the abominations that be done in the midst thereof. □

(44)

Bloom's elaborated account of these relations between belated poets and their precursors was derived from his reading of Freud's account of defence mechanisms set out in *The Anxiety of Influence*:

■ *Poetic Influence – when it involves two strong, authentic poets, – always proceeds by a misreading of the prior poet, an act of creative correction that is actually and necessarily a misinterpretation. The history of fruitful poetic influence, which is to say the main tradition of Western poetry since the Renaissance, is a history of anxiety and self-saving caricature, of distortion, of perverse, wilful revisionism without which modern poetry as such could not exist.* □

(Bloom 1973, 30; italics in original)

By the early 1970s the idea that Freudian accounts of the divided self were relevant to the narratives of the fall into division in Blake's prophecies was not uncommon, if sometimes rather unimaginatively employed in seeing Blake as simply prefiguring Freud. From as early as Damon's *Blake Dictionary*, casual references to Freudian terminology had been used to translate Blake's mythology (see George 1980, 17). Blake had also been a signal presence in attacks on sexual repression in the counter-culture of the 1960s, like Norman O. Brown's *Life against Death* (1959) and *Love's Body* (1966). Among an array of other prophets of sexual and psychic liberation, *Love's Body* sees Blake as lamenting a fall from a polymorphous sexuality that refuses distinctions between self and other, life and death, into a world dominated by the anxieties of the ego. Little of Brown's work, although saturated with Blake, offers any close analysis of the working through of these ideas in the poetry, but they were picked up by literary studies like Morton D. Paley's *Energy and the Imagination* (1970). For Paley, following Brown, 'Blake envisions, not revolution *and* sexual freedom, but a revolution which is libidinal in nature' (Paley 1970, 16). Paley's study went beyond most of those written within the paradigm of Romanticism by giving this libidinal energy joint billing with the imagination, but his concern with the development of Blake's thought pushed him towards *The Marriage of Heaven and Hell* and the prophecies rather than a sustained analysis of *Songs*.

The first full-length psychoanalytical study of Blake took the approach of Freud's former disciple C. G. Jung, predictably enough perhaps given the strong tendency within criticism since Frye to read the poet in terms of archetypes. June K. Singer's *The Unholy Bible* (1970) reads Blake in terms of the tropes that Jung believed structured the collective unconscious shared by all human beings. Singer's study understands poems like 'Cradle Song' as dimly recognising 'the emerging contents of the unconscious which appeared as sensual demands' (Singer 1973, 26). Brenda Webster followed the Jungian track in *Blake's Prophetic Psychology* (1983), but provided a symptomatic reading that saw Blake in flight from female sexuality: 'Blake's anal eroticism and homosocial bonding led him to fear a powerful female sexuality' (Webster 1983, 144). Diana Hume George's *Blake and Freud* (1980) does not provide a diagnosis of Blake, but instead returns to the idea that he was developing his own ideas about the role of the subconscious in the formation of identity in *Songs*. George argues that Blake's ideas not only 'anticipated Freud's, but that his mapping of psychic processes actually subsumes Freud's in several identifiable respects'. Her approach acknowledged the revisionist Freudianism of figures like Brown and Marcuse, but also began to direct them towards a discussion of the gender issues that we will return to in our next section (George 1980, 17, 18). In general terms, George's approach does not impose Freudian terms on Blake, but thinks about the relationship between the insights of Blake and Freud. Her analysis of the relations between Innocence and Experience, for instance, begins with an account of 'Infant Sorrow' as an exploration of Freudian birth trauma:

■ My mother groand! my father wept.
Into the dangerous world I leapt:
Helpless, naked, piping loud;
Like a fiend hid in a cloud.

Struggling in my fathers hands:
Striving against my swadling bands:
Bound and weary I thought best
To sulk upon my mothers breast. □

(E28)

The scenario seems to anticipate Freud's account of the libidinous demands of the newborn child, but whereas the psychoanalyst grew increasingly negative about the destructiveness of the infant libido, Blake's emphasis is on its perversion by the categories of Experience. The newborn of 'Infant Sorrow' is a fiend only because his parents restrain his energy in swaddling bands. His struggling and striving are not negative in themselves. Rather his inability to break free is the inhibiting and destructive event. *Songs of Innocence* is primarily concerned with familial situations that are nurturing rather than repressive of these libidinous drives. The children in the poems, for their part, are full of fears that they cannot fully comprehend, but hark back to the trauma of separation and anticipate punishment for Oedipal desires within the family romance. *Songs of Experience*, for George, is primarily concerned with the repressive situation whereby parental figures 'become the restrainers of youthful sexuality and individuation' (98). 'To Tirzah' she reads as a brutal expression of the necessity of separation from the family:

■ Thou Mother of my Mortal part.
With cruelty didst mould my Heart.
And with false self-decieving tears,
Didst bind my Nostrils Eyes & Ears.

Didst close my Tongue in senseless clay
And me to mortal life betray:
The Death of Jesus set me free,
Then what have I to do with thee? □

(ll. 9–16, E30)

The harshness of the poem seems to participate in Freud's sense of the narcissism of parental love generating resentment in the girl child for being born a woman, and in the boy a bitterness born out of the castration complex originating in the fear of harbouring desire towards the mother (98).

George shows several examples of 'latent tenderness yielding latent brutality' in *Experience*, revealing Blake's understanding of the Freudian processes of repression and sublimation that shape libidinal impulses into the forms of civilisation. Perhaps the primary example of this creation of the superego is 'Thou shalt not', written over every door in 'The Garden of Love':

■ I went to the Garden of Love,
And saw what I never had seen:
A Chapel was built in the midst,
Where I used to play on the green. □

(ll. 1–4, E26; George 1980, 102)

For George (104) these lines are the recognition of the prohibition against incest – 'the mother is an erotic garden of love' – and the child's dawning understanding that he must sublimate his feelings into a respectful worship at a distance, generating the resentment that pervades *Songs of Experience*. Only a very few speakers in the poems seem to understand the processes that they feel tightening their grip upon them. Among them is the boy in 'A Little Boy Lost', a speaker who comes to perceive that his affection is not given freely:

■ And Father, how can I love you,
Or any of my brothers more?
I love you like the little bird
That picks up crumbs around the door. □

(ll. 5–8, E28)

'What passes for love', as George notes (107), 'is dependence and fear'. One very distinctive aspect of George's book for its time was the fact that it extended the analysis of the sexual dialectic in the poems to thinking about 'feminine psychology'. Whereas writers like Brown saw the libidinal aspects of Blake's writing in terms of an undifferentiated human form of wholeness, George was participating in a turn towards rethinking the distinctions between male and female experience in the poems. By the late 1970s, feminist criticism was questioning the widespread assumption that Blake ought to be understood only in terms of a visionary company of masculine poets.

EARLY FEMINIST CRITICISM

Anne K. Mellor described the essays gathered in her *Romanticism and Feminism* (1988) as a sign of 'the coming of age of a feminist criticism of the major texts of the English Romantic period' (Mellor 1988b, 3). None of the essays in Mellor's book discusses *Songs* or any other of Blake's works in any detail, but she and a number of other critics had already made major contributions in the area. Perhaps the first essay to raise these issues seriously was Irene Tayler's 'The Woman Scaly' (1973). Like many feminist accounts that have followed, the essay focuses on the negative figure of 'the Female Will' that emerges in *Jerusalem*. Tayler read the figure as a metaphor of the 'jealousy, selfishness, and ruthless will to power that grows in the heart of the possessed object'. In 'The Female as Metaphor in William Blake's Poetry' (1977), Susan Fox returns to the figure of 'the Female Will' and sees in it Blake's inability to escape the destructive attitudes to women of his time. 'The Female Will' is a misogynistic identification of a feminine principle with the material world, projecting the traditional gendering of Nature onto women, but Fox understands it as primarily a development of the later poetry. In *Songs of Innocence* 'the positive internal powers of the realm are female' (Fox 1977, 509). Nature there seems nurturing and imbued with spiritual potentialities. Where male adults are constructive, they appear at the boundaries. Otherwise they are either helpless or actively pernicious figures. Even so, the roles assigned to women are severely restricted, for instance, to traditional ideas of nurture. Even in *Innocence*, no female figure seems to have the power 'to initiate her own salvation'. Overall, Fox judged the 'philosophical principle of mutuality' found in the poetry to be 'undermined by stereotypical metaphors of femaleness' (513, 507).

Mellor's work has continually argued that Blake's representation of women remains habitually sexist, especially in his prophetic books, even where he seems to celebrate a 'Human Form Divine' that transcends sexual divisions:

■ Blake's theoretical commitment to androgyny in his prophetic books is thus undermined by the habitual equation of the female with the subordinate or the perversely dominant. □

(Mellor 1982–3, 148)

In her essay in the same special number of *Blake: An Illustrated Quarterly* as Mellor's, Alicia Ostriker sees the early Blake as 'the vigorous, self-confident advocate of gratified desire'. 'London', for Ostriker, gives a critique of the gendered inequalities that curbed the energies of desire in men and women alike; it is:

■ Blake's most condensed indictment of the gender arrangements in a society where Love is ruled by Law and consequently dies; where virtuous females are pure, modest, and programmed for frigidity, so that healthy males require whores; where whores have ample cause to curse; and where their curses have the practical effect of infecting young families with venereal disease as well as with the more metaphoric plague of unacknowledged guilt. □

(Ostriker 1982–3, 157)

Any assumption that *Songs* offers a feminist perspective was firmly rebutted by Mellor in 'Blake's *Songs of Innocence and of Experience*: A Feminist Perspective' (1988). Mellor develops Fox's account of the way women there are confined to 'an exclusively private and domestic sphere, while his males move in the public sphere' (Mellor 1988a, 4).

Women in the poems are primarily carers, nurses, and mothers, Mellor points out. If they are permissive and affirming, they are also 'politically conservative' in so far as they are never allowed to challenge the status quo. So, argues Mellor, the mother in 'The Little Black Boy' encourages her child to accept 'social discrimination, suffering, and even death as both inevitable and finally rendered nugatory by the all-embracing and redemptive love of God'. When it comes to Ostriker's question of gratified desire, Mellor (7) suggests the women in *Songs* are 'eager, welcoming, uninhibited, always available', that is, primarily defined in relation to the gratification of male desire, 'passive but giving' as she puts it, noting how frequently the designs place women physically in roles where they are lying or sitting. The identification of women with Nature in the poems had been a cardinal idea of Blake criticism up to this time, whatever its methodology. Compared with this confined role for his female characters, Mellor points out, the male figures in *Songs* seem capable of adapting beyond biological determinism. Men in *Songs* are privileged both to inhabit the domestic sphere, with its associated virtues of pity, love, and peace, and also to access a wider world where they can act as guardians and guides. To give a specific example provided by Mellor, in both the Frontispiece and the 'Introduction' to *Innocence* the poet seems inspired by a male child, displacing the traditionally female muse by a male personification of the imaginative faculty. Where women do become more powerful figures – in the world of Experience – they become 'life-denying' like the harlot in 'London'. When they are allowed to express themselves in any kind of public sphere, Mellor argues, Blake seems to present women as newly vicious, prototypes of what he called 'the Female Will' in his later prophecies. From this perspective, the polymorphous ideas of sexuality celebrated by Brown and others look like an anxiety about female sexuality, paradoxically echoing Bloom's idea that Blake saw 'sexual love as regression, a drive back to ocean' (Bloom 1975, 11). Mellor cites Brenda Webster's Jungian reading of Blake as profoundly disturbed by female sexuality, in flight from what he perceived as the horror of Nature (Mellor 1988a, 14).

In contrast to these readings of a Blake terrified by female sexuality, Diana Hume George had ended her book with a discussion that addressed a question Blake had asked himself in his 1818 version of *The Gates of Paradise*: 'Is She also the Divine Image?' (George 1980, 186–8; E263).[5] George acknowledged that Blake found himself increasingly caught up in the identification of the feminine with Nature, even as he tried to make it clear these roles were capable of being transcended by individuals (191). Effectively, he forgets one of his own first principles, the possibility of every form being capable of redemption, and comes to utterly identify women in this world with this deadening principle of the Female Will (196). More generally, however, George sees Blake as battling against sexual repression and the reification of the gender roles prescribed by society. She rejects Fox's claims about Blake's representation of women in the 1790s by arguing that they confuse description of the way gendered identities come into being with prescription. George sees Blake's greatness lying in his 'full acknowledgment of unconscious thought processes and of the role of sexuality in human personality' (205). Where George believes he actually went *beyond* Freud is in refusing biology as the ultimate determinant:

■ His bitter lack of reverence for nature made it easier for him to be less deterministic in imagining new values for femininity, even if it also bound him to revile the aspect of femininity that had also been associated with the natural. □

(227)

Debate around these issues of gender and sexual identity has become increasingly central to Blake criticism since George's groundbreaking book, stimulating some of the most interesting studies of recent years, discussed in Chapter 9.

CHAPTER EIGHT

Blake's Composite Art in the 1980s and 1990s: Textuality and the Materiality of the Book

This chapter examines a sea change in Blake criticism that saw an intensifying move away from reading in terms of a Blakean system primarily identified with the mythos of the prophetic books. In the 1970s, literary criticism in the Anglo-American world started to be influenced by what became known as 'deconstruction', the critical movement associated with the French philosopher Jacques Derrida and the Belgian literary critic Paul de Man, who wrote from within the American academy. Whereas earlier critical trends had tended to understand poetry as an iconic whole, deconstruction placed the emphasis on the play of the signifier, the way the text generated a network of traces that could never be stabilised into something as definite as 'meaning'. Although this tendency, more generally, was not usually interested to recover any stable intention in the text, certainly not as its meaning as such, deconstructive responses to Blake were rather different, not least because they often understood the illuminated books to be actively encouraging an open-ended engagement with the text in Blake's reader. So Paul de Man reportedly took the view that 'Blake's privileging of writing makes him less interesting to deconstruction, because it makes his work less resistant to its strategies' (quoted in Mitchell 1986, 91). In one way, deconstructive criticism's emphasis on Blake's textuality meshed with and deepened the thematic interest in play found in more traditional critics like Glen and Leader, discussed in the previous chapter.

For many readers, deconstruction seemed to make the stability of the text dissolve in alarming fashion, although in certain regards it might be understood as a form of radical empiricism, resisting any attempt to idealise the text into a reified object beyond the words on the page, which stubbornly refuse to be reduced into meaning.

A similar paradox might be found, we would suggest, in the other major critical development discussed in this chapter: the approach to *Songs* as an illuminated book rather than a collection of poems with their illustrations. In the second part of this chapter, we discuss two aspects of this development. One is the issue of the relationship between the verbal and the visual in *Songs*, focusing on the disagreement between Jean Hagstrum (1970) and W. J. T. Mitchell (1970 and 1978) about Blake's 'composite art'. Despite their disagreement about the relationship between visual and verbal in the illuminated books, in many ways Hagstrum and Mitchell continued to agree with an idea of the ultimate unity of the illuminated book that was to come increasingly under attack from those who thought of textuality, especially in Blake's hands, as resistant to any ultimate resolution. This chapter's second section ends with a discussion of the key examples from *Songs* brought forward in Mitchell's *Blake's Composite Art* (1978), but we also suggest some of the ways those instances are capable of being understood in terms of their radical indeterminacy in relation to any higher unity.

At the same time that this disagreement about the relationship between the verbal and visual was going on, there were some crucial developments in thinking about Blake's books as material objects and the processes that brought them into being. This necessarily strengthened the idea of *Songs* as a work of composite art as it brought to the centre of the debate the role of William Blake as engraver and printmaker we laid out in Chapter 1. An important step in this development was the publication of Robert Essick's *William Blake Printmaker* (1980). Our final section in this chapter looks at the consequences for criticism of *Songs* of thinking about the collection as an illuminated book produced by a distinctive reproductive process. Work in this direction had stretched back at least to the researches of Ruthven Todd in the 1940s, but literary criticism has increasingly taken it into account since the publication of Joseph Viscomi's very influential *Blake and the Idea of the Book* (1990). Central to Viscomi's work was the idea of the *edition* as a critical category, that is, placing emphasis on how and when groups of *Songs* were printed rather than single copies of the book, which criticism had previously often understood to be unique objects. One of the ironies of Viscomi's book, intended or otherwise, is its tendency to perpetuate the idea of a unity of conception at any particular printing, beyond the materiality of the book, potentially at odds, for instance, with Essick's idea of the materiality of reproductive processes as resistant to such Romantic transcendence (see Chapter 7). Even so, Essick and Viscomi, together with Morris Eaves, have collaborated on one of the key developments in bringing Blake's *Songs* to readers in their original 'composite' form. The William Blake Archive at www.blakearchive.org is putting individual copies online in very high quality resolution to enable viewers to see something of the minute particularities of the different copies of *Songs* as printed by Blake himself, without, of course, being able to get away from the fact that it is involved in yet another form of remediation, however much it might seem to promise some form of direct access.

BLAKE AND TEXTUALITY

Deconstruction had begun to appear as a significant critical movement in the American academy in the 1970s. The signature event for Blake and deconstruction was a conference held at the University of Santa Cruz in 1982. The collection of essays *Unnam'd Forms: Blake and Textuality* (1986) edited by Nelson Hilton and Thomas A. Vogler was a published version of its proceedings. 'Textuality' in this circumstance implied the complex traces made by any linguistic sign as it entered into the intertextual web of language. Rather than seeking necessarily to nail down any particular associations as the meaning of a text, this playful relationship with textuality was interested in looking at the way words were continually opening out onto other possibilities. Blake criticism has often understood him to be encouraging this kind of proliferation of meaning. Indeed, it has often been seen as fundamental to the structure of *Songs* as a collection and the way it seems to offer multiple, overlapping, but also sometimes contradictory relationships, for instance, between poems or between the verbal and the visual aspects of poems.

In the *Unnam'd Forms* collection, the most sustained reading of any poem from *Songs* was provided by Gavin Edwards' essay on '"performative" utterances'. Focusing primarily on 'London', Edwards was concerned with the poem's exploration of the kind of utterance that executes what it describes. Edwards begins by pointing out that Blake's poem 'includes a whole range of acts of vocalization and scription: sighs and charters, and marks as well as curses and bans' (Edwards 1986, 27). He picks out four key words that have often been remarked upon in earlier criticism of the poem: 'charter'd', 'ban', 'curse', and 'mark'. All these words can act as performatives, in the sense that they can perform the actions to which they refer, as in the sentence 'I curse you!' Edwards points out that these performatives often play an important part in legal processes and religious ritual. We can think of 'I now pronounce you man and wife'. The example is relevant to 'London' since Edwards is concerned with the poem's interrogation of the overlapping domains of Church and Law in his society. The words Edwards lists are not primarily used performatively in 'London', in the sense that Blake does not write a curse or a charter, but function as 'deactivated performatives' – a phrase Edwards takes from the deconstructionist critic Barbara Johnson, as he acknowledges (28). The point Edwards is making is that these words bear within them the trace of performative utterance in 'congealed form'. In one sense, they present the intention of the utterance as already achieved outside the text:

■ The achievement of the poem is to register such acts as the imposition of arbitrary labels that are nevertheless not external to those who receive them; as marks inscribed by authority that are also signs of an inward condition, marks 'of weakness and of woe'. □

(29)

There is one active performative in the poem, Edwards notes, and that is the marking done by the 'I' of Blake's poem. If the sense of the word is restricted only to its sense of 'observation', this seems a strange assertion, but central to Edwards's deconstructive method is the idea that the trace of its other uses cannot escape the reader, not least because the word also appears in the poem as the physical markings on those its speaker observes. The result of the tension between these two uses of 'mark' for Edwards is that it opens up an instability in the use of the first-person singular, the 'I' of the poem. 'I' describes the first person in the act of writing, but is also what Edwards calls 'the act of scription'. 'I' names us, everyone, as subjects, making us part of a discursive domain with positions ready made for us, even as it seems to credit us with individuality. As a result, a typical deconstructive aporia or space opens up within which, as Edwards (31) puts it, 'the subject of the act of writing and the subject of what is written never finally coincide or separate'.

Edwards reconnects with the work of Glen and Thompson we discussed in Chapter 7 by suggesting that 'London' is about the experience of finding one's self never autonomous and always already scripted, as it were, by prior authorities, whether it be in the Church or via the other legal instruments mentioned in the poem, 'situations in which one accedes to a kind of freedom, an identity as a human subject and center of initiative, by virtue of one's subjection to a name' (33). Perhaps where Edwards's method departs most obviously from

Glen and Thompson is in his reading of the poem's much-debated penultimate stanza:

■ How the Chimney-sweepers cry
Every blackning Church appalls,
And the hapless Soldiers sigh
Runs in blood down Palace walls. □

(ll. 9–12, E27)

Whereas charters and curses are ritual utterances that can effect material change, Edwards argues that the various cries and sighs in the final stanza seem powerless, but prolix in their metaphorical possibilities:

■ The variety of critical interpretations put upon the lines testifies to their ineradicably unstable and multiple significance, an instability and multiplicity that it has been the ideological function of literary criticism to resolve, conceal, or condemn. □

(35)

Where traditional literary criticism, in the eyes of Edwards, would be involved in explaining away this variety, as it were, deconstructive criticism is involved in endlessly reopening perspectives. Resistance seems to reside primarily in the refusal of language itself to reproduce stable discursive positions, despite all the attempts of social authority to assert them.

Nelson Hilton, another major contributor to the Santa Cruz conference, took up the pursuit of the playful signifier in *Songs* with particularly infectious glee. Hilton's *Literal Imagination: Blake's Vision of Words* (1983) is a joyous account of the proliferation of particular clusters of metaphorical possibilities across Blake's writing. In Hilton's hands, no pun seems impossible when looking at the lexicon of *Songs*, and after reading *Literal Imagination*, Blake's poems become newly enlivened by a range of semantic possibilities that he may or may not have consciously intended. Starting out from Yeats's description of Blake as 'a literal realist of the imagination' (Yeats 1903b, 182), Hilton's method militates against translating difficult words into some prior symbolic or abstract meaning (Hilton 1983, 1–2). Hilton's typically paradoxical version of literalism, on the contrary, focuses on particular patterns of words in the poetry to the point where stability of meaning dissolves. For Hilton this process is not an irresponsible inattention to the author's intentions, but rather a redoubled attention to the words as he engraved them on the page. Traditional critics often close up these possibilities in order to deliver a coherent meaning, as they see it; Hilton's readings continually show us their working methods, as it were, rather than just presenting us with a final calculation. Where Blake's literalism is visionary for Hilton, is in its focus upon a verbal point at which 'each sense, each golden "bit" of information, opens a dimension, making the word like the rugged diamond in Blake's *Milton*, "open all within"' (28.37, E126).

Hilton's method necessarily takes him in pursuit of the unchaining of words across Blake's entire output, but one example (63–7) at least partially focused on *Songs* is the variations rung by Blake on the words 'chains' and 'charter'd' in 'London' and elsewhere, taking them far beyond the particular associations explored by E. P. Thompson (see Chapter 7). Hilton begins by noting that the fragment 'King Edward the Third' in *Poetical Sketches* opens with the king praising 'Liberty, the charter'd right of Englishmen', contrasting their situation with their French enemies who 'fight in chains, invisible chains, but heavy: | Their minds are fetter'd' (E424). King Edward assumes a stable binary between English liberties and French tyranny. The grounds of the assumption implode as the fragment progresses. For Hilton the questions opened up by the play, once his followers begin to criticise Edward's ambition, are: how do the king's men know they are not bound and what is the nature of these chains unseen? Similar questions, Hilton suggests, confront the reader in 'London', where the chains binding the fettered French in 'Edward the Third' now seem to have descended upon Londoners. Circling around the poem's pivotal verb phrase 'I hear', Hilton asks what we do hear in the phrases before it. Is 'mind-forg'd', earlier in the last line, a reference to forgery or the work of the smith? In the question, the idea of manly English liberties seems to be hammered into the tyranny of the beaten links of chain. Do we follow up the associations with metal work in 'mind-forg'd' into the near homophone 'mine', or stick with 'mind'? Do we hear the word 'man' from the first line of the final stanza in the 'manacles' of the last? The text for Hilton performs a deconstruction that enjoins us to hear things in strange, synaesthetic ways that confuse the senses. Thus the aural and visual are confused in the sigh that runs in blood or the cry that casts a pall in the third stanza. In the final stanza, we hear not the curse, as one might expect, but instead how it 'blasts' the new-born infant's 'tear', a word whose rhyme sends us back to 'hear'. The cluster 'hear–curse–tear' now seems to merge into the final word of the poem, 'hearse', which appears in an oxymoron, 'marriage hearse'. The world of 'London' now seems to be one where it is almost impossible to experience sight and sound cohering into distinct sensations.

Hilton's next step draws on the Edwards essay we discussed above. 'London' seems, he argues, to insist on the impossibility of the links (another pun on chain) fitting mind or language in any natural sense to an external world. Contrary to the nostalgia for the oral power of the prophet that Bloom's account in *Poetry and Repression* saw in the poem (see Chapter 6), Hilton suggests:

> ■ We might rather conclude that 'London' offers an affirming and self-deconstructing text, one that implicitly urges the reader to allow his or her eye to wander through its chartered lines, marking its marks, and hearing its 'every voice'. □

From this perspective, 'London' offers 'proliferated chains of association'; now liberating rather than constricting in the way they reel off from 'mind-forg'd' (Hilton 1983, 65–6). The next link in this chain of associations Hilton finds in *Songs* is 'Earth's Answer':

> ■ Break this heavy chain,
> That does freeze my bones around
> Selfish! Vain!
> Eternal bane!
> That free love with bondage bound. □

(ll. 21–5, E19)

For Hilton the sexual possibilities of 'free love' in the poem seem bound up with what he calls 'the free intercourse of signification'. The syntactical complexity of the poem's third stanza, according to Hilton, effectively shows language dissolving 'univocal syntax and meaning, as the various constructions in themselves contest the heavy chain' (67):

> ■ Selfish father of men
> Cruel jealous selfish fear
> Can delight
> Chain'd in night
> The virgins of youth and morning bear. □

(ll. 11–15, E 18–19)

Feminist criticism would soon be suggesting that there were further traces in these lines, ones that opened up the possibility that 'free love' might involve certain sorts of enslavement for women in Blake's society (see Chapter 9).

What Hilton does point out is that questions of cause and effect, the links in the chain that seem to produce one thing out of another, are left deeply uncertain in Blake's poetry. We can note, for instance, the question of whether 'men' and/or 'fear' are the subjects of a single sentence in which 'delight' is the verb. Or is 'delight' the personified subject of a sentence in which it has to bear the weight of 'chain'd' virgins? These suggestions of ours scarcely exhaust the possibilities, which begin to proliferate as soon as one attends to the 'literal' text, in Hilton's sense, rather than plugging it into some notion of a Blakean system or trying to resolve it into a unified meaning. As it is, instead of dwelling on the question of syntax in *Songs*, Hilton goes on to pursue the 'chain' metaphor into Blake's prophetic books, but more recently one critic has returned to the question of Blake's syntax in *Songs* and the undecidability of relations of cause and effect it can produce.

In his essay 'Blake and the Syntax of Sentiment: An Essay on "Blaking" Understanding' (2006), James Chandler used the question of syntax to think about the relationship between *Songs* and the sentimental tradition that was such an important part of eighteenth-century culture. Writing after the historical turn in Blake criticism that followed McGann's *Romantic Ideology*, Chandler considers Blakean indeterminacy in its historical context, that is, as a feature of his rhetoric derived from developments in the culture(s) of his time. The context is not used to tie Blake down to a determinate historical meaning, but to think about where his proliferating textuality might have come from and how it works in relation to its precursors. Although critics like Bloom laboured mightily to place Blake in the visionary company of major Romantic poets, Chandler notes that Frye long ago placed Blake in 'the Age of Sensibility' that preceded Romanticism as such (Chandler 2006, 102). For Chandler, this culture is specifically identified with ideas of 'moral sentiment' associated with the philosopher Adam Smith's *Theory of Moral Sentiments* (1759), and his essay shows how Blake's writing attempts to unravel the basic syntax of this thinking, specifically, the rendering of specific situations into general cases such as Smith imagined necessary to make sympathy between individuals possible.

To argue his case, Chandler takes us to 'A Poison Tree' and adverts to John Brenkman's reading of the poem we discussed in the previous chapter. Chandler notes that the two readings that Brenkman proposed pivoted around 'the apple bright' at the centre of the poem. One reading is a moral fable about the ethics of not holding in one's wrath, which, Chandler observes (111), was the basis for various sentimental plots, including Laurence Sterne's in his novella *Sentimental Journey*. The second is the chilling possibility that the 'gladness' expressed in the final line is actually a kind of gloating at the death of the foe killed by the poisoned fruit. These contradictory plots are left by Blake as 'suspended and unresolved' (109) in the poem. The process of creating 'moral sentiment' by making a general case out of a particular emotional nexus works in Blake's poem instead 'to decompose sentiment into passion and sense' (110). Where Smith was concerned with the way that sympathy worked in society to produce a certain kind of moral subject, able to act as an individual with ethical certitude, Blake suggests, instead, a much less cohesive story of the way sympathy works. At this point, Chandler adduces the question of syntax and its relation to cause and effect. In order to explain the issue he introduces the trope of 'hypallage', which he understands in terms of the rhetorical reversal of cause and effect, explicitly discussed by Sterne in *Tristram Shandy* as putting the cart before the horse. Chandler suggests (112) it is used by Blake in *Songs* to thwart assumptions about the orderly progress of passion into moral sentiment. Chandler turns to 'The Shepherd', one of the lyrics from *Songs* rarely discussed by critics, to illustrate his case:

■ How sweet is the Shepherds sweet lot,
From the morn to the evening he strays:
He shall follow his sheep all the day
And his tongue shall be filled with praise.

For he hears the lambs innocent call
And he hears the ewes tender reply,
He is watchful while they are at peace,
For they know when their shepherd is nigh. □

(E7)

While it is easy to read the poem as an entirely conventional stock of tropes, Chandler shows that serious attention to the syntax of the poem reveals that it inverts our normal assumptions about the shepherd's relationship to his flock. The shepherd follows the sheep in Blake's poem, not the other way around, and it is he who strays and then heeds the call of his flock. More fundamentally, though, than reimagining this familiar scenario, syntax in this poem turns 'exactly on questions of causality and exchange' (113). The omission of the punctuating apostrophe in the opening lines of each of the first two stanzas allows a syntactical ambiguity of the kind Hilton delighted in. For it allows 'call' in the second stanza to be both a noun modified by 'innocent' and an alternative reading in which 'call' becomes a verb, 'innocent' an adjective modifying 'lambs', and even 'tender', with its economic associations, to be a verb, rather than a sentimental adjective modifying 'reply'. The syntax resists any resolution of the scenario into a familiar moral sentiment about the responsibility of the shepherd for his flock. The thorny economic possibility kept in play by Chandler's reading is especially important as it functions to remind its readers of the commercial society whose moral mechanisms Smith was trying to articulate into a coherent form. In Blake's poem, by contrast, traditional relations between the shepherd and his flock now seem invested, if we may be allowed the pun, in a commercial process of tendering ethics out to the highest bidders.

COMPOSITE ART

The deconstructive readings of Blake's textuality discussed in the preceding section were given impetus not only by new ideas about language circulating in the academy, but also by recent developments in thinking about relations between the verbal and the visual in Blake's illuminated books. These relations were coming to be seen not in terms of the visual illustration of a verbal text, but in terms of something altogether more complex. The term 'composite art', as we pointed out in Chapter 1, was first used to describe the illuminated books by Jean Hagstrum in his *William Blake: Poet and Painter* (1964). When W. J. T. Mitchell chose the term as the title of his own study *Blake's Composite Art* (1978), he was signalling Hagstrum's role as the antagonist for his own thinking about the relation between text and design in the illuminated books. Their disagreement was first set out in their essays 'Blake's Composite Art' and 'Blake and the Sister Arts Tradition' in David Erdman and John E. Grant's *Blake's Visionary Forms Dramatic* (1970). Hagstrum's work centred on the 'sister arts' or more narrowly the 'ut pictura poesis' [as is painting so is poetry] tradition that thought poetry and painting ought to 'combine forces in order to lead the beholder beyond themselves to nature, or nature's God, or the mind of man'. For Hagstrum, Blake aims at the third of these objectives: 'His Forms are displayed in order to bring us to what his predecessors called "ideal" reality and what he himself called the "Intellectual or Mental"' (Hagstrum 1970, 90). For Mitchell, quite the contrary is the case. The division between the two media does not co-operate to represent 'invisible, abstract, transcendent reality' (Mitchell 1978, 38). Instead one is constantly made aware of the fact that the verbal and the visual do not easily match onto each other. As the word 'composite' might well suggest, the relationship is not of any kind of natural complementarity, but of something brought together as part of a process of artifice.

Mitchell begins his book-length study *Blake's Composite Art* by noticing that in *Songs* there are many instances of the two media operating not as matching aspects of a joint process but as one where the two media are subordinate one to the other (Mitchell 1978, 4). He takes the frontispiece to *Experience* as the most obvious manifestation of this phenomenon, that is, the presence in the illuminated books of 'illustrations which do not illustrate':

■ The figure of a young man carrying a child on his head in the frontispiece to *Songs of Experience*, for instance, is mentioned nowhere in *Songs*, nor for that matter anywhere else in Blake's writing. □

(4–5)

In this situation, Mitchell argues, the design forces us 'to concentrate on the picture *as a picture in the world of pictures*, rather than seeing it as a visual translation of matters already dealt with in words' (5). Of course, it is not difficult to find connections between the frontispiece and other designs in *Songs*. Mitchell gives as an obvious correlate the figure looking up at the child on a cloud in the frontispiece to *Songs of Innocence*. And, what is more, this design does have 'an explicit verbal equivalent' in so far as it serves as an illustration to the song of the Piper 'piping down the valleys wild' in the 'Introduction', but this provides no 'direct verbal translation' to the *Experience* frontispiece:

■ It is clear that the two frontispieces function not just as companion pieces with similar compositions but as 'contraries' whose differences are as important as their similarities. Any words we find to describe the frontispiece to *Experience* will have to involve transformations and reversals of the language discovered in the poem and illustration which introduce *Songs of Innocence*. □

(5)

Mitchell insists that the relationships between text and design are rarely explicit or obvious in *Songs*, but must 'be arrived at by a series of associations, transformations, and creative inferences'. Much more than 'simple matching or translation of visual signs into verbal' (6), these relationships set the reader to work to compose meanings. And the relationships are further complicated by references to visual representations beyond the text, including, for instance, representations of St Christopher in religious painting, encouraged by precisely the fact that the frontispiece to *Experience* has no proximate verbal referent (8). A few years later, critics of a deconstructive turn, like Nelson Hilton, would point to this kind of relationship as part of the complexity of traces set into action by the intermediality of *Songs*.

Far from the 'balance' that critics like Frye and Hagstrum find in the interplay of the verbal and visual, Mitchell sees 'two equally compelling art forms, each clamoring for primary attention' (13). He identifies three major tendencies in eighteenth-century pictorialism, each of which Blake resists in defiance of any idea of the unity of the different media. These principles are:

(a) *translatability*, a conviction that the differences between the media are ultimately superficial;
(b) *transferability* of techniques from one medium to another such that painting is viewed as not merely similar to poetry but able to borrow techniques from its sister art;
(c) where differences were acknowledged, the issue of unity was resurrected via the idea of *complementarity*.

Mitchell (21) carefully distinguishes Blake's practice from each of these principles as follows:

(a) In contrast to the practice of most eighteenth-century illustrators, Blake provides 'not a plausible visualization of the scene described in the text but rather a symbolic recreation of the ideas embodied in that scene' (Mitchell 1978, 20).
(b) Blake rejects the notion of 'a homogeneous nature' that lay behind eighteenth-century confidence in transferability. Whereas poetry was widely praised in the period for its ability to invoke pictures in the mind, Blake's poetry is primarily dramatic.
(c) His poems also use settings that resist visualisation. The valleys wild and echoing greens in *Songs*, for instance, are not given with the landscape artist's investment in nuances of light and shade. Many of the poems, in fact, involve visual paradoxes like the 'hapless Soldiers sigh', a sound that becomes a sight as it 'Runs in blood down palace walls'.

Hagstrum's essay in *Visionary Forms Dramatic* insisted on the presence of three aspects of eighteenth-century pictorialism in Blake's illuminated books: (a) 'verbal icons'; (b) 'picture gallery form'; and (c) others including 'visualizable personification' (85). Mitchell acknowledges the presence of all three features, but argues that in Blake they usually work in ways that serve to mark his unconventionality. His use of visual icons, for instance, most often provides an image that is strangely difficult to visualise, even in poems where they seem to provide the central motif. Mitchell mentions the tree implanted in the human brain in 'The Human Abstract', but we might think also about 'The Poison Tree' and the logical impossibilities of its central figure of 'the apple bright' discussed by Brenkman and Hilton. If the 'sister arts' tradition was committed to making poetry visual, the other side of the equation was thinking of painting in poetical terms. The narrative aspects of Hogarth's output are one instance of such poetical devices in the visual arts mentioned by Mitchell, but even where Blake seems to arrange his visual material into sequences, as in some of the figures arranged as marginal frames around individual songs, they do not seem to show any narrative unfolding in time (25).

Blake's 'composite art', as Mitchell sees it, is not designed to give the fullest possible picture of an objective world. Instead of the idea of one art adding to the other, Mitchell suggests, Blake thinks of them as 'multiplied by one another to give a product larger than the sum of the parts, which might include, but not be limited by, the world of space and time' (31). In certain regards, this proliferation seems to anticipate the spiralling out of meaning that was to be celebrated by critics like Hilton in the 1980s, but the notion of a higher unity is ultimately smuggled into Mitchell's analysis as Blake's desire to 'dramatize the interaction of the apparent dualities in our experience of the world and to embody the strivings of those dualities for unification' (33). Few of the deconstructive critics discussed earlier in this chapter would have been in sympathy with this idea of a larger unity. For Mitchell 'the contrariety of poem and picture reflects the world of the reader as a place of apparent separation of temporal and spatial, mental and physical phenomena', but the human imagination can provide the connection for Mitchell, at least at this stage in his career, just as it provided the key for many critics who followed Frye. More recent criticism has tended to stress the indeterminacy of these relations, what Stephen Leo Carr, writing in the *Unnam'd Forms* collection, described as 'the radical variability ... embedded in the material processes of producing illuminated prints' (Carr 1986, 182). This interest in material processes has become a key aspect of Blake criticism in recent years, especially since the advent of Viscomi's *Blake and the Idea of the Book* (1993), but before turning to the specific contributions of this work, it is worth noting that it is predicated on the idea of a basic unity founded in the 'integrality of the acts of writing and drawing' (Viscomi 1993, 25). Deeply opposed to assumptions about the uniqueness of different copies of *Songs* made by critics like Carr, Viscomi was also hostile to their idea of the indeterminacy of the Blake text. For Viscomi's work is committed to finding 'the place of origin, the place where idea and image are *found*' (40).

BLAKE AND THE BOOK

The question of how Blake produced his illuminated books has been one of the liveliest areas of debate in recent years. Often based on experimental attempts to replicate Blake's methods in the print workshop, these critical controversies can seem to depend on arcane details, to the uninitiated. In this section, we aim to bring out the key issues of these debates, especially in relation to *Songs*, and to give a sense as to why they matter in terms of criticism, rather than simply as arguments about technique. Early work in relation to Blake's method of combining the verbal and the visual in *Songs* was done by Ruthven Todd (1948), who argued that Blake must have used the transfer method to create the illuminated books, that is, he must have written his text on paper coated with gum Arabic using stop-out varnish, placed the paper on the plate, and then achieved a transfer effect by applying pressure. The designs would then have been drawn directly on the plate using the varnish. A major breakthrough in discrediting this theory came with Robert Essick's *William Blake Printmaker* (1980). Essick showed that Blake would much more likely have written backwards directly onto the plate, a method that would have resisted the division between the verbal and visual arts by making the two aspects of the illuminated books part of a single process. Essick's debunking of Todd was further elaborated in Viscomi's *Blake and the Idea of the Book* (1990), which insisted that Blake's techniques resisted any division between conception and execution. This development of Essick's thesis was only one of many important contributions to the understanding of Blake's illuminated books provided by Viscomi. Chief among the others was the refutation of the idea that Blake intended each copy of *Songs* and the other illuminated books to be unique. Viscomi showed that many of the variations between copies, key for critics like Carr, were accidental results of the process of reproduction that could not be understood in terms of Blake's intentions, such as misregistrations of the copper plate on the paper in the printing process.

Not everyone has accepted the version of the production of the illuminated books propounded by Essick and Viscomi. The most coherent oppositional voice has been Michael Phillips, who gave the most elaborated version of his position in *William Blake: the Creation of the Songs* (2000). Whereas Viscomi's *Blake and the Idea of the Book* may be

said to practise a form of technical determinism, the practical possibilities of the print shop ultimately conditioning the range of meanings
potentially generated by the books, Phillips sees *Songs* not only as the
product of the available forms of print production – about which he
disagrees with Essick and Viscomi – but also as the result of a complex
relationship with the poet's situation in London. Beginning with the
origins of *Songs* in *Poetical Sketches*, as we noted in Chapter 1, Phillips
understands even *Innocence* as the product of this urban milieu. 'The
Garden of Love', for instance, may be a response to local property
developers announcing Subscriptions for the erection of a chapel on
the village green known as the Lawn. Like Stanley Gardner's work
(1998, 130), on which Phillips draws in this instance, the effect is to
make the version of pastoral at work in *Songs* one that is constantly
aware of the disjunctions between conventional idyll and Blake's
everyday experience.

Whereas the idea of the book propounded by Essick and Viscomi
lays great store by the unity of conception and execution, admittedly
grounded in Blake's various comments on the subject, for Phillips,
on the contrary, 'when composing [Blake] often ran into difficulty
and only rarely was satisfied to leave fair copy unaltered' (Phillips
2000, 111). Viscomi acknowledges the relevant evidence from *Poetical
Sketches*, and from the notebooks for *Experience*, but understands *Songs*
as exceptional in this regard when it comes to the larger picture of
Blake's composite art. Phillips also suggests that the processes of production were much more laborious and difficult than Viscomi's printing in editions seems to allow. Other critics, including those more
generally in sympathy with Viscomi than Phillips, have pointed out
that Viscomi's editions theory only really applies to the initial process of printing (Gourlay 1995). Hand-coloured books could have been
finished with a buyer in mind or for other reasons. Blake's ordering of
the printed pages, too, is not necessarily as closed a matter as Viscomi
sometimes makes it seem:

■ Collective finishing as well as printing appears to have occurred, but
unlike printing, finishing and assembling could take place at any time, and
revision, reassembling, and refinishing were always possible. □
(Gourlay 1995, 34)

The question of which differences matter has been made more difficult by Viscomi's work, but it does not mean they can be ignored, and
different copies will always need to be consulted to make judgements
about significance.

For Phillips a major point in the production of the *Songs* is the period over 1792–3 when he sees a voice of overt political protest emerging in the manuscript songs intended for *Experience*. The word 'charter'd' in 'London', for instance, traced to Paine's writing by many critics, as we have seen, is for Phillips very specifically the product of its appearance in Part II of *Rights of Man*, published in the first months of 1792. This radical turn in *Songs* is then weighed against the counter-current represented by the loyalist reaction against the French Revolution, which gathered pace from the formation of the Association for the Protection of Property against Republicans and Levellers in November 1792. In this chronology, the question of the colour-printing process that has been a major bone of contention between Essick and Viscomi, on the one hand, and Phillips, on the other, has had an important place. Phillips partly justifies his advocacy of the 'double-pull' method of colour-printing in historical terms as a turn towards a more connoisseurial mode of production:

■ Prints that required this level of skill and individual artistic finish to produce posed no threat politically because their cost precluded circulation to all but the very few who could afford them. □

(Phillips 2000, 113)

For Viscomi, Blake's reconfiguration of the illuminated books towards such an audience is a much later phenomenon, the product of the depletion of stocks built up in the 1790s, and the emergence of the idea of his books in more pictorial terms than the original idea of them as a composite art.

As we write, the balance of opinion appears largely on Essick and Viscomi's side in relation to the question of colour-printing, but the idea of the uniqueness of the various copies has been a stubborn one to shake in criticism of *Songs*, and the illuminated books more generally. The decision to alter colouring or the order of plates in assembling a book implies a change in attitude, as does allowing some accidentals to stand and others not. Saree Makdisi (2003), whose work will be examined in more detail in the next chapter, draws different conclusions than Viscomi from the latter's emphasis on the unity of execution and conception. Any copy of *Songs* is the product of a process in which variability is immanent rather than a logic derived from the idea of a determining prototype (Makdisi 2003, 192). For others the fact that differences could be introduced into editions when they were being coloured or assembled in a particular order meant that individual copies of the book could have been tailored to particular buyers in ways understood in terms other than simply a commercial transaction. From this perspective, it remains important to take account of 'the personal nature of Blake's relationship with those we know obtained copies from him' (Phillips 2000, 111). This opens up the possibility that 'the passing on of Blake's books, as well as the qualities of the books themselves, might manifest their value' (Haggarty 2010, 15).

Until very recently it has been impossible to compare different copies without making trips to the widely dispersed libraries which currently own them, and even then it is difficult to line plates up next to each other for comparison. This problem has to some extent been solved by the online Blake archive, edited by Essick, Viscomi, and Morris Eaves. Their editorial principles have allowed for multiple copies to be displayed, with the capability of searching for text and image within the archive. The reproductions are excellent, and the editors seek constantly to use new digital technology to improve the quality of the image, to the point of showing the misregistrations and other 'accidental' variations of the production process. Even so, Essick himself has suggested that the main contribution of the archive may be 'more to do with the issues it raises, in terms of editorial theory and concepts of representation, than its utility in support of traditional types of textual and iconographic research' (quoted in Kraus 2002, 171). The more access that is given to reproductions of the illuminated books, the more do we see their uniqueness in relation to conventional ideas of the book and more familiar forms of reproduction; but there are other tensions within the project that are more worrying for Essick and his collaborators. Paradoxically, just as the archive seems to promise more and more direct access to the books themselves, as it were, so it seems also 'actively to entice processes of translation, mutation, proliferation into other media' (Clark, Connolly, and Whittaker 2012, 2). The centrifugal energy that *Songs* has always generated, beloved of the deconstructive critics discussed in the first section of this chapter, seems at odds with what some have described as the 'monumental' aspects of the archive with its implications of storage and preservation. Shirley Dent, for instance, detects a tension between the site's polite requests for its users to respect the copyright of the various museums and institutions that have allowed the Archive to house digital versions of their treasures, and the desire of cybernauts to cut and paste images from the site for their own creative purposes (Dent 2012, 58, 67). According to Roger Whitson, 'for Digital Blake to truly make a transformative difference, it must reconceptualise the relationship between literature and the media, transform the theory of materiality that favours originality, and contest the space of the university' (Whitson 2012, 42).

As we will see at the end of the next chapter, so pervasive has the centrifugal creativity of *Songs* been across a range of media that the study of its reception and influence has now become a focus of critical attention in its own right. This includes claims that the collection ought to considered less in terms of the idea of a book than as a Local Area Network open to be reconfigured and reimagined by readers in ways that live up to Blake's resistance to the logic of the forms of production available to him in his own time (Saklofske 2011).

CHAPTER 9

Worlding Blake Today: 'Past, Present and Future Sees'

There is by now an incredibly rich diversity of criticism discussing Blake's *Songs*. This chapter attempts to say something about the most striking recent developments, but these continue to multiply in ways that are scarcely predictable, changing and reconfiguring our understanding of what remains Blake's best-known work. The first part of the chapter returns to some of the gender issues discussed in Chapter 7. The feminist interventions of the 1970s and 1980s have influenced approaches that are now a central part of Blake criticism, encouraged by the way the texts seem to challenge crude binaries, but also at times get tangled in their own attempts to think a way beyond fixed identities. Gender studies of Blake have often taken an historical approach since the 1990s, locating Blake in relation to debates in his time about the emancipation of women (Bruder 1997), homosexuality (Hobson 2000), or eighteenth-century medical discourses surrounding the body (Connolly 2002). Much of this work revisits the issue of embodiment, which Bloom and earlier critics were so confident that Blake wished to transcend. Now criticism is much more likely to explore the consequences of a perception that 'for Blake the ideal human is not a disembodied spirit', but with a sense of the complexities involved (Connolly 2002, xv). As Connolly herself persuasively argues, Blake 'at once reviles and glorifies the human body' (vii).

The penultimate section of this chapter looks at recent attempts to place Blake in terms of a complex ethical relationship to the world around him. Two recent developments in worldwide literary criticism, eco-criticism and post-colonialism, have pushed Blake studies forward in this regard. In certain respects, the Romantic eco-criticism of recent years has struggled to come to terms with a writer who said in his annotations on William Wordsworth's *Poems* (1815):

■ Natural Objects always did & now do Weaken deaden & obliterate Imagination in Me Wordsworth must know that what he Writes Valuable is Not to be found in Nature. □

(E665)

Certainly Jonathan Bate and other influential eco-critics seem more comfortable with Wordsworth than Blake. But there are signs of developments within eco-criticism that share some of Blake's scepticism about a reified Nature, and these are discussed here. The other aspect of what we have called 'worlding Blake' has been a reassessment of 'English Blake', as Bernard Blackstone called him in 1949, in relation to the global context of his time. Saree Makdisi's account returns to the idea of Blake as a prophet against empire by looking at him as a writer who fundamentally challenges the ideas of western authority that were gaining hegemony during his career. The issue for Makdisi is not simply one of the criticism of imperialism discussed by Erdman and others, but also Blake's resistance to a more fundamental set of assumptions about subjectivity that allowed colonial peoples to be regarded as objects that could be legitimately conquered and governed.

Blake's poetry has become much more widely known over the past century or so. Although a great deal of scholarly effort goes into disentangling the density of his prophetic works, it is perhaps *Songs* that has had most influence on other writers and artists, especially in popular culture. Given the deferred nature of the emergence of Blake's *Songs* into the public sphere, described in our guide's first four chapters, 'from the point of view of the study of reception Blake is a late nineteenth-century and twentieth-century poet, important to the understanding of Swinburne, Yeats and Joyce, Ginsberg and Ted Hughes' (Larrissy 1999, 10). Larrissy himself offered a detailed account of Blake's importance to such writers in his *Blake and Modern Literature* (2006), arguing that:

■ he was central in the retrospective construction of a Romanticism that was acceptable to the twentieth century, that he assisted in the gestation of innovative writing in the modern period, and that this kind of centrality is continuing into the twenty-first century. □

(Larrissy 2006, 1)

Attention to reworkings of *Songs* has gone beyond looking at the literary inheritance explored by Larrissy and others to thinking also about the influence of Blake's lyrics in contexts as different as Benjamin

Britten's settings of *Songs* and the music and songs of Jah Wobble, as the final section of this chapter shows.

GENDER, IDENTITY, AND THE BODY

Anne Mellor's (1993, 22) claim that 'Blake shared his culture's denigration of the feminine gender' has produced a wealth of responses, confirming and denying her perspective. For Harold Bloom and feminist critics like Brenda Webster alike, this attitude was primarily located in hostility to the biological body (see Chapter 7). Most recent feminist criticism has been drawn instead to the contradictions of Blake's poetry in relation to corporeality and broader gender issues. For Tristanne J. Connolly in *William Blake and the Body* (2002), his attitudes to the body are seen as complex and even contradictory, not least in relation to the various processes of birth explored and depicted in the visual and verbal art. While much of her excellent study is concerned with the various forms of splitting and fusion going on in the late prophecies, she has some very illuminating things to say about *Songs*. In her discussion of the anatomical practices of late eighteenth-century visual artists, for instance, Connolly notes how in the illuminations of poems like 'Laughing Song', 'Nurse's Song', and 'The Little Girl Lost' Blake shows clothes 'clinging to the body and revealing its shape' (Connolly 2002, 45). This was an aspect of Blake's visual repertoire that troubled Coleridge, who identified 'the ambiguity of the Drapery' as one of the 'faults' of *Songs* (*BR* 336; see Chapter 2 for more on Coleridge's response to Blake). The exaggerated musculature of Blake's figures stands out against the softening tendencies of artists of the time such as Sir Joshua Reynolds, but Connolly is far from seeing Blake as simply celebrating physical form. Like many others who have discussed this issue, she puts the poem Blake added to *Songs* c. 1803, 'To Tirzah', at the centre of her discussion of the issue.

Connolly sees 'To Tirzah' as 'a major connecting point between Blake's negative feelings about the body and the feminine'. She reads the accusations of the speaker as reworking Jesus's question to his mother at the wedding at Cana: 'Woman, what have I to do with thee? Mine hour is not yet come' (John 2:4). Jesus performs the miracle for his mother, providing a disturbing contrast with this question, just as the questions in 'To Tirzah' seem at odds with those songs that celebrate the physical body. In the Bible, Tirzah is one of the daughters of Zelophehad, who seek an inheritance from their father, perhaps identifying Blake's figure with a female desire for material things that is seen as transgressive, but Connolly acknowledges Nelson Hilton's reading of the poem in terms of the complexities of point of view in *Songs* (Hilton 1999, 108). The speaker of 'To Tirzah' may well be one of the overly righteous, whose own confidence condemns him as a blinkered moralist, as Hilton suggests. Even so, Connolly points out, the poem necessarily draws attention to a more problematic aspect of embodiment than the enthusiasm of many of the other songs. Hilton, she notes, argues that the poem ought not to be seen as any kind of a rejection of sexual pleasure. Connolly returns to the poem's first stanza to open up a rather different perspective on this issue:

■ Whate'er is Born of Mortal Birth,
Must be consumed with the Earth
To rise from Generation free;
Then what have I to do with thee? □

The crux of Connolly's reading of the poem is not so much sexual pleasure as 'generation', that is, 'the pain of childbirth on a female partner, or the pain of mortality on a resulting child' (Connolly 2002, 98–9). Exploring Blake's representation of Tirzah in the later prophecies, Connolly shows her to be a female principle that wishes 'to bind human forms in order to have control over them'. This analysis of 'To Tirzah' strongly implies that the later gendered anxiety over 'generation' is not so powerfully present in the earlier versions of *Songs* (which did not include the poem). Compared with the focus in the poems Blake wrote in or after 1794 on 'the failure of procreation' or 'bizarre variations on birth', as Connolly puts it (125), *Songs* seems populated by children who for the most part experience birth from the womb, rather than the contorted nativities of the later prophecies. The two poems 'closest to the moment' of birth, in Connolly's eyes, are 'Infant Joy' and 'Infant Sorrow'. 'Infant Sorrow' seems to take a Calvinistic view of birth as something like a fall into generation; 'nothing but birth', Connolly writes, 'has occurred to deface the innocence of the fiendish child who immediately causes pain to his or her parents' (126). From the child's perspective, though, it is the world that is 'dangerous'. The relationship between parent and child is characterised by strife with the father and 'bound and weary' sulking on the breast of the mother:

■ Like Blake's later family relationships, this one seems a tangle of unfathomable motivations, secret desires, and frustrations. Are the parents restricting the child who should be free, or is the child torturing the parents? Is the child really a fiend or does it only appear so to its parents? □

(126)

In 'Infant Joy' the arrival of the child immediately poses a question for the parent: 'What shall I call thee?' The answer seems to be the exuberance of the child, 'Joy', the experience of the joy of another re-creating the joy in oneself. The children here seem to Connolly 'embodied aspects of their parents' personalities, and their embodiment is contagious, causing others to become what they behold' (126). Childhood and, especially, childbirth seems to be far from the reciprocal experience of playful joy found in the poem, by Glen and others (see Chapter 7).

Connolly implies that this pair of poems pre-figures the idea of entrapment within the cycle of reproduction found in Blake's later illuminated books, but she does not offer a sustained reading of these issues as they play out in *Songs* as a collection. In a contribution to the lively collection of essays gathered in Helen Bruder's *Women Reading William Blake* (2006), Susan Wolfson explicitly identifies the period from *Songs of Innocence* and the combined *Songs*, roughly 1789–94, as key to the emergence of 'female sexuality as Blakean metafigure for the complexities, and sometimes outright contradictions, of reading "experience"' (Wolfson 2006, 261). Wolfson's analysis begins with 'The Little Girl Lost' from *Innocence*, a poem that seems to invite a reading in terms of a liberation that will turn the girl's desert into a garden, 'the visionary playcard' as Wolfson puts it, 'rising from the grave, from isolation to union, from barrenness to fertility' (262). From this perspective, the poem seems a masculine fantasy, where parental, especially maternal, control must be escaped to allow heterosexual pleasure, but the question that this begs for Wolfson's analysis is the degree of jeopardy in the poem. Are the little girl's dangers only the product of an Experienced reader's anxieties and so to be discounted as her or our mind-forged manacles? Or do we see dangers that she cannot? And are the dangers more specific because of the gender of the wandering child? It is these ambiguities, from Wolfson's perspective, which make it understandable that Blake moved the poem to *Experience*, a collection where the question of the relation of the gender differential to the question of liberation is especially acute. So, in 'Earth's Answer' to the voice of the Bard in the 'Introduction' to *Experience*, there seems to be a straightforward identification of free love with liberty:

■ Break this heavy chain,
That does freeze my bones around
Selfish! vain!
Eternal bane!
That free love with bondage bound. □

(ll. 21–5, E19)

The last line, so often read straightforwardly as an ungendered celebration of free love, 'lets slip a suggestion that for a female speaker in 1794
free love is bondage of some kind'. It is an implication that Wolfson
sees rippling out across *Experience*, on the single plate that contains 'My
Pretty Rose Tree', 'Ah! Sun-Flower', and 'The Lilly', in 'London', and
also in 'The Sick Rose'. Harold Bloom blamed the rose 'for refusing man'
(quoted in Wolfson 2006, 267), but in a reading that underplays the
menace associated with the phallic worm in the poem. As Wolfson puts
it, the rose seems 'sick if she does, sick if she doesn't'. The poem becomes
the kind of ideological knot Brenkman identified in 'A Poison Tree' (see
Chapter 7), but focused for Wolfson very particularly on the impossibilities presented to women in the context of Experience:

> ■ Staging the deformations of living in a culture that fears what it prizes,
> Blake's female figures shape general questions about innocence and
> experience, repression and liberation, but in terms that convey processes
> and prejudices that fall into drastic differentials of gender, no less then
> than now. □

(267)

Wolfson's reading, perhaps generously, sees Blake at least glimps-
ing the contradictions of a feminine situation. More recently, criticism
has begun to explore other sexual identities in *Songs* that go beyond
the straightforward assertion of masculine desire as a form of liberation. Although by no means the first study to look at the complex
nature of sexuality in Blake's work, Christopher Hobson's *Blake and
Homosexuality* (2000) played a major role in reconfiguring discussions
of sexuality in the poetry. For Hobson, early Blake is a staunchly mas-
culinist poet, who shows little sign of the sympathy for same-sex desire
found in the later prophecies. The idea of the 'improvement of sensual
enjoyment' (*Marriage* pl. 14, E39) that seems to be celebrated in several *Songs* is predicated on a notion of 'heterosexual desire as implicitly
superior to other kinds of sexuality' (Hobson 2000, 23). Female desire,
as many feminist critics have pointed out, seems to exist in a positive
light mainly, perhaps only, in relation to the fulfilment of male fan-
tasies in the poems. Behind this set of assumptions in Blake, Hobson
argues, is a powerful ideological position derived from ideas of man-
liness associated with republican notions of virtue. Hobson's book is
primarily concerned with developments in the historical context that
challenged and altered Blake's assumptions after *Songs*, but his interest
in the diverse configurations of sexuality found in the later prophecies
reopened the question of desire in relation to the earlier poems for
other critics. Many of these were gathered together in the volume

Queer Blake (2010) edited by Bruder and Connolly. In certain respects this volume picks up and develops a longstanding interest in poly-morphous perversity found in Blake enthusiasts from the 1960s like Norman O. Brown (see Chapter 7). Germaine Greer's essay in *Women Reading William Blake* (2006) acknowledges the Blakean idea of 'grati-fication [...] dissociated from reproduction [...] free from any identi-fication with any particular way of sex', although this kind of critical perspective has most often been developed towards the question of Blake's anxiety about 'generation', as we have seen (Greer 2006, 4). In *Queer Blake* the editors ask us whether we should instead think about the sado-masochistic imaginings of poems like 'The Garden of Love' or 'My Pretty Rose Tree', where 'her thorns were my only delight' (Bruder and Connolly 2010, 6). Within the collection, Steve Clark picks up and develops work he did prior to Hobson in his *Sordid Images: the Poetry of Masculine Desire* (1994). There Clark had explored the way desire in Blake tended to float without any 'relation to a specific individual' (Bruder and Connolly 2010, 1). In his essay for *Queer Blake*, 'Blake's Sentimentalism as (Peri)Performative', Clark develops this idea in a series of comparisons between Blake and the poet Robert Merry, who had come to public notice under the pseudonym Della Crusca, writing flirtatious poetry in the pages of *The World* newspaper at the end of the 1780s. Merry was widely regarded by his contemporaries as effemi-nate in the silky gloss of his imagery. Clark makes a powerful case for thinking of Blake's notebook poetry as merging out of a dialogue with a Della Cruscan aesthetic, 'a flirtation of self with self, conducted via the mediation of an anonymous recipient, in epistolary form', and in the process lays open a path for future research about thinking about desire in the lyrics in *Songs* as Della Cruscan (Clark 1994, 170). In this regard, as in many others, the recent interest in Blake and sexual identity reveals a range of literary contexts once interdicted by a per-ceived need to place his work within a strong line of male poets. Robert Merry would not have made it into Bloom's visionary company, but Blake now seems more complex for reading his poetry in the context of Merry's. No doubt other intertextual relations for *Songs* will be dis-covered as the canon of scholarly understanding of the poetry of the Romantic period continues to expand and diversify.

WORLDING BLAKE

Among the most obvious developments in literary criticism over recent years has been the emergence of eco-criticism. Given the widespread and persistent identification of the period's poetry with Nature it is no surprise that major works were published on Romanticism and the environment by scholars such as Karl Kroeber (1994) and Jonathan Bate (1991 and 2000). Interestingly neither of these studies had much to say about Blake, either in general or in relation to *Songs* in particular, probably because of his hostility to 'things of Vegetative & Generative Nature', a quotation from Blake's commentary on his painting *The Vision of the Last Judgment* used by Bate in *The Song of the Earth* (Bate 2000, 245; E555). An early exception to this omission was Mark Lussier's *Romantic Dynamics* (1999), which contains a whole chapter on Blake, including some thoughtful comments on the way 'imagination must supplement reason at the point of coincidence between mind and matter, acting as a catalyst for the coalescence of reality'. This insight, for Lussier, is essential to a perception of mental processes as other than 'pure mechanism' (Lussier 1999, 56). From this perspective Nature is not reified as other, but 'only emerges in the complementary relations of mind's imaginative presence'. Rather than Blake's position on the natural world, then, it is Blake's epistemology that Lussier sees as remarkably close to that of ecologists, a point he elaborates upon with a reading of the 'Introduction' and 'Earth's Answer' at the beginning of *Experience*:

■ To borrow freely from several discourses, the symbolic order (phallic in structure) attempts to regulate the earth's body to keep it from acting upon its natural desire, which is to live and love. Blake, a keen student of mythologies, read empirical philosophy as an expression of empire, a colonizing and consuming ideology that, in past manifestations, had cloven the individual from nature through symbolic intervention. □

(57)

This last point touches upon the work of Saree Makdisi that I will return to later in this section, but before shifting on to the question of empire I want to talk about some more recent eco-criticism that has seen Blake as a useful presence in critiquing ideas of nature existing for itself, beyond human imagining, or what has become known as 'deep ecology'.

In *Imagining Nature: Blake's Environmental Poetics* (2002), Kevin Hutchings distances himself from assumptions about Nature as a distinct whole that can be imagined beyond forms of human discourse. His point is not that there is no non-human domain, but that its alterity can only be approached 'through language and the social discourses organizing its conventional usage'. For Hutchings, Nature is necessarily bound up not only in non-human processes, but also in what he calls 'human power relations' (Hutchings 2002, 8). Consequently, he is impatient with those aspects of the work of critics like Bate and Kroeber that present nature as transcending issues of power in the name of what is perceived as the separate and more pressing question of ecological disaster (9–10). A version of Hutchings's concern that eco-criticism may too often naively celebrate 'green and wild spaces' (10), plays its part in Ashton Nichols's suggestion that eco-criticism is sometimes too ready to identify nature with the non-urban and define it against human culture. The point for Nichols is that 'nature' is a human idea by virtue of it being a word at all. While he acknowledges that critics like Bate have made it clear they are not seeking a renunciation of 'metropolitan modernity', he senses in much Romantic eco-criticism a hostility to the urban places created by the industrial revolution. As a consequence, these spaces are simply ignored rather than reinhab-ited in new ways (Nichols 2011, 23). The idea of 'nature for its sake' is understood by Nichols as a powerful impulse within an ideology of 'pastoral' romanticism (170). 'One element of Romanticism', Nichols thinks, has always been drawn to the view that 'nature is somehow opposed to urbanity, the wild is what the city gets rid of, human cul-ture is the enemy of nature' (xxi). Following the Australian eco-critic Kate Rigby, who argues that 'the challenge is not to flee to the coun-try but to reinhabit the world as it is given to us [...] in the midst of those places, however urbanized, in which we dwell, tarry, or stray' (quoted in Nichols 2011, 171), Nicholls, instead, wishes to resituate the advocacy of the non-human 'in order to include the human – the city, the suburb, and the urban, urbanature – in all discussions of ways that this planet (and its finite space) should be cared for and shared by human beings in the future' (170). It is this kind of reimagining that Nichols finds in Blake's *Songs*, especially in 'The Tyger', although he offers no sustained reading of any of the poems, nor does he reflect more broadly on the idea of pastoral at work in the collection as whole. Given the emphasis in the research of Gardner and Phillips on the pas-toral in *Songs* as something that existed for Blake within his urban sur-roundings in London, there seems an opportunity to rethink poems like 'The Ecchoing Green' with the kind of eco-criticism being sug-gested by Nichols.

Timothy Morton's scepticism about contemporary eco-criticism develops in a different direction, more in tune with the critique of 'deep ecology' offered by Hutchings. Morton's concern about 'deep ecology' is not so much that it excludes the urban as that it shows a tendency to imagine it can simply dream away difference and so deaden our sensitivity to the question of our relations with the non-human. 'Dark ecology', as Morton terms it, 'tells us we can't escape from our minds' (Morton 2007, 201). For Morton, nature is what keeps returning us to an awareness of our mortality, 'an inert, horrifying presence, and a mechanical repetition' (202). He illustrates his point partly through a reading of Blake's 'The Fly':

■ Little Fly
Thy summers play,
My thoughtless hand
Has brush'd away.

Am not I
A fly like thee?
And art not thou
A man like me?

For I dance
And drink & sing:
Till some blind hand
Shall brush my wing.

If thought is life
And strength & breath.
And the want
Of thought is death;

Then am I
A happy fly,
If I live,
Or if I die. □

(E23–4)

As it happens, Hutchings selected this poem as 'a profound medita-tion on the difference between human and non-human identity' (Hutchings 2002, 83). Hutchings praises the poem's unsettling multi-perspectivism, but Morton takes the analysis further and sees 'The Fly' as even more disturbing in its implications. On the one hand, argues Morton, this poem 'condemns us to be no better than flies [...] caught in the cycle of life and death'. One the other, the poem achieves an identification with the fly beyond what Morton calls 'the dreamy qual-ity of immersion in nature'. This dreaminess is dispelled in the kind of identification imagined in Blake's poem:

■ If we identify with the fly, we dispel the dream. We have lost nature, but gained a collective. The beautiful soul wakens to his conscious determi-nation. □

Blake's reversible poems allow us to 'glimpse humans through non-human eyes' (Morton 2007, 202). In the process, Morton sees a valuable admission that creates a space from which ecological thinking can begin:

■ So we have bottomed out, which is only the beginning of the rest of our ecological life. It is a strange ground, discernible in and as our experience of groundlessness. We have admitted that yes, we have a mind and that this mind fantasizes about nature in the struggle to think itself out of the history it has created. □

(203)

For Morton, Blake is aligned with a pattern of thought sceptical of 'deep ecology', constantly working towards sympathy out of an awareness of our position within a state of Experience that cannot simply be transcended.

Saree Makdisi's version of the issue of worlding Blake starts from the historical issue of imperial domination in his time, but whereas scholars like Erdman looked at the particularities of Blake's attacks on Empire, Makdisi sees in Blake a more fundamental rejection of the modes of thinking that made imperialism possible, a rejection with consequences for political conceptions of self and other that still persist today. Although he places a great deal of emphasis on ideas of 'participation in a community open to all', Makdisi's sense of 'an as yet unimaginable history of freedom' in some regards anticipates Morton's scepticism about difference as something that can be simply transcended. As with many critics writing after McGann's intervention on the topic (1986), 'indeterminacy' becomes a key term in Makdisi's account of Blake, 'whose very openness encourages multiple and even contradictory readings of the same passage' (Makdisi 2003, 160). Makdisi makes this claim in a reading of 'Ah! Sun-flower' from *Experience*:

■ Ah Sun-flower! weary of time,
Who countest the steps of the Sun:
Seeking after that sweet golden clime
When the travellers journey is done.

Where the youth pined away with desire,
And the pale virgin shrouded in snow:
Arise from their graves and aspire,
Where my Sun-flower wishes to go. □

(E25)

The paradox identified by Makdisi in the poem is that the end point of each linear day 'marks both the location where the youth and virgin arise from their graves, and the location where they aspire (to go)'. They wish to be where they already are, a situation which creates what Makdisi calls 'a gap, the no-time in between, a no-time in which the distinction between past and present breaks down' (160). For Makdisi, Blake's poetry attempts to teach its readers to exist in this space rather than seek to close this 'gap'. Nowhere is this idea of a gap more obviously at work in Makdisi's idea of Blake than in the relationship between words and images in *Songs* and elsewhere:

■ Much of the experience of reading one of the illuminated books, then, invokes alternating between reading words and reading images, and turning back and forth through the plates, tracing and retracing different interpretive paths through the gap between words and images. □
(Makdisi 2003, 163)

Makdisi makes the point that reading 'The Little Black Boy' of *Innocence* with 'The Chimney Sweeper' is very different from reading the poem on its own. Skin colour and identity are at issue in both poems, although in racial terms in one and in terms of class and occupation in the other. Reading the poems together makes it difficult to accept the charge of racism levelled against 'The Little Black Boy', as the other poem reminds the readers that 'becoming "white" is not simply a matter of "race" in the narrow sense, and in any case, both need to be read with some measure of irony, since both subvert parental wisdom' (165). Makdisi extends this point to the question of 'the path of reading that the reader has developed in tracing and retracing various paths between words and images through *Songs of Innocence*'. The potential variety of these paths means that 'the "same" plate can become other to itself – that is, no longer identical to itself – in the sense that it gradually becomes more difficult, even impossible, to think of it as a single, definite stable identity' (165). The point can be extended to the identities of *Innocence* and *Experience*:

■ The stable self-containment of a single illuminated book is superseded by the wide virtual network of traces among different plates, different copies, different illuminated books – virtual because it is not necessarily activated and, even when it is, not always activated in the same way. □
(168)

If aspects of this analysis seem to build out from the approaches discussed in our Chapter 8, in terms of both the play of textuality and relations between the verbal and visual in *Songs*, what is most distinctive about Makdisi's account is his relationship of Blake's method to the historical juncture of the industrial revolution. For Makdisi what is crucial about Blake is his resistance to forms of reproduction associated with work-time discipline. Repetition of the Blakean kind is very different from 'repetition in any ordinary sense': 'It multiplies the text and amplifies its significance rather than merely replicating it.'

Makdisi's wider argument is that Blakean repetition dislodges a logic of original and copy fundamental to the rhetoric of European superiority that legitimated imperialism. Makdisi sees in Blake a notion of human unity *'along with* all its differences' (246), articulated most clearly in 'The Divine Image' from *Songs of Innocence*:

■ To Mercy, Pity, Peace, and Love,
All pray in their distress:
And to these virtues of delight
Return their thankfulness.

For Mercy, Pity, Peace, and Love,
Is God, our father dear:
And Mercy, Pity, Peace, and Love,
Is Man his child and care.

For Mercy has a human heart,
Pity, a human face,
And Love, the human form divine,
And Peace, the human dress.

Then every man of every clime,
That prays in his distress,
Prays to the human form divine,
Love Mercy Pity Peace.

And all must love the human form,
In heathen, turk or jew.
Where Mercy, Love & Pity dwell,
There God is dwelling too. □

(E12–13)

Written at a time of intense political and military investment in non-European cultures, these lines for Makdisi represent 'a radical challenge to the emergent cultural politics of British imperialism' (247). What is distinctive about the poem is its suggestion that it is precisely 'the infinite variety of humankind that makes it "alike"' (248). What Makdisi calls 'being in common' is constituted by *'heterogeneity'* (author's italics).

There is no assumption of some primary original against which all varieties must be measured.

RE-MEDIATING BLAKE: RECEPTION CRITICISM

Over the last two decades our knowledge of the context in which Blake's *Songs* emerged has developed immeasurably. We know much more now about the material processes of producing the illuminated books. The researches of Keri Davies and Martha Keith Schuchard (2004) have revealed that Blake's mother was a Moravian, and opened up a whole new context for understanding his use of religious symbolism. Another development has taken criticism in what might seem a diametrically opposed direction, into the reception history of *Songs*. Chapters 2 to 4 of this book explore the responses of Blake's contemporaries and near-contemporaries. One way that Makdisi's sense of the proliferating virtual pathways available in the illuminated books has been manifested over time is in the work of other artists and writers who have responded to Blake. Over the past decade or so, literary criticism has paid increasing attention to this question of reception as a legitimate object of study, often placing it in a globalised context, revealing just how far *Songs of Innocence and of Experience* has been disseminated since the neglected origins discussed in our guide's early chapters.

An important early contribution to this development was *Radical Blake: Influence and Afterlife from 1827* (2002), co-written by Shirley Dent and Jason Whittaker. The book traces Blake's influence on its earliest mediators, including the early nineteenth-century Swedenborgians James John Garth Wilkinson and Charles Augustus Tulk, discussed in Chapter 3. Among the most interesting of the lines of reception explored in *Radical Blake* is the tradition of 'Metropolitan Blake', for which 'London' has been a key text. Dent and Whittaker see the earliest of these metropolitan readings of Blake as Gilchrist's *Life* (see Chapter 4), whose sense of a city criss-crossed by visionary possibilities they contrast with the response of the poet James Thomson (see Chapter 4). Thomson's long essay 'The Poems of William Blake', published in 1866, ended with the following rewriting of 'London':

■ He came to the desert of London town,
    Grey miles long;
He wandered up and he wandered down,
    Singing a quiet song.

He came to the desert of London town,
    Mirk miles broad;
He wandered up and he wandered down,
    Ever alone with God.

There were thousands and thousands of human kind
    In this desert of brick and stone:
But some were deaf and some were blind,
    And he was there alone.
At length the good hour came; he died,
    As he had lived, alone:
He was not missed from the desert wide,
    Perhaps he was found at the Throne. □

(Thomson 1896a, 268–9)

Dent and Whittaker see this poem inhabiting the same territory as *The City of Dreadful Night* (1874), Thomson's most famous work, where the metropolis is 'a place of negative creation [...] the overriding image is of the isolated individual, entrapped within a vacuum of self-knowledge and self-creation'. Ironically, perhaps, it is not this bleak vision of the materialistic metropolis that has dominated twentieth-century reimaginings of Blake's 'London'. Instead his account of London in *Songs* and elsewhere has spawned a line of novels that Dent and Whittaker describe as 'visionary London fiction', the work of novelists like Peter Ackroyd, himself a Blake biographer, Angela Carter, and Iain Sinclair. In this fiction, those aspects of Blake's 'London' often identified by critics as symbolist 'become a postmodern phantasmagoria that pushes against the very bounds of material reality' (Dent and Whittaker 2002, 53–4).

Following *Radical Blake*, a slew of reception studies has appeared, although again the tradition has roots, this time in Deborah Dorfman's *Blake in the Nineteenth Century* (1969). More recent examples include Edward Larrissy's *William Blake and Modern Literature* (2006), Steve Clark and Jason Whittaker's *Blake, Modernity and Popular Culture* (2007), Donald Ault and Roger Whitson's *William Blake and Visual Culture* (2007), and Colin Trodd's *Visions of Blake: William Blake in the Art World, 1830–1930* (2012). To a certain extent Blake has become a 'brand', as Mark Lussier has suggested, although studies of the phenomenon suggest that it by no means has the kind of stable image that ad men might like. In this regard, reception does seem to exploit the indeterminacy of Blake's texts, producing the phenomenon that Whittaker has dubbed 'zoamorphosis, the process of flux within the Blakean text that refuses an original ideal meaning' (Whittaker 2012, 211). Of course, this kind of proliferation of readings is a fact of all texts, but Whittaker, like Makdisi and many others, thinks that the disposition of Blake's work positively encourages it. Within the diversity of responses, Whittaker suggests, some patterns can be discerned, 'whereby the parent text generates a multiplicity of variants through succeeding introductions of visions, some of which survive and become the dominant meme for a while, others which disappear very quickly or lie dormant for a time' (211). A 'meme' is a word Whittaker adapts from Richard Dawkins's *The Selfish Gene* (1976) to denote a unit of cultural replication or trans- mission that propagates itself by imitation. In Whittaker's application of the concept, it represents a version of Blake that gains cultural trac- tion for a particular period. Larrissy's work has suggested that serious study of Blake begins in 'that period of pre-modernism when the flu- idity and tentativeness of states of mind is being increasingly empha- sized' (Larrissy, 2006, 23). In this period, Blake's claim in his sub-title to *Songs* to be 'shewing the two contrary states of the human soul' is picked up in Yeats right down to the pairing of poems in his collec- tions (Larrissy 2006, 2–3; see also Chapter 5). The visionary aspects of Blake's writing were developed very literally by Allen Ginsberg, who claimed to have heard Blake reciting 'Ah! Sun-flower' and 'The Sick Rose' after reading a copy of *Songs* (Larrissy 2006, 115–16). Other patterns in the literary reception of Blake have been discernible more recently, including the meme of visionary London traced by Dent and Whittaker in novels since the 1960s. Whether this particular aspect of *Songs* is becoming a worn out trope for novelists is a question that remains to be answered, but it is likely to be replaced by other aspects coming to the fore for future generations, including, for example, the ecological and/or urbanatural possibilities of its pastoral elements.

The trajectory of reception has anyway been rather different in other art forms. Take music, for instance, and the sustained engagement with *Songs* made by Benjamin Britten. Keri Davies has explored the body of work that began with the 1935 version of 'A Poison Tree', in a recent essay 'Blake set to Music'. Davies notes Britten's tendency to dwell on the tragic aspects of *Experience*. A very different sense of Blake, stress- ing the freedom from restraint, informs the settings in Jah Wobble's *The Inspiration of William Blake* (1996), animated by a desire to 'take the memory of Blake from the proms and the Tory Party conference, and give him to the people' (Wobble, quoted in Davies 2012, 199). Davies notes in his essay that Blake has become mainstream in popular music: 'part of a common currency', although how users value that currency has differed a great deal (200). David Fallon notes that for popular music he tends to be 'an alluring figure for rebellion and excess', a route to an alternative vision that at least imagines itself outside of the mainstream (Fallon 2012, 248). Even within this 'meme', to use Whittaker's term, Fallon's analysis throws up some variations depending on the artists in question. Given the Gothic orientation of Nick Cave's music, for instance, his emphasis on poems like 'Infant Sorrow' and 'Little Boy Lost' is unsurprising. Within this dark vision, with its touches of black comedy, 'visionary innocence', as Fallon puts it, 'becomes its crazed perversion' (Fallon 2012, 250). Much more in tune with ideas of Blake the visionary, perhaps, although working its own distinctive take on the tradition, has been the body of work produced by Julian Cope, described by Fallon as 'informed by fervent punk heathenism and a commitment to matriarchal religion as an oppositional source of cultural values' (251). The track from *The Black Sheep* CD called 'Psychedelic Odin' is a self-conscious reworking of 'The Little Black Boy':

■ My mother bore me in the Northern Void,
And I am white, but O! my heart is black,
Black as the devil's, and a soul to avoid,
For Southern Death Cults broke me on their rack. □

Clearly committed to the idea that Blake was fundamentally opposed to the patriarchal deity he called Nobodaddy in some of his manuscript poems (E471, 499, 500), the song narrates a history of religion whereby Norse mythology represented a temporary refuge from the stifling morality of Christianity.

Despite the differences of emphasis in the reworkings of *Songs* discussed by Fallon, he finds Blake's appeal to 'alternative songwriters' to lie in their perception of the poetry's urgency and sensory overload (Fallon 2012, 262). Of course, this idea of rebelliousness within popular music might itself be understood as a particular Blake 'brand'. A very different context for reception was brought to the attention of Anglo-American scholars by the collection *The Reception of Blake in the Orient* (2006), edited by Steve Clark and Masashi Suzuki. The collection reveals that Blake was a presence in Japanese literary and philosophical circles from as early as the 1890s, not very long after he came to notice in such circles in Britain. Translations by Ariake Kanbara and Choko Ikuta early in the twentieth century provided important early introductions to *Songs*. Clark and Suzuki reveal that Ikuta's translation of 'The Sick Rose' had a powerful impact on the poet Rofu Miki, who wrote his own 'Yameru Bara' ['the sick rose'] as a response. One aspect of this reception that the editors identify is the absence of some of the assumptions that dominated and perhaps distorted early twenti-eth-century receptions in English, including, for instance, the binaries madness/sanity or orthodoxy/heresy. What they reveal is a distinctive and robust history of reception of Blake, as the editors put it, 'whole and on his own terms, in a way perhaps not matched in the West until Northrop Frye's *Fearful Symmetry*' (Clark and Suzuki 2006, 9). Within Blake's *Jerusalem*, 'bright Japan' represents a limit of expansion, as Barnard Turner points out in his essay on the influence of Blake on the novels of Oe Kenzaburo, but there now seems no limit to where Blake criticism might go in either literal or metaphorical terms (Turner 2006, 246; E170). English-language scholars have scarcely examined the question, for instance, of Blake's reception within continental European criticism, perhaps with the exception of Georges Bataille's *Literature and Evil* (1957). This remains part of the meaning of Blake's *Songs* that has yet to emerge, what Clark and Suzuki (2006, 2) call 'the interpretative horizons of future audiences' that remain virtual within the poems and illuminations themselves, and call forth chapters of this book that cannot yet be written. One thing these reception stud-ies make obvious, to echo a point made recently by Steven Goldsmith, is that readers still find it 'exciting, even viscerally exciting, to read William Blake' (Goldsmith 2013, 1)

Notes

CHAPTER ONE

1. We extrapolate here from the appendix to Viscomi (1993, 376–81).
2. For recent treatments of *Poetical Sketches*, see Wolfson (1997); on *An Island in the Moon*, see Newman (2007), Rawlinson (2002), and Mee (2009).
3. www.bl.uk/onlinegallery/ttp/blake/accessible/introduction.html.
4. For details of these poems, see Table II in Erdman and Moore (1973, 53–58), and Phillips (2000, 32–94).
5. Geoffrey Keynes made a decisive intervention in this regard when, in his three-volume *Writings of William Blake* (1925), he not only included texts gleaned from the notebook (Dante Gabriel Rossetti had taken the initiative on this point in 1863 – see Chapter 4) but also recorded Blake's deletions and additions. Aghast, Joseph Wicksteed writes in 1928: 'The "Songs" are the Poet's own selection and are without any question the right selection. They are his exhibition, his palace, his book, whereas the MS. is his workshop; and though it is an inestimable privilege to have the opportunity of looking through the window at Blake as he works, and though we cannot afford to throw away one scrap that fell from his hand, we do a manifest injustice by exhibiting his chips side by side with his masterpieces' (Wicksteed 1928, 42).
6. Not all these reviews were positive. Writing in *The Examiner*, the critic Robert Hunt calls Blake's illustrations for *The Grave* 'absurd' and 'libidinou[s]', and judges the paintings and catalogue for his 1809 exhibition to be the work of 'an unfortunate lunatic' (*The Examiner*, 7 August 1809 and 17 September 1809, quoted in *BR* 258–61, 282–5).
7. Printing the plate borders: i.e. Blake left visible the edges of the copperplate as a frame within the paper page, where previously he would have wiped the plate borders free of ink before printing.
8. This 'Order' was first printed by Muir at the close of his facsimile edition of Blake's *Marriage of Heaven and Hell*; it was reproduced and its order followed by Sampson in *Blake's Poetical Works* in 1905 (see Sampson 1905, 70–1).

CHAPTER TWO

1. On the prices at which Blake sold his books, see Bentley (1999). Blake spoke of his 'horror of money' to Henry Crabb Robinson in 1826: see *BR* 435, 704.
2. On the significance of the ways in which Blake sold his books, see further, Haggarty (2010, 19–23).

3. For an accessible and more complete list of early reprintings of Blake's *Songs*, see *BR* appendix.
4. On Blake and eighteenth-century poetics, see further Murray (1974).
5. On the secularisation and recuperation of 'poetic enthusiasm' at the time and more broadly, see Clark (1997, 64–7). Ellis and Yeats also comment on this issue at E-Y, I.48.
6. The mutual implication of Blake's genius and his madness is also suggested by the poet and reviewer Robert Southey, who in the 1840s reflected on Blake as '[t]hat painter of great but insane genius' ([Robert Southey], *The Doctor, &c* [1847], cited by *BR* 300; see also *BR* 310).
7. Robinson found the translation of his article 'In most respects well done, but in one or two instances, the Sense of the verse was mistaken' (diary entry for 28 April 1811, communicated in personal correspondence with the authors by Tim Whelan).
8. With thanks to James Vigus and Karen Junod for these translations.
9. Crabb Robinson also appears to have given Wordsworth a manuscript copy of Blake's poems, perhaps including the *Songs* (see *BR* 436–7).
10. We do, however, have records of Blake's reactions to some of Wordsworth's writings: see *BR* 437–8, and E665–7.

CHAPTER THREE

1. Allan Cunningham wrote to John Linnell on 20 July 1829, 'I know Blakes character for I knew the man,' but there is no indication elsewhere that the two were acquainted (*BR* 497).
2. Cunningham's quotation is derived from James Thomson's poem 'Winter', in *The Seasons* (1726) (l. 432).
3. On the authorship of the *London University Magazine* article, see Dorfman (1969, 42–3nn.), and Lines (1999).

CHAPTER FOUR

1. Such a view is reiterated by reviewers of the *Life*: see Dorfman (1969, 83–4), and Hoover (1974).
2. On Christina Rossetti's response to *Songs*, see Harrison (1998, 149–52).
3. Swinburne substitutes 'fears' for 'tears' in his transcription of this poem, as well as altering punctuation, spelling, and case.
4. Dorfman discusses Swinburne's suppression of Blake's Christianity in connection with the textual emendations he made to the 'Introduction' to *Songs of Experience*, in *A Critical Essay*: see D 133; S 117. For Swinburne's comments on Blake and de Sade, see S 158n.
5. The importance of 'a concrete work of art' to Aestheticism is suggested by Prettejohn (2007, 2–3).
6. See Burlington Fine Arts Club (1876), catalogue entries 309 and 312 (books), and 273, 274–5, 277, and 278 (pictures).

CHAPTER FIVE

1. On Joyce's response to Blake, see further, Gleckner (1982, 135–63), and Larrissy (2006, 56–69).
2. On Blake's influence on Yeats, see further, Adams (1955).
3. www.english.uga.edu/~nhilton/ee/home.html.
4. In Blake's poem *Tiriel* (c. 1789), Mnetha is the aged mother of one of the other characters, Har.
5. For more on Blake and correspondences, see Thomson (1896a, 261); Rix (2007, 63–4); and Raine (1969, vol. I).
6. A similar account of Blake's automatic writing is given by Berger (1907). On the issue of Blake's automatism more largely, see Haggarty (2010).

CHAPTER SIX

1. For more recent and more detailed work on Blake and Lavater, see Erle (2010).

CHAPTER SEVEN

1. See, for instance, the reprints in Frye (ed.) (1966) and Bottrall (1970).
2. This aspect of Ostriker's work draws upon Josephine Miles (1957, 79).
3. Wagenknecht (1973, 14–15) is quite explicit in saying that to compare Blake with Barbauld and Wollstonecraft would be to devalue his work: 'To see Blake thus, against the background of Spenser and Milton rather than of Barbauld and Wollstonecraft, is not only to clarify meaning but to imply evaluation as well, if only because to restore Blake to the company he surely keeps is obliquely to reinforce my thesis.'
4. Brenkman's reading of *Songs* in terms of the Frankfurt School has been extended by Williams (1998).
5. *Gates of Paradise* was a small emblem book of engravings, originally issued in 1793 with the sub-title *For Children*. The 1818 version appeared with the sub-title *For the Sexes*, suggesting something of Blake's self-consciousness regarding the issues discussed in this section.

Bibliography

WORKS CITED

An asterisk marks key critical sources discussed at length in the chapters.

WORKS OF BLAKE CRITICISM CITED THROUGHOUT

*Bentley, G. E., Jr (1975) *William Blake: The Critical Heritage* (London and Boston: Routledge & Kegan Paul), This contains obituaries as well as other key critical responses; see esp. Ch. 3.
_____ (1977) *Blake Books* (Oxford: Clarendon Press).
_____ (2001) *The Stranger from Paradise: A Biography of William Blake* (New Haven and London: Yale University Press). The major recent biography.
*_____ (2004) *Blake Records*, 2nd edn (New Haven, CT: Yale University Press). This contains transcriptions of criticism from Blake's contemporaries, see Ch. 2, and early biographies, see Ch. 3.
*Bottrall, M. (ed.) (1970) *William Blake, Songs of Innocence and Experience: A Casebook* (London: Macmillan). A wonderful resource for both contemporary and posthumous criticism.
Dent, S. and J. Whittaker (2002) *Radical Blake: Influence and Afterlife from 1827* (Basingstoke: Palgrave Macmillan).
Dorfman, D. (1969) *Blake in the Nineteenth Century: His Reputation as a Poet from Gilchrist to Yeats* (New Haven and London: Yale University Press).
*Erdman, D. V. (1977) *Blake: Prophet Against Empire: A Poet's Interpretation of his Own Times*, 3rd edn (Princeton, NJ: Princeton University Press). The classic historical study of Blake, see Ch. 6.
Erdman, D. V. (ed.) (1982) *The Complete Poetry and Prose of William Blake*, rev. edn (Berkeley and Los Angeles: University of California Press). Foreword by H. Bloom.
Essick, R. N. (1980) *William Blake, Printmaker* (Princeton, NJ: Princeton University Press).
*Frye, N. (1947) *Fearful Symmetry: A Study of William Blake* (Princeton, NJ: Princeton University Press). See especially Ch. 6.
*Gilchrist, A. (1998) *The Life of William Blake*, ed. W. G. Robertson (Mineola, NY: Dover Publications).
Mee, J. (1992) *Dangerous Enthusiasm: William Blake and the Culture of Radicalism in the 1790s* (Oxford: Oxford University Press).
Phillips, Michael (2000) *William Blake: The Creation of the Songs from Manuscript to Illuminated Printing* (London: The British Library) See esp. Ch. 1.
Stevenson, W. H. (2007) *Blake: The Complete Poems*, 3rd edn (Harlow: Pearson Education).

Trodd, C. (2012) *Visions of Blake: William Blake in the Art World, 1830–1930* (Liverpool: Liverpool University Press).

Viscomi, J. (1993) *Blake and the Idea of the Book* (Princeton, NJ: Princeton University Press) See esp. Chs 1 and 8.

*Wittreich, J. A., Jr (ed.) (1970) *Nineteenth-Century Accounts of William Blake* (Gainesville, FL: Scholars' Facsimiles and Reprints).

WORKS CITED BY CHAPTER

Chapter 1   Producing *Songs*: 'In a Book that All May Read'

The crucial sources for this chapter are Phillips (2000) and Viscomi (1993), details above.

Bentley, G. E., Jr (1958) 'A. S. Mathew, Patron of Blake and Flaxman', *Notes and Queries* 203, pp. 168–78.

Damon, S. F. (1924) *William Blake, His Philosophy and Symbols* (London, Bombay, Sydney: Constable).

England, M. (1970) 'The Satiric Blake: Apprenticeship at the Haymarket?' in D. V. Erdman and J. E. Grant (eds), *Blake's Visionary Forms Dramatic* (Princeton, NJ: Princeton University Press).

*Erdman, D. V. and D. K. Moore (eds) (1973) *The Notebook of William Blake: A Photographic and Typographic Facsimile* (Oxford: Clarendon Press).

Essick, R. N. and J. Viscomi (2001) 'An Inquiry into Blake's Method of Color Printing', *Blake / An Illustrated Quarterly* 35 (Winter), pp. 73–102.

Glen, H. (1983) *Vision and Disenchantment: Blake's Songs and Wordsworth's Lyrical Ballads* (Cambridge: Cambridge University Press).

Haggarty, S. (2010) *Blake's Gifts: Poetry and the Politics of Exchange* (Cambridge: Cambridge University Press).

Hecimovich, G. (2008) *Puzzling the Reader: Riddles in Nineteenth-Century British Literature* (New York: P. Lang).

Hedley, D. (2003) *Coleridge, Philosophy, and Religion: Aids to Reflection and the Mirror of the Spirit* (Cambridge: Cambridge University Press).

McGann, J. J. (1983a) *A Critique of Modern Textual Criticism* (Chicago; London: University of Chicago Press).

Mee, Jon (2009) '"A Little Less Conversation, A Little More Action": Mutuality, Converse and Mental Fight', in S. Haggarty and J. Mee (eds), *Blake and Conflict* (Basingstoke: Palgrave Macmillan).

Mitchell, W. J. T. (1978) *Blake's Composite Art: A Study of the Illuminated Poetry* (Princeton, NJ: Princeton University Press).

Newman, S. (2007) 'Ballads and the Problem of Lyric Violence in Blake and Wordsworth', in *Ballad Collection, Lyric, and the Canon: the Call of the Popular from the Restoration to the New Criticism* (Philadelphia: University of Pennsylvania Press).

Phillips, M. (1994) 'Blake and the Terror 1792–93', *The Library*, 6th ser, 26.4 (December), pp. 263–97.

Rawlinson, N. (2002) 'Talking of Virtuous Cats: *An Island in the Moon*', in *William Blake's Comic Vision* (Basingstoke: Palgrave Macmillan).

Wicksteed, J. (1928) *Blake's Innocence and Experience: A Study of the Songs and Manuscripts 'Shewing the Two Contrary States of the Human Soul'* (London and Toronto: J. M. Dent & Sons; New York: E. P. Dutton).

Wolfson, S. (1997) 'Sketching Verbal Form: Blake's *Poetical Sketches*', in *Formal Charges: The Shaping of Poetry in British Romanticism* (Stanford, CA: Stanford University Press).

Chapter 2   Blake's Contemporaries on *Songs*: Simplicity, Madness, Genius, and Swedenborgianism

Contemporary responses by Malkin, Crabb Robinson, Wordsworth, Coleridge, Lamb, and Hazlitt are all most easily consulted in *Bentley's *Blake Records*, details above.

Bentley, G. E., Jr (1999) 'What Is the Price of Experience?: William Blake and the Economics of Illuminated Printing', *University of Toronto Quarterly* 68, pp. 617–41.

Clark, T. (1997) *The Theory of Inspiration: Composition as a Crisis of Subjectivity in Romantic and Post-Romantic Writing* (Manchester: Manchester University Press).

Davies, K. (1999) 'Miss Bliss: A Blake Collector of 1794', in S. Clark and D. Worrall (eds), *Blake in the Nineties* (Basingstoke: Macmillan).

Goldstein, J. (1987) *Console and Classify: The French Psychiatric Profession in the Nineteenth Century* (Cambridge: Cambridge University Press).

Haggarty, S. (2010) *Blake's Gifts: Poetry and the Politics of Exchange* (Cambridge: Cambridge University Press).

Hazlitt, W. (1821) 'On Vulgarity and Affectation', in *Table-Talk; or, Original Essays* (London: John Warren).

Jackson, H. J. (2004) '"Swedenborg's *Meaning* is the truth": Coleridge, Tulk, and Swedenborg', in S. McNeilly (ed.), *Essays on Swedenborg and Literature: In Search of the Absolute* (London: The Swedenborg Society).

Johnson, S. (2009) *Lives of the English Poets*, ed. G. Birkbeck Hill, 3 vols (London: Faber & Faber).

Junod, K. (2012) 'Crabb Robinson, Blake, and Perthes's Vaterländisches Museum (1810–1811)', *European Romantic Review* 23.4, pp. 435–51.

Lamb, C. (1987) 'The Praise of Chimney-Sweepers', in *Elia; and The Last Essays of Elia*, ed. J. Bate, The World's Classics series (Oxford: Oxford University Press).

McCalman, I. (1999) 'Enthusiasm', in I. McCalman et al. (eds), *The Oxford Companion to the Romantic Age* (Oxford: Oxford University Press).

*Montgomery, J. (ed.) (1824) *The Chimney-Sweeper's Friend, and Climbing-Boy's Album* (London).

Murray, R. (1974) 'Blake and the Ideal of Simplicity', *Studies in Romanticism* 13.2, pp. 89–104.

Plotz, J. A. (2000) *Romanticism and the Vocation of Childhood* (Basingstoke: Macmillan).

Rix, R. (2007) *William Blake and the Cultures of Radical Christianity* (Farnham: Ashgate).

Wu, D. (2008) *William Hazlitt: The First Modern Man* (Oxford: Oxford University Press).

Chapter 3   Reviving Blake in the 1820s and 1830s: Obituaries, Biographies, and the First New Editions.

Obituaries can be found in *Bentley's *Critical Heritage* volume, details above. The Cunningham and Smith sources given below are also reproduced in *Blake Records*.

Auden, W. H. (1969) *Collected Shorter Poems, 1927–1957*, rev. edn (London: Faber & Faber).

*Cunningham, A. (1830) *The Lives of the Most Eminent British Painters, Sculptors and Architects*, 2nd edn (London: J. Murray), vol. II.

Elliott, C. (2009) 'William Blake and America: Freedom and Violence in the Atlantic World', *Comparative American Studies* 7.3 (September), pp. 209–24.

Evans, F. H. (1912) *James John Garth Wilkinson, An Introduction* (London: New Church Press). Repr. 1936.

Lines, R. (1999) '"The Inventions of William Blake, Painter and Poet": An early appreciation of Blake's genius', *Journal of the Blake Society at St James* 4, pp. 56–65.

Palmer, A. H. (ed.) (1972) *The Life and Letters of Samuel Palmer, Painter and Etcher*, intro. R. Lister and K. Raine, rev. edn (London: E. & J. Stevens).

Robinson, H. C. (1938) *On Books and Their Writers*, ed. E. J. Morley, 3 vols (London: J. M. Dent and Sons).

Rossetti, W. M. (1906) *Some Reminiscences of William Michael Rossetti*, 2 vols (London: Brown Langham).

*Smith, J. T. (1828) *Nollekens and His Times*, 2 vols (London: Henry Colburn).

Swinburne, A. C. (1959–62) *The Swinburne Letters*, ed. C. Y. Lang, 6 vols (New Haven, CT: Yale University Press).

Thomson, J. (1896b) 'A Strange Book', in *Biographical and Critical Studies* (London: Reeves & Turner; Bertram Dobell).

Tulk, C. A. (ed.) (c. 1843) William Blake, *Songs of Innocence and Experience* (London: C. A. Tulk).

Wilkinson, C. J. (1911) *James John Garth Wilkinson: A Memoir of his Life, with a Selection from his Letters* (London: Kegan Paul, Trench, Trübner).

*Wilkinson, J. J. G. (1839) 'Preface', in J. J. G. Wilkinson (ed.), William Blake, *Songs of Innocence and of Experience* (London: W. Pickering).

Chapter 4   Enshrining Blake in the 1860s and 1870s: Pre-Raphaelitism, Aestheticism, and Counter-Attack

[Allingham, W.] (1860) 'Preface', in Giraldus (ed.), *Nightingale Valley: A Collection, including a Great Number of the Choicest Lyrics and Short Poems in the English Language* (London: Bell & Daldy).

Armstrong, I. (2012) 'The Pre-Raphaelites and Literature', in E. Prettejohn (ed.), *The Cambridge Companion to the Pre-Raphaelites* (Cambridge: Cambridge University Press).

Burlington Fine Arts Club (1876) *Exhibition of the Works of William Blake: Born 1757: Died 1827* (London: Spottiswoode). Conway, M. D. (1868) 'William Blake: A Critical Essay. By Algernon Charles Swinburne', *The Fortnightly Review* 3, new series (January–June), pp. 216–20.

*[Crawfurd, O.] (1874) 'William Blake: Artist, Poet and Mystic', *New Quarterly Magazine* (April), pp. 466–501.

Cruise, C. (2012) 'Pre-Raphaelite Drawing', in E. Prettejohn (ed.), *The Cambridge Companion to the Pre-Raphaelites* (Cambridge: Cambridge University Press).

Dent, S. (2007) 'Anne Gilchrist and *The Life of William Blake*', in H. P. Bruder (ed.), *Women Reading William Blake* (Basingstoke: Palgrave Macmillan).

Ferguson-Wagstaffe, S. (2006) '"Points of Contact": Blake and Whitman', *Romantic Circles Praxis Series*, special issue: *Sullen Fires Across the Atlantic: Essays in Transatlantic Romanticism* (November).

*Gilchrist, A. (1863) *The Life of William Blake: 'Pictor Ignotus'*, ed. A. Gilchrist with the assistance of D. G. and W. M. Rossetti, 2 vols (London: Macmillan).

Gilchrist, H. H. (ed.) (1887) *Anne Gilchrist: Her Life and Writings* (London: T. Fisher Unwin).

Harper, G. M. (1953) 'Blake's "Nebuchadnezzar" in "The City of Dreadful Night"', *Studies in Philology* 50.1, pp. 68–80.

Harrison, A. H. (1998) *Victorian Poets and the Politics of Culture: Discourse and Ideology* (Charlottesville and London: University Press of Virginia).

*Hewlett, H. G. (1876) 'Imperfect Genius: Blake', *Contemporary Review* 28 (October), pp. 756–84.

Hoover, S. R. (1974) 'The Public Reception of Gilchrist's *Life of Blake*', *Blake Newsletter* 29–30, special issue: *Blake Among Victorians* 8.1–2 (Summer–Fall), pp. 26–31.

Housman, L. (1893) 'Introduction', in L. Housman (ed.), *Selections from the Writings of William Blake* (London: Kegan Paul, Trench, Trübner).

McGann, J. J. (1998) 'Rossetti's Iconic Page', in G. Bornstein and T. Tinkle (eds), *The Iconic Page in Manuscript, Print, and Digital Culture* (Ann Arbor: University of Michigan Press). Repr. in 2001.

—— (2003) 'Introduction', in D. G. Rossetti, *Collected Poetry and Prose*, ed. J. J. McGann (New Haven and London: Yale University Press).

—— (2012) 'The Poetry of Dante Gabriel Rossetti (1828–1882)', in E. Prettejohn (ed.), *The Cambridge Companion to the Pre-Raphaelites* (Cambridge: Cambridge University Press).

Paley, M. D. (1974) 'The Critical Reception of *A Critical Essay*', *Blake Newsletter* 29–30, special issue: *Blake Among Victorians* 8.1–2 (Summer–Fall), pp. 32–7.

*Patmore, C. (1889) 'Blake', in *Principle in Art. Religio Poetae* (London: Duckworth). Repr. in 1913.

Prettejohn, E. (2007) *Art for Art's Sake: Aestheticism in Victorian Painting* (New Haven and London: Yale University Press).

Reynolds, J. (1997) *Discourses on Art*, ed. R. R. Wark (London and New Haven: Yale University Press).

Rooksby, R. (1997) *A. C. Swinburne: A Poet's Life* (Aldershot: Scolar Press).

*Rossetti, W. M. (1874) 'Prefatory Memoir', in W. M. Rossetti (ed.), *The Poetical Works of William Blake, Lyrical and Miscellaneous*, The Aldine Edition of the British Poets (London: George Bell and Sons).

*Scott, W. B. (1876) 'Introductory Remarks', in Burlington Fine Arts Club, *Exhibition of the Works of William Blake: Born 1757: Died 1827* (London: Spottiswoode).

*Smetham, J. (1880) 'Essay on Blake', in A. Gilchrist, *The Life of William Blake: 'Pictor Ignotus'*, ed. A. Gilchrist with the assistance of D. G. and W. M. Rossetti, 2 vols, 2nd edn (London: Macmillan).

*Swinburne, A. C. (1868) *William Blake: A Critical Essay* (London: John Camden Hotten).

—— (1959–62) *The Swinburne Letters*, ed. C. Y. Lang, 6 vols (New Haven, CT: Yale University Press).

Symons, A. (1907) *William Blake* (London: Jonathan Cape).

*Thomson, J. (1896a) 'The Poems of William Blake', in *Biographical and Critical Studies* (London: Reeves & Turner; Bertram Dobell).

*—— (1896b) 'A Strange Book', in *Biographical and Critical Studies* (London: Reeves & Turner; Bertram Dobell).

Chapter 5   Blake and the Moderns: Symbolism and Scholarship

Adams, H. (1955) *Blake and Yeats: The Contrary Vision* (Ithaca, NY: Cornell University Press).

Benson, A. C. (1896) 'William Blake', in *Essays* (London: W. Heinemann).

Berger, P. (1907) *William Blake: mysticisme et poésie* (Paris).

Bloom, H. (1970) *Yeats* (New York: Oxford University Press).

Cowley, M. (1969) 'S. Foster Damon: The New England Voice', in A. Rosenfeld (ed.), *William Blake: Essays for S. Foster Damon* (Providence, RI: Brown University Press).

*Damon, S. F. (1924) *William Blake, His Philosophy and Symbols* (London, Bombay, Sydney: Constable).

____ (1967–8) 'How I Discovered Blake', in *Blake Newsletter* 1 (Winter), pp. 2–3.

*Eliot, T. S. (1997a) 'Blake', in *The Sacred Wood: Essays on Poetry and Criticism* (London: Faber & Faber).

____ (1997b) 'Tradition and the Individual Talent', in *The Sacred Wood: Essays on Poetry and Criticism* (London: Faber & Faber).

Ellis, E. J. (1893) 'Introduction', in E. J. Ellis (ed.), *Facsimile of the Original Outlines Before Colouring of The Songs of Innocence and of Experience Executed by William Blake* (London: Bernard Quaritch).

*Ellis, E. J., and W. B. Yeats (1893) *The Works of William Blake, Poetical, Symbolic, and Critical*, 3 vols (London: Bernard Quaritch).

Fletcher, I. (1974) 'John Todhunter's Lectures on Blake', *Blake Newsletter* 29–30, special issue: *Blake Among Victorians* 8.1–2 (Summer–Fall), pp. 4–14.

Frye, N. (1963) 'Yeats and the Language of Symbolism', in *Fables of Identity: Studies in Poetic Mythology* (New York: Harcourt, Brace, & World).

Gleckner, R. F. (1982) 'Joyce's Blake: Paths of Influence', in R. J. Bertholf and A. S. Levitt (eds), *William Blake and the Moderns* (Albany, NY: State University of New York Press).

Haggarty, S. (2010) *Blake's Gifts: Poetry and the Politics of Exchange* (Cambridge: Cambridge University Press).

*Joyce, J. (1959) ['William Blake'], in E. Mason and R. Ellmann (eds), *The Critical Writings of James Joyce* (London: Faber & Faber).

*Keynes, G. (ed.) (1925) *The Writings of William Blake*, 3 vols (London: Nonesuch Press).

Larrissy, E. (2006) *Blake and Modern Literature* (Basingstoke: Palgrave Macmillan).

Murry, J. M. (1933) *William Blake* (London: Jonathan Cape).

Palgrave, F. T. (ed.) (1991) *The Golden Treasury of the Best Songs and Lyrical Poems in the English Language*, ed. C. Ricks, Penguin Classics (Harmondsworth: Penguin).

Quiller-Couch, A. (ed.) (1900) *The Oxford Book of English Verse, 1250–1900* (Oxford: Clarendon Press).

Raine, K. (1969) *Blake and Tradition*, 2 vols (London: Routledge & Kegan Paul).

____ (1986) 'Yeats's Debt to Blake', in *Yeats the Initiate* (London: G. Allen & Unwin; Mountrath: The Dolmen Press).

Rix, R. (2007) *William Blake and the Cultures of Radical Christianity* (Farnham: Ashgate).

Rossetti, W. M. (1874) 'Prefatory Memoir', in W. M. Rossetti (ed.), *The Poetical Works of William Blake, Lyrical and Miscellaneous*, The Aldine Edition of the British Poets (London: George Bell and Sons).

Rudd, M. (1953) *Divided Image: A Study of William Blake and W. B. Yeats* (London: Routledge & Kegan Paul).

*Sampson, J. (ed.) (1905) *The Poetical Works of William Blake* (Oxford: Clarendon Press).

Shepherd, R. H. (ed.) (1866) *Songs of Innocence and Experience, with Other Poems* (London: B. M. Pickering).

____ (1874) *The Poems of William Blake: Comprising Songs of Innocence and of Experience with Poetical Sketches and some copyright poems not in any other edition* (London: B. M. Pickering).

Symons, A. (1907) *William Blake* (London: Jonathan Cape).

Thomson, J. (1896a) 'The Poems of William Blake', in *Biographical and Critical Studies* (London: Reeves & Turner; Bertram Dobell).

*Todhunter, J. (1972) 'Lecture VII, 31 October 1872, Songs of Innocence', *Blake Newsletter* 29–30, special issue: *Blake Among Victorians* 8.1–2 (Summer–Fall), pp. 6–8.

*___ (1974) 'Lecture XVIII, 12 March 1874, William Blake', *Blake Newsletter* 29–30, special issue: *Blake Among Victorians* 8.1–2 (Summer–Fall), pp. 13–14.

White, H. C. (1927) *The Mysticism of William Blake* (Madison: University of Wisconsin Press).

Wicksteed, J. (1928) *Blake's Innocence and Experience: A Study of the Songs and Manuscripts 'Shewing the Two Contrary States of the Human Soul'* (London and Toronto: J. M. Dent & Sons; New York: E. P. Dutton).

Williams, N. C. (2006) 'Introduction: Understanding Blake', in N. C. Williams (ed.), *Palgrave Advances in William Blake Studies* (Basingstoke: Palgrave Macmillan).

Yeats, W. B. (1903a) 'The Symbolism of Poetry', in *Ideas of Good and Evil* (London: A. H. Bullen).

___ (1903b) 'William Blake and his Illustrations to *The Divine Comedy*', in *Ideas of Good and Evil* (London: A. H. Bullen).

*___ (1903c) 'William Blake and the Imagination', in *Ideas of Good and Evil* (London: A. H. Bullen).

___ (1999) *Autobiographies*, Volume III of *The Collected Works of W. B. Yeats*, ed. W. H. O'Donnell and D. N. Archibald (New York: Scribner).

Chapter 6   The Post-War Foundations: System, Myth, and History

*Bloom, H. (1963) *Blake's Apocalypse: A Study in Poetic Argument* (London: Victor Gollancz).

*Bronowski, Jacob (1943) *William Blake: A Man Without a Mask* (London: Secker & Warburg).

___ (1972) *William Blake and the Age of Revolution* (London: Routledge).

Brown, Norman O. (1959) *Life against Death: The Pyschoanalytical Meaning of History* (London: Routledge & Kegan Paul).

___ (1966) *Love's Body* (New York: Random House).

Crehan, S. (1984) *Blake in Context* (Dublin: Gill and Macmillan Humanities Press).

Erdman, D. V. (1953) 'Blake's Early Swedenborgianism: A Twentieth-Century Legend', *Comparative Literature* 5, pp. 247–57.

Erle, S. (2010) *Blake, Lavater and Physiognomy*, Studies in Comparative Literature 21 (London: Legenda).

Essick, R. N. (1991) 'William Blake, Thomas Paine, and Biblical Revolution', *Studies in Romanticism* 30, pp. 189–212.

Frye, N. (1957) *The Anatomy of Criticism: Four Essays* (Princeton, NJ: Princeton University Press).

*___ (2004) *Fearful Symmetry: A Study of William Blake*, ed. N. Halmi, with an introduction by I. Singer, vol. 5 of *The Works of Northrop Frye* (Toronto: University of Toronto Press).

___ (1976) *Spiritus Mundi: Essays on Literature, Myth, and Society* (Bloomington, IN: University of Indiana Press).

Harper, G. M. (1961) *The Neoplatonism of William Blake* (Chapel Hill, NC: University of North Carolina Press).

Hirst, D. (1964) *Hidden Riches: Traditional Symbolism from the Renaissance to Blake* (London: Eyre & Spottiswoode).

Hobson, C. Z. (1998) 'The Myth of Blake's "Orc Cycle"', in J. DiSalvo, G. A. Rosso, and C. Z. Hobson (eds), *Blake, Politics, and History* (New York: Garland).

Lowery, M. R. (1940) *The Windows of the Morning: A Critical Study of William Blake's Poetical sketches, 1783* (New Haven, CT: Yale University Press).

*Makdisi, S. (2003) *William Blake and the Impossible History of the 1790s* (Chicago, IL: University of Chicago Press).

Pedley, C. (1991) 'Blake's "Tyger" and Contemporary Journalism', *British Journal of Eighteenth Century Studies* 14, pp. 45–9.

*Raine, K. (1969) *Blake and Tradition*, 2 vols (London: Routledge & Kegan Paul).

Salusinszky, I. (1987) *Criticism in Society: Interviews with Jacques Derrida, Northrop Frye, Harold Bloom, Geoffrey Hartman, Frank Kermode, Edward Said, Barbara Johnson, Frank Lentricchia, and J. Hillis Miller*, 2 vols (London, Methuen).

*Schorer, M. (1946) *William Blake: The Politics of Vision* (New York: H. Holt).

Chapter 7   Freedom and Repression in the 1960s and 1970s: Form, Ideology, and Gender

Abrams, M. H. (1973) *Natural Supernaturalism: Tradition and Revolution in Romantic Literature* (New York and London: W. W. Norton).

Adams, H. (1963) *William Blake: A Reading of the Shorter Poems* (Seattle: University of Washington Press).

—— (1986) 'Blake and the Philosophy of Literary Symbolism', in N. Hilton (ed.), *Essential Articles for the Study of William Blake* (Hamden, CT: Archon).

Bateson, F. W. (1906) *William Blake: A Critical Essay* (London).

Bloom, H. (1973) *The Anxiety of Influence: A Theory of Poetry* (New York: Oxford University Press).

—— (1975) *A Map of Misreading* (New York: Oxford University Press).

—— (1976) *Poetry and Repression: Revisionism from Blake to Stevens* (New Haven, CT: Yale University Press).

*Brenkman, J. (1987) *Culture and Domination* (Ithaca, NY and London: Cornell University Press).

Burke, E. (1791) *Reflections on the Revolution in France*, 11th edn (London: J. Dodsley).

Crehan, S. (1984) *Blake in Context* (Dublin: Gill and Macmillan Humanities Press).

*Essick, R. N. (1989) *William Blake and the Language of Adam* (Oxford: Oxford University Press).

Ferber, M. (1985) *The Social Vision of William Blake* (Princeton, NJ: Princeton University Press).

*Fox, S. (1977) 'The Female as Metaphor in William Blake's Poetry', *Critical Enquiry* 3, pp. 507–19.

Frye, N. (ed.) (1966) *Blake: A Collection of Critical Essays* (Englewood Cliffs, NJ: Prentice Hall International).

*George, D. H. (1980) *Blake and Freud* (Ithaca, NY: Cornell University Press).

Gillham, D. G. (1966) *Blake's Contrary States: The 'Songs of Innocence and of Experience' as Dramatic Poems* (Cambridge: Cambridge University Press).

Gleckner, R. F. (1957) 'Point of View and Context in Blake's Songs', *Bulletin of the New York Public Library* 61, pp. 531–6.

*_____ (1959) *The Piper and the Bard* (Detroit, MI: Wayne State University Press).

*_____ (1969) 'Blake's Verbal Technique', in A. H. Rosenfeld (ed.), *William Blake: Essays for S. Foster Damon* (Providence, RI: Brown University Press).

*_____ (1974) 'Most Holy Forms of Thought: Some Observations on Blake and Language', *English Literary History* 4, pp. 555–77.

*Glen, H. (1983) *Vision and Disenchantment: Blake's Songs and Wordsworth's Lyrical Ballads* (Cambridge: Cambridge University Press).

Hirsch, E. D. (1964) *Innocence and Experience: An Introduction to Blake* (New Haven, CT: Yale University Press).

Holloway, J. (1968) *Blake: The Lyric Poetry* (London: Edward Arnold).

Leader, Z. (1981) *Reading Blake Songs* (London: Routledge & Kegan Paul).

*Mellor, A. K. (1982–3) 'Blake's Portrayal of Women', *Blake – an Illustrated Quarterly* (Winter), pp. 148–55.

*_____ (1988a) 'Blake's *Songs of Innocence and of Experience*: A Feminist Perspective', *Nineteenth-Century Studies* 2, pp. 1–17.

_____ (1988b) 'Introduction', in A. K. Mellor (ed.), *Romanticism and Feminism* (Bloomington: Indiana University Press).

Miles, J. (1957) *Eras and Modes in English Poetry* (Berkeley: University of California Press).

*Ostriker, A. (1965) *Vision and Verse in William Blake* (Madison, WI: University of Wisconsin Press).

_____ (1982–3) 'Desire Gratified and Ungratified: William Blake and Sexuality', *Blake – an Illustrated Quarterly* (Winter), pp. 156–65.

Paine, T. (1985) *Rights of Man*, intro. E. Foner with notes by H. Collins (London: Penguin).

*Paley, M. D. (1970) *Energy and the Imagination: A Study of the Development of Blake's Thought* (Oxford: Oxford University Press).

Singer, J. K. (1973) *The Unholy Bible: A Psychological Interpretation of William Blake* (New York: Harper Colophon Books).

Tayler, I. (1973) 'The Woman Scaly', *Bulletin of the Midwest Modern Language Association* 6.1, pp. 74–87.

Thompson, E. P. (1968) *The Making of the English Working Class*, rev. edn (Harmondsworth: Penguin).

_____ (1978) 'London', in M. Phillips (ed.), *Interpreting Blake* (Cambridge: Cambridge University Press).

*Wagenknecht, D. (1973) *Blake's Night: William Blake and the Idea of Pastoral* (Cambridge, MA: Belknap Press).

*Webster, B. (1983) *Blake's Prophetic Psychology* (London: Macmillan).

Williams, N. C. (1998) *Ideology and Utopia in the Poetry of William Blake* (Cambridge: Cambridge University Press).

Chapter 8   Blake's Composite Art in the 1980s and 1990s: Textuality and the Materiality of the Book

Carr, S. L. (1986) '*The Book of Urizen* and the Horizon of the Book', in N. Hilton and T. A. Vogler (eds), *Unnam'd Forms: Blake and Textuality* (Berkeley: University of California Press).

*Chandler, J. (2006) 'Blake and the Syntax of Sentiment: An Essay on "Blaking" Understanding', in Steve Clark and David Worrall (eds), *Blake, Nation and Empire* (Basingstoke: Palgrave Macmillan).

Clark, S., T. Connolly, and J. Whittaker (2012) 'Introduction', in S. Clark, T. Connolly, and J. Whittaker (eds), *Blake 2.0: William Blake in Twentieth-Century Art, Music, and Culture* (Basingstoke: Palgrave Macmillan).

Dent, S. (2012) '"Rob & Plunder … Translate & Copy & Buy & Sell & Criticise, but not Make": Blake and Copyright Today', in S. Clark, T. Connolly, and J. Whittaker (eds), *Blake 2.0: William Blake in Twentieth-Century Art, Music, and Culture* (Basingstoke: Palgrave Macmillan).

*Edwards, G. (1986) 'Repeating the Same Dull Round', in N. Hilton and T. A. Vogler (eds), *Unnam'd Forms: Blake and Textuality* (Berkeley: University of California Press).

Gardner, S. (1998) *The Tyger, The Lamb and the Terrible Desart* (London: Cygnus Arts).

Gourlay, A. S. (1995) Review of Joseph Viscomi, *Blake and the Idea of the Book', Blake – an Illustrated Quarterly* 29.1 (Summer), pp. 31–5.

Haggarty, S. (2010) *Blake's Gifts: Poetry and the Politics of Exchange* (Cambridge: Cambridge University Press).

*Hagstrum, J. (1964) *William Blake, Poet and Painter* (Chicago, IL: Chicago University Press).

_____ (1970) 'Blake and the Sister Arts Tradition', in D. V. Erdman and J. E. Grant (eds), *Blake's Visionary Forms Dramatic* (Princeton, NJ: Princeton University Press).

*Hilton, N. (1983) *Literal Imagination: Blake's Vision of Words* (Berkeley, CA: University of California Press).

*Hilton, N., and T. A. Vogler (1986) *Unnam'd Forms: Blake and Textuality* (Berkeley, CA: University of California Press).

Kraus, K. (2002) '"Once Only Imagined": An Interview with Morris Eaves, Robert N. Essick, and Joseph Viscomi on the Past, Present, and Future of Blake Studies', *Studies in Romanticism* 41, pp. 143–99.

Makdisi, S. (2003) *William Blake and the Impossible History of the 1790s* (Chicago, IL: University of Chicago Press).

McGann, J. J. (1983b) *Romantic Ideology: A Critical Investigation* (Chicago, IL: University of Chicago Press).

Mitchell, W. J. T. (1970) 'Blake's Composite Art', in D. V. Erdman and J. E. Grant (eds), *Blake's Visionary Forms Dramatic* (Princeton, NJ: Princeton University Press).

*_____ (1978) *Blake's Composite Art: A Study of the Illuminated Poetry* (Princeton, NJ: Princeton University Press).

_____ (1986) 'Visible Language: Blake's Wond'rous Art of Writing', in M. Eaves and M. Fischer (eds), *Romanticism and Contemporary Criticism* (Ithaca, NY: Cornell University Press).

Rothenberg, M. A. (1993) *Rethinking Blake's Textuality* (Columbia, NY: University of Columbia Press).

Saklofske, Jon. (2011) 'Remediating William Blake: Unbinding the Network Architectures of Blake's Songs', *European Romantic Review* 22.3, pp. 381–8.

Thomson, J. (1896a) 'The Poems of William Blake', in *Biographical and Critical Studies* (London: Reeves & Turner; Bertram Dobell).

Todd, R. (1948) *The Techniques of William Blake's Illuminated Painting* (Woodstock, VT: W. E. Rudge).

Whitson, R. (2012) 'Digital Blake 2.0', in S. Clark, T. Connolly, and J. Whittaker (eds), *Blake 2.0: William Blake in Twentieth-Century Art, Music, and Culture* (Basingstoke: Palgrave Macmillan).

Yeats, W. B. (1903b) 'William Blake and his Illustrations to *The Divine Comedy*', in *Ideas of Good and Evil* (London: A. H. Bullen).

Chapter 9   Worlding Blake Today: 'Past, Present and Future Sees'

Ault, D., and R. Whitson (2007) *William Blake and Visual Culture*, special issue of *ImageText* 3.2.

Bataille, G. (2012) *Literature and Evil*, trans. Alastair Hamilton (London: Penguin Classics).

Bate, J. (1991) *Romantic Ecology: Wordsworth and the Environmental Tradition* (London and New York: Routledge).

*____ (2000) *The Song of the Earth* (London: Picador).

Blackstone, B. (1949) *English Blake* (Cambridge: Cambridge University Press).

Bruder, Helen P. (1997) *William Blake and the Daughters of Albion* (Basingstoke: Macmillan).

*____ (ed.) (2006) *Women Reading William Blake* (Basingstoke: Palgrave Macmillan).

*Bruder, H. P., and T. Connolly (eds) (2010) *Queer Blake* (Basingstoke: Palgrave Macmillan).

Clark, S. (1994) *Sordid Images: The Poetry of Masculine Desire* (London: Routledge).

____ (2010) 'Blake's Sentimentalism as (Peri)Performative', in H. P. Bruder and Tristanne Connolly (eds), *Queer Blake* (Basingstoke: Palgrave Macmillan).

Clark, S., T. Connolly, and J. Whittaker (2012) 'Introduction', in S. Clark, T. Connolly, and J. Whittaker (eds), *Blake 2.0: William Blake in Twentieth-Century Art, Music, and Culture* (Basingstoke: Palgrave Macmillan).

Clark, S., and M. Suzuki (2006) 'Introduction', in S. Clark and M. Suzuki (eds), *The Reception of Blake in the Orient* (New York and London: Continuum).

Clark, S., and D. Worrall (eds) (2006) *Blake, Nation and Empire* (Basingstoke: Palgrave Macmillan).

*Connolly, T. (2002) *William Blake and the Body* (Basingstoke: Palgrave Macmillan).

Davies, K. (2012) 'Blake Set to Music', in S. Clark, T. Connolly, and J. Whittaker (eds), *Blake 2.0: William Blake in Twentieth-Century Art, Music, and Culture* (Basingstoke: Palgrave Macmillan).

Davies, K., and M. K. Schuchard (2004) 'Recovering the Lost Moravian History of William Blake's Family', *Blake – an Illustrated Quarterly* 38.1 (Summer), pp. 36–42.

Fallon, D. (2012) '"Hear the Drunken Archangel Sing": Blakean Notes in 1990s Pop Music', in S. Clark, T. Connolly, and J. Whittaker (eds), *Blake 2.0: William Blake in Twentieth-Century Art, Music, and Culture* (Basingstoke: Palgrave Macmillan).

*Goldsmith, S. (2013) *Blake's Agitation: Criticism and the Emotions* (Baltimore, MD: The Johns Hopkins Press).

Greer, G. (2006) '"No Earthly Parents I confess": The Clod, the Pebble and Catherine Blake', in H. P. Bruder (ed.), *Women Reading William Blake* (Basingstoke: Palgrave Macmillan).

Hilton, N. (1999) 'What has *Songs* to do with Hymns?' in S. Clark and D. Worrall (eds), *Blake in the Nineties* (Basingstoke: Macmillan).

Hobson, C. Z. (2000) *Blake and Homosexuality* (Basingstoke: Macmillan).

*Hutchings, K. (2002) *Imagining Nature: Blake's Environmental Poetics* (Montreal and Kingston: McGill-Queen's University Press).

*Kroeber, K. (1994) *Ecological Literary Criticism: Romantic Imagining and the Biology of Mind* (New York: Columbia University Press).

Larrissy, E. (1999) 'Introduction', in E. Larrissy (ed.), *Romanticism and Postmodernism* (Cambridge: Cambridge University Press).

Larrissy, E. (2006) *Blake and Modern Literature* (Basingstoke: Palgrave Macmillan).

*Lussier, M. S. (1999) *Romantic Dynamics: The Poetics of Physicality* (Basingstoke: Macmillan).

*McGann, J. J. (1986) 'The Idea of an Indeterminate Text: Blake's Bible of Hell and Dr Alexander Geddes', *Studies in Romanticism* 25, pp. 303–24.

*Makdisi, S. (2003) *William Blake and the Impossible History of the 1790s* (Chicago, IL: University of Chicago Press).

Mellor, A. K. (1993) *Romanticism and Gender* (London: Routledge).

*Morton, T. (2007) *Ecology without Nature: Rethinking Environmental Aesthetics* (Cambridge, MA: Harvard University Press).

Nichols, A. (2011) *Beyond Romantic Ecocriticism: Towards Urbanatural Roosting* (Basingstoke: Palgrave Macmillan).

Turner, B. (2006) 'Oe Kenzaburo's Reading of Blake: An Anglophonic Perspective', in S. Clark and M. Suzuki (eds), *The Reception of Blake in the Orient* (New York and London: Continuum).

Whittaker, J. (2012) 'Zoamorphosis: 250 Years of Blake Mutations', in M. Crosby, T. Patenaude, and A. Whitehead (eds), *Re-Envisioning Blake* (Basingstoke: Palgrave Macmillan).

*Wolfson, S. (2006) 'The Strange Difference of Female "Experience"', in H. P. Bruder, *Women Reading William Blake* (Basingstoke: Palgrave Macmillan).

DIGITAL SOURCES

*The British Library (n.d.) *The Notebook of William Blake*: www.bl.uk/onlinegallery/ttp/blake/accessible/introduction.html.

*Eaves, M., R. N. Essick, and J. Viscomi (eds) (2008) *The William Blake Archive*: www.blakearchive.org.

Hilton, N. (ed.) (n.d.) *eE on-line Blake Concordance*, in *Blake Digital Text Project*: www.english.uga.edu/~nhilton/ee/home.html.

Index